750
Cook. dessert

The Great American Chocolate Contest Cookbook

The
Great American

Contest Cookbook

■ ■ ■

150 of the Best Chocolate
Recipes from the National Recipe Contest

■ ■ ■

T. K. Woods

Hearst Books / New York

Library of Congress Cataloging-in-Publication Data

Woods, T. K., 1959–
    The great American chocolate contest cookbook : 150 of the best chocolate recipes from the national recipe contest / T. K. Woods.
        p.   cm.
    Includes index.
    ISBN 0–688–13395–9
    1. Cookery (Chocolate)   2. Desserts.   I. Title.
TX767.C5W66   1995
    641.6'374—dc20   95–15000
                                             CIP

Printed in the United States of America

2   3   4   5   6   7   8   9   10

BOOK DESIGN BY RICHARD ORIOLO

*This book is completed with great love
in memory of my father,
Lyle Creston Woods.*

Acknowledgments

■ ■ ■

It takes a lot of people to run a contest and even more people to create a cookbook. First of all, my gratitude to all the people who entered The Great American Chocolate Contest. Chocolate lovers from all over the country were generous enough to put their favorite recipes on paper and share them with us. Thank you.

Elizabeth Howard, Chocolate Heaven Assistant Chocolatier, has been my right arm and sometimes my left brain during the intensive process of running a national recipe contest and the development of the cookbook. Wise beyond her twenty-something years, she combines intellect and creativity with a passion for excellence, and her constant support kept me sane at times when I thought chocolate was consuming me. The book benefits so much from her contribution. We both wish to thank Charlotte Willour, who connected us. Char was my fourth- and fifth-grade teacher in Arlington Heights, Illinois, to whom I dedicated *The Great American Meatloaf Contest Cookbook*. How and why Char introduced us is a long story that you can hear in minute detail by contacting me at Chocolate Heaven/World Meatloaf Headquarters.

Thank you to the chefs and students of the Culinary Arts Department at Newbury College in Brookline, Massachusetts, who prepared many, many, many chocolate desserts for one of the final chocolate tastings. A special thank you to George Anbinder and Janet Lightizer, who accepted this project and supervised it from beginning to end. Thanks also to Chef/Instructor Terence Janericco and his students Joshua Appleby, Kathy Belyea, Tim Castler, Steven Della Croce, Tim Eaton, Lisa Ford, Pascale Guillaume, Theresa Hilliard, Nicholas Karasoulos, George Kouloheras, Peter Kourafalos, Rosalie Lentini, Carine Marius, Michael McCaffery,

Brendan McCarthy, Thu Nguyon, and Jeremy Reardon. You all deserve an "A" on this final.

A thank you also goes to Felicia's Catering, Hyde Park, Boston, for whipping up about thirty recipes in one day.

My thanks to the wonderful chocophiles from all over the United States, Canada, and even Great Britain who donated their palates to taste the chocolate recipes, including: Dawn and Denny (and Madelynn) Bain, Eliza Bartlett, Susan Beaupre, Terry Belli and Terri Bogage, Denise Booker and Don Hendrick (and Jesse), Denise Henson-Brosler and Eric Brosler (and Alexander and Madelaine), Tim Buie, Eric Chelman and Joan Chelman, Liz Coxon, Lauren Gilligan, Rachael Howard, Craig Hughes, Jim Hundreiser, Sue Farrell, Chuck and Mary Kilo, Kirsten Kissmeyer, Jane Lindsey, Wendy Mandel, Nuala McGrath, Maureen McLaughlin, Rob Nager, Brian Owens, Nixie Raymond, Leigh and Mike Slattery, Rob Smollen, Jeannie Verrando, Lori Weiss, Rosa Werthwein, and Jeni Yamada and Phil Hanff assisted by Aaron, Adam and Jason Yamada-Hanff and Mitsuye Yamada. And thanks to the Tri Deltas at Boston University, who believe chocolate should never go to waste and kindly helped with the removal of chocolate leftovers.

My neighbors to the right and left and across the street from my Chocolate House have always been enthusiastic supporters and consumers of the chocolate creations. My thanks to the O'Connors, David I. Walsh, the Elmuts, and Sarah Fiorillo and to Marie Boylan for keeping me apprised of the latest mysteries that even include chocolate.

And a special thanks to Janell and Gary Kohls, who opened their warm and loving home to a displaced writer and made their laserprinter always available when I was without one. Their kindness and great capacity for caring I've been fortunate enough to experience in a special friendship these past twenty-five years.

Megan Newman is an editor *extraordinaire*, and her incessant caring for everything she does is one more reason this book was a privilege to do. The William Morrow team of professionals, from copy editor to art director to the special sales people, deserves a well-earned thanks.

I was bombarded by tons of love and support from the Woods family (especially my mom, Patricia Woods) and the Buie family. Although they are dispersed throughout the United States, distance did not prevent their presence from sustaining me through the sadness and the joy of this year.

Speaking of family, Tim Buie could not move in his own house without bumping into chocolate. This guy made midnight runs to the store for semisweet morsels, hunted relentlessly for obscure ingredients, and cleaned thousands of dishes and pans. And he doesn't even like chocolate. Thank you, Tim, for your patience and wonderful encouragement.

Let's not forget the Chocolate Contest mascots, Penny, Scruffy, Tiffany, and Atticus, who avoided all chocolate but still helped keep the kitchen floors crumb-free.

Reviewing these paragraphs, I have learned this is not just a book or a contest, it has been a chocolate experience. And this chocolate experience has taught me that I am a very lucky woman.

Contents

■ ■ ■

Introduction:
In the Beginning . . .
There Was Chocolate

■ ■ ■

In the beginning was the word
and the word was Chocolate.
*And, it was good.**

*C*hocolate. The little kid in all of us bursts out at the mention of the word. *Chaalklot.* The image of a dark fudgy substance oozes from the word double-dipped in memories. I've been in love with chocolate since my time on this planet began. That's why the *ahhh* is emphasized—*chAHHHclot.* "Can you pahk the chahhhclot cah in the Hahvahd Yahhd," they say in Massachusetts. "Chklit," the word whips from chocolate-loving Chicagoans. "Chahhhhhklahhht," Southerners luxuriously drawl. "Ch-ch-ch-oc-c-c-l-l-l-i-t, youbetcha," they declare in Minnesota. "Cherklit" they say in Indiana, and "Charklit" in St. Louis. "Carob," they say in California—what?

That which we call chocolate pronounced any other way would taste as sweet.

---

*As seen on a T-shirt worn by Craig Hughes, a brilliant computer software engineer who is currently working on "chocolate virtual reality" and whose mom created the Millionaire's Shortbread on page 83. The T-shirt is created by High Cotton, Inc., Bluffton, South Carolina, and was inspired by the Bible.

Chocolate-Covered Memories

When I was little, I remember eating a brown spider thinking it was chocolate with legs walking right to me, a gift from the chocolate god. After my stomach was pumped and my IQ checked, I learned that chocolate couldn't walk, but it could fly. It would come in the form of my Great Aunt Hundee (my mother's eighty-something-year-old aunt), a wonderful, silver-blue coiffed, six-foot-tall spirit who would fly in from Bloomington, Illinois, for a much-awaited family visit. With great drama, as I stood patiently by, she would fling open her blue American Tourister suitcase, and out of the meticulously packed garments would spring clouds of Estée Lauder perfume, bars of Dove soap, and a precious Hershey bar. Together she and I would eat the candy bar square by square. A Hershey chocolate bar has never tasted the same without the smell of Estée Lauder and Dove soap, the sparkle of Aunt Hundee's blue eyes, and her laugh as thick and rich as chocolate.

Those are just two of my chocolate memories. There are as many pounds of them as I have eaten over these years. That hardly qualifies me to produce a chocolate cookbook. And in fact I did not write this entire book. More than one hundred great Americans from all over the United States have shared recipes to create the ultimate chocolate cookbook. Through the forum of The Great American Chocolate National Recipe Contest™ people shared their deepest, darkest chocolate recipes without constraint. A nonsponsored cooking contest is a rare event. *Nonsponsored* means the contestant doesn't have to use any particular brand name product or ingredient, just chocolate in one form or another. Chocolate without strings. So here we are with about fifteen different categories from cakes to pies to cookies. Included in this cookbook are old-fashioned recipes passed down from generation to generation and new, innovative chocolate recipes. Even chocolate salsas and chocolate entrees and chocolate soup were contributed by contestants influenced by Mexican cooking. Wow. I've tasted all these recipes, so many times I know each recipe as if it were an old friend.

In fact, contestants from the Great American Meatloaf Contests (1991 and 1992) would come up to me at book signings and introduce themselves by asking, "Guess who I am?" I always knew them by their recipe. They are lifetime members of a special group known as meatloavers. The chocolate lovers who are in this cook-book are recognized the same way: "You are Mary Ann Lee from Marco Island, and you created 'The Brownie of Seville' recipe" (page 74).

Testing 999 Chocolate Recipes: It Was a Tough Job, but Someone Had to Do It

I was envied by every person who knew I was running a chocolate contest and receiving hundreds and hundreds (into the thousands) of cherished chocolate recipes. Occupation? I would be asked on forms or credit applications (chocolate contest–running can be expensive). "Uh . . . chocolate," I would respond.

I would get calls: "Are you FAT yet?" "Are you sick of chocolate?" What do you think about when you're testing nearly one thousand chocolate recipes? Oh, you think about broccoli and salads with vinaigrette. Really. And you wonder what's on *Oprah* today. And you wonder if you'll be able to watch it while the chocolate cakes are baking, or should you (guilt, guilt) clean up? And you wonder if you should get cable in the kitchen. And you wonder if you have any friends anymore since you haven't been out with anyone for weeks. And you listen to a lot of talk radio and wonder who these people are who call and how do they have the time to call? And then you find yourself reaching for the phone to argue with the show's host. And you wonder if you'll ever read anything ever again that doesn't have the word *chocolate* in it. And when someone does suggest going to a movie, you wonder if they'll take you to see *Like Water for Chocolate*. And you wonder if your kitchen will ever stop looking like the back room of Willy Wonka's factory. And then you wonder if the Oompa Loompas in the film *Willy Wonka and the Chocolate Factory* possibly could have appeared in *The Wizard of Oz* (when you're raised in Kansas, everything has a *Wizard of Oz* connection). And then you wonder . . . did I already put a cup of sugar in this recipe? Do over.

Recipe testing takes tons of concentration and pounds of patience. I did discover cha-cha music is inspiring while making chocolate recipes—cho-co-late cha-cha-cha. And, as an inveterate nibbler surrounded by every brand of candy bar beckoning "just a bite," I prevented unconscious nibbling by chewing spearmint gum. Try it if you too are plagued by nibbling habits.

Choco-phobia

There was a curse in my family. No one baked with chocolate. My mother is a fabulous gourmet cook who had a television cooking show when TV was fresh and live in the Tri-City region of Iowa. She was offered a lifetime contract with WGN television in Chicago—which she gave up to have four children, she would remind us when we were in trouble. Despite her love of cooking, she hated the touch and feel of flour and chocolate made her nervous. So we never had any home-baked cakes or cookies. But before I'm pitied, while other kids were eating Spam, we were dining on duck à l'orange, salmon en papillote, and coquilles St. Jacques. It was enough to drive anyone to take French classes just to pronounce what we had for dinner every night.

What was even weirder about the lack of chocolate in the house was the fact that my father worked with chocolate manufacturers and baking companies. His company provided the necessary ingredients to emulsify and enrich foods, including chocolate. Actually, we were never quite sure what my father did. At career day, I had difficulty describing that he was "vice president of something to do with food." But the samples of chocolate we received from his clients and/or colleagues clarified the question deliciously.

A Dream Comes True

One morning, my father casually mentioned to my mother to expect a delivery of Bun candy bars (chocolate-covered patties filled with a creamy center and peanuts) from the candy bar's plant manager, a friend of my dad's.

We had just arrived home from school, all except my little brother, who was always home sick. At the age of seven, he hated to miss Graham Kerr's *The Galloping Gourmet*. He greeted us, dancing in his Dr. Denton's, screaming (despite the alleged sore throat), "Candy men came in a big truck and dumped hundreds of millions of candy bars in the basement." We all raced for the basement to see the floor covered with box after box of candy bars. One box was spilled over to reveal candy bars with different colored wrappings indicating plain, maple, and peanut butter flavors. Big bars, little bars, every bar chocolate-covered. My mother screamed behind us, "Just one before dinner, I mean it," as we plunged into the opened box, grabbing handfuls of candy, unwrapping them, and stuffing our mouths with maple-nut, peanut-butter–nut, and creamy plain. "Just one . . ." Her pleas faded in the screams and shouts. No one listened and no one ate dinner that night.

Naturally, someone had gotten the orders for a grocery store chain and the Woods family, of Arlington Heights, Illinois, mixed up. They never bothered to pick up the order. We were left with thousands of candy bars. We took gobs in our lunch bags to share with friends. Everyone came home with us to eat candy and watch *The Three Stooges.* And no one could leave our house without having some Bun candy bars shoved in their pockets or purses. "Please take a Bun," was our trademark offer to the mailman, the gas station attendant, and strangers on the street. I was very popular for a week in my neighborhood. And everyone met back at our house for a Bun after a big game of kick-the-can. With a shelf life of one thousand years, the Bun bars stayed in large bowls around our house for almost a year, through Christmas and Halloween. Everyone knew what they were going to eat at our house.

It took me two years to eat a candy bar again after the Bun barrage. And, twenty-five years later, I finally worked through my fear of cooking with chocolate thanks to The Great American Chocolate National Recipe Contest.™

How The Great American Chocolate National Recipe Contest ™ Was Judged

The contest was judged by everyday people identified as chocophiles, who donated their taste buds for a worthy cause. Some are experienced cooks, others are experienced eaters, and the results were a very fair representation of people tasting, evaluating, and scoring according to the rules. The chocophiles come from all parts of the United States, and chocolate recipes were tested in their respective categories without the judges knowing who the contestants were or where they lived. Chocophiles ranged in age from young, younger, youngest, and can-I-be-younger-than-her? When you're testing chocolate, we all become the same age. Carpenters, teachers, salespeople, physicians, students, writers, artists, corporate executives, office managers, social workers, lawyers, computer software geniuses, mothers, fathers, the working, and the retired all came together without much arm-twisting. There is a magic when you invite people to come taste chocolate. Few RSVPs were returned with a decline. Chocolate parties are a definite win/win situation.

Using an unbiased point system, the judges evaluated the recipes. Cash prizes were awarded to the prize winners in each category, and each contestant whose recipe was selected from hundreds of entries and published in the cookbook is an official Honorary Great American Chocolate National Recipe Contest™ Award Winner (referred to as an H.G.A.C.N.R.C.A.W. at Chocolate Heaven), and they received prizes for their contributions.

How to Use This Cookbook

All the recipes are kitchen-tested and may be somewhat modified from the contestant's original recipe for ease of use. However, we did attempt to maintain the integrity of the original recipe and either explain ingredients or steps or offer suggestions for more convenient substitutes. The important point is that *recipes are guidelines*. Baking powder, baking soda, and the like have their chemical reasons for being in a recipe, but flavorings are generally optional. If you don't like cinnamon, then don't use the spice even if it is specified, or substitute another spice.

Experiment with the recipe and vary it according to your tastes or your family's preferences. We always ended up somehow adding more chocolate in one way or another. I suggest you write your light-bulb ideas for modifications right in the cookbook next to the recipe. I know it's considered sacrilege to recommend defacing a book, but my hieroglyphs in a number of my cookbooks give them that personal touch. Plus, people seem to hesitate at "borrowing" a marked copy.

Advice for the Kitchen Maverick

Because I Said So! There are rules when it comes to cooking chocolate. And, as much as I am a plop-the-slop-in-the-pan-and-hope-for-the-best type of cook, there are reasons for the rules. For those of you who, like me, hate rules and tend to be belligerent rule-breakers in the kitchen, let's call them guidelines, helpful hints, tips . . . just make sure you do it.

My father, a wonderful man who came from the Captain Von Trapp school of disciplinarians, believed in the child psychology of "do or die." As a child, I did not know there was a question "Why?" until the hormones went wacko and I went through my rebellious years. When a rule or dictum was handed down from Dad Olympus and you dared to ask "Why?," the answer "Because I said so" usually halted further inquiry. I have found cookbooks to sometimes sound like my dad.

I used to watch *Leave It to Beaver* (reruns, okay?) and think, gee, Wally and the Beaver have their dad sit on their twin beds and explain to them why they have to do something or learn something. So, gee, cookbook readers, when I tell you to do something that seems pretty firm, I'll always try to explain why in a Ward Cleaver kind of way. Then, if you still won't do it . . . don't come crying to me when you're chocolate burns, your cake falls, or the cookie crumbles. And, like Ward and my dad, I may not have all the answers. You may just have to discover a thing or two on your own. But I'll do my best to anticipate and protect you as much as possible.

Read the introductions to the chapters for advice. Everyone reads the introductions to chapters about as avidly as they read term papers on nuclear fusion. But you will get some tried-and-true advice and guidelines that will help you in that particular chocolate category.

Speaking of nuclear fusion, baking is chemistry. Even though I avoided this class for fear of flunking, chocolate has taught me that science can be fun, and if more schools combined home economics and science classes, we'd have more scientists emerging who are also great cooks. But as in science, if you alter the proportions of, say, baking powder or baking soda, flour, sugar, and other important ingredients, you can create Chocostein monsters that are really frightening.

Get an oven thermometer. Let me repeat that. Get an oven thermometer. Why? Most ovens are not calibrated properly. In English: Home ovens have a great tendency to run hot or cold. So when you turn the dial to 350 degrees, the oven may actually be 400 or 300 degrees. An oven thermometer placed in the oven will give you the proper registration. I actually use two, because I'm paranoid. But I find an older oven thermometer that has fallen a few hundred times from the rack isn't accurate anymore. Go figure. Also, having knocked my thermometer to the bottom of the oven a few times, I have a tip: Take some picture-hanging wire or other thin wire and secure the thermometer to the rack in a convenient location. Remove it when you are cleaning the oven.

Since most ovens have cold and hot spots, turn the baking item halfway through the cooking time for even baking, especially to avoid the Leaning Tower of Pisa effect in cake baking.

Ingredient Information

Kinds of Chocolate Used in This Book

Here are some brief descriptions of the kinds of chocolate you will see used in this book.

Unsweetened Chocolate: Looks can be deceiving, and almost every person who is introduced to chocolate baking experiences the bitter truth with one bite into an unsweetened baking bar. It must be mixed with other ingredients to make it palatable. The U.S. Chocolate Police (The United States Standards of Identity) require the chocolate to contain between 50 percent and 58 percent cocoa liquor. Cocoa liquor comes from ground cocoa nibs (the "meat" of the cocoa bean without the husk) and is not sweet.

Bittersweet Baking Chocolate: To make bittersweet chocolate, sugar is added to unsweetened chocolate, but the result is not as sweet as a candy bar. This chocolate melts well for use in baking and is especially good for dipping and garnishing because no additional sugar is really needed. Baker's German's chocolate is an example.

Semisweet Chocolate: This is an American version of the European-style bittersweet chocolate, but it is usually slightly sweeter. This chocolate is available for baking and is produced by different manufacturers in the form of chips or morsels. Both bittersweet and semisweet chocolate contain at least 35 percent cocoa liquor.

Milk Chocolate: Although used primarily for eating, milk chocolate is becoming popular in baking, especially in the form of chocolate chips or as an ingredient in addition to other chocolate. The cocoa liquor content is at least 10 percent and is combined with dry milk products. The equivalent of 1 cup of milk is contained in a standard candy bar like a Hershey's Plain Milk Chocolate bar. Unlike the other forms of chocolate, milk chocolate may not store well over a long period of time. That's why that old smooshed Snickers bar stuck to the bottom of your purse since last summer just won't satisfy you.

White Chocolate: More than you really want to know about white chocolate is in the introduction to the chapter on page 273. Simply, it is not chocolate, hence the title of the chapter: "The Great White Lie—White Chocolate Cakes, Candy, and Desserts." Cocoa butter, sugar, powdered milk, and sometimes vanilla come together to create a smooth and versatile product for use in baking and candy making.

Chocolate Brands

In recipes not specifying a particular brand, we used Baker's chocolate. Available in the four I-states (Iowa, Idaho, Illinois, and Indiana) and nationwide, it is a convenient chocolate to use and is consistent in quality. Contestants may specify or suggest a variety of other chocolates, which may make a difference in their particular recipe. But use the ingredients that are available to you. If you wish to experiment with some of the European-produced chocolate, you are encouraged to try the amazing variety available in such recipes as Terri's Terrific Truffles with Almonds (page 232).

For white chocolate, we recommend you use a quality brand of white chocolate for ease of use and flavor. This is explained in more detail in the white chocolate chapter (see page 273). With the growing popularity of white chocolate, it is being manufactured and distributed more widely and is available at grocery stores throughout the United States.

When it came to chocolate chips, unless the contestant specified a particular brand, for consistency in testing and judging, we used Nestlé's.

Storing Chocolate

Store chocolate tightly wrapped and in a dark, cool place (no more than 75 degrees). Do not store chocolate in the refrigerator. The cold temperature may make the cocoa butter separate from the cocoa liquor, producing a "bloom," or white coloration on the chocolate.

Chocolate has a long shelf life. Finer quality chocolates (with high cocoa butter content and a longer manufacturing process, such as Valrhona or Lindt), like fine wine, actually improve with age, but this probably won't apply to your package of chocolate chips.

Chocolate is like an odor sponge and will pick up flavors surrounding it. So don't store your chocolate in the garlic keeper. Garlic and chocolate don't mix.

Every Christmas when I was growing up, a great and loving friend of my parents used to send us homemade goodies, each carefully and individually wrapped and beautifully presented in coffee cans. The chocolate-layered, peanut butter–filled candies and chocolate-covered almonds were too beautiful to eat. And most of the time we didn't. Because each of these fabulous chocolate-covered gems tasted like mothballs. Sometimes I would just suffer and eat the candy, closing my eyes (and nose) and imagining the chocolate taste like a mirage through the haze of mothball flavor.

It was not easy to write our thank-you notes each Christmas. My little brother had the direct approach: "Thank you for sending all these cans filled with really nice looking candies, but why do they taste like mothballs?" A rewrite was commanded.

Deducing that our friend probably stored the old coffee cans she used as candy containers in the wool closet stocked with moth protection, we sent her beautiful boxes to fill with her wonderful candies. The next year the candy arrived packaged in the brightly colored boxes we had given her. We were thrilled and madly unwrapped the candies and shoved them in our mouths. "Yuuuuuck!" was the universal utterance. She had apparently stored the beautiful boxes in the same closet where the snowy white Mount Killabunch-of-Moths certainly existed.

For the Chocolate Know-It-All

There is a section on page 13 called "More than You Ever Really Wanted to Know About Chocolate," which you may wish to peruse just in case you're in a Cliff Claven type of mood (now that I live in Boston, everything has a *Cheers* connection) and care to impress your friends with too much knowledge about a topic they really only want to eat.

Enjoy

Chocolate is also pronounced "fun." So have some chocolate and have some fun. From the chocolate lovers who contributed their recipes in this cookbook and all of us at Chocolate Heaven: Create, eat, and enjoy.

Chocolate-Loving Yours,
T. K. WOODS

More Than You Ever Really Wanted to Know About Chocolate

■ ■ ■

Great Moments in Chocolate History

1502—Columbus discovers the cocoa bean, which is used by natives in South America in a bitter chocolate beverage. Columbus takes the cocoa concoction back to Ferdinand and Isabella, who declare it disgusting.

1519—Montezuma, emperor of the Aztecs, introduces the Spanish explorer Cortés to his chocolate beverage known as *xocolatl* (pronounced "zo-co-lah-til" and meaning "bitter water"), which is served in golden goblets and consumed before a visit to the harems. Women are not allowed to drink this beverage, which may account for women's present-day passion for chocolate.

1615—Chocolate debuts in France when Anne of Austria, daughter of Philip III of Spain, marries Louis XIII of France and brings her favorite beverage with her.

1670s—Chocolate drinking is hot! Chocolate houses become favorite hangouts and gambling centers in London.

1700s—Quaker families the Cadburys, Frys, and Rowntrees (creator of the Kit-Kat bar) in England become chocolate producers in the hopes of replacing alcohol consumption with chocolate drinking.

1727—Hans Sloan of Switzerland invents milk chocolate.

1779—The first American chocolate company is founded by Dr. James Baker, and a factory is established in Milton, Massachusetts. The company is named Walter Baker and Company.

1828—Coenraad van Houten from Holland invents the press removing excess cocoa butter and creating cocoa powder. This revolutionizes chocolate production.

1847—Fry & Sons in England produces the first eating chocolates.

1852—Samuel German, an American and an employee of the Baker's company, adds sugar to bitter chocolate and creates German's Sweet Chocolate.

1875—Daniel Peter and Henri Nestlé of Vevey, Switzerland, produce milk chocolate for eating on a wide scale.

1894—Milton Snavely Hershey mass-produces America's first inexpensive and individually wrapped chocolate bar.

1907—Hershey's releases its first chocolate Kiss, which involves a patented process of inserting the signature blue and white slip inside the foil wrapping.

1912—The Whitman's Sampler of fine chocolates is first marketed in its recognizable yellow box, used by many kids thereafter for marbles, old crayons, and other precious pieces of junk.

1922—The Eskimo Pie, a chocolate-covered ice cream bar, is marketed. It was originally called the I-Scream Bar.

1930—Mrs. Ruth Wakefield of the Toll House Inn in Massachusetts, trying to melt bits of chocolate in cookie dough, accidentally creates the now famous tollhouse cookie and launches a demand for semisweet bits or morsels.

1994–1995—The Great American Chocolate National Recipe Contest™, one of the first nonsponsored national recipe contests, attracts creative recipes featuring chocolate in all its finest forms.

What Is Chocolate?

Since the magical myth of chocolate milk coming from a chocolate cow was first shattered, I have been fascinated with chocolate beginnings. Many a book report was done on this subject in school.

Cocoa beans are really seeds produced by the cacao tree, or *Theobroma cacoa*. Most of the world's cacao trees are located in the Ivory Coast, Ecuador, Brazil, and Ghana. *Theobroma* means "food of the gods." This is a precious and precarious food. As chocolate is temperamental in cooking, it is also temperamental in growing. The trees take up to seven years to mature. The pods have to be carefully harvested primarily by hand because the slightest damage can kill the tree. Like coffee beans, cocoa beans are affected by the slightest fluctuation in temperature.

Once the cocoa pods have been harvested by hand, they are opened and the fruit of the pods is allowed to ferment, which increases the character and flavor of the cocoa bean. After fermentation, the beans are dried and sorted. They are then sent around the world to their respective processing establishments, for example, Hershey, Pennsylvania, or Callebaut, Belgium, or the Rhone Valley in France, where mouthwatering Valrhona chocolate is produced. There, the beans are roasted to the desired flavor.

After roasting, the shell of the cocoa bean is removed, leaving the meat, known as the nib. The nibs are then crushed to create two substances: chocolate liquor and cocoa butter. The chocolate liquor is then mixed back with the cocoa butter (other, less expensive fats may sometimes be used instead) in combination with milk products, sugar, and vanilla. The mixture is then further ground in a process known as conching, which grinds the chocolate to a smooth texture. Some manufacturers conch the chocolate for only twelve hours and others conch for up to seven days, adding more cocoa butter to increase the quality and smoothness. More cocoa butter content and the longer the conching period, the higher the grade and quality of the chocolate. And, if you really want to know, the reason they called it conching is that the implement originally used for stirring the chocolate resembled a conch shell.

According to the Chocolate Manufacturers Association, in the United States an average of 11 pounds of chocolate is eaten per person per year, and this figure applies just to candy bars and chocolate confections, not the chocolate chips and chocolate used in baking. This chocostatistic has increased from 8 pounds a person just a few years ago. But we do not hold the title for top consumer: Twelve other countries consume more chocolate than the United States, including France, Great Britain, Norway, and Switzerland, which is the top consumer at 21.7 pounds per person. That's why the name of the country is really pronounced "Sweetzerland." If you ever have the opportunity to try European chocolate—for example, Belgian chocolate—you'll understand why the Europeans are the champion chocolate eaters of the world.

And whenever you eat some chocolate or use a pound of chocolate in your baking, think of this: It took approximately 400 cocoa beans to make that one pound of chocolate just for you. But don't feel guilty, you deserve it.

Chocolate Is Bad for You . . . and Other Great Myths

■ ■ ■

*"If I had my life to live over again,
I'd eat more chocolate."*

—motto at Chocolate Heaven

Chocolate is loaded with caffeine. Wrong! A milk chocolate bar (1.5 ounces) has about 9 milligrams of caffeine compared with a cup of coffee, which has about 115 milligrams. Suspected culprit for spreading this rumor: Juan Valdez, who really wanted to be a cocoa bean grower.

Chocolate causes cavities. Wrong! Not brushing causes cavities. In fact, a number of studies have found that chocolate may actually inhibit tooth decay. There is a substance in cocoa that prevents the breakdown of sucrose into glucose and fructose, which both encourage bacteria growth, the real cause of tooth decay.

Chocolate is an aphrodisiac. Do you think I'm going to blow this myth? I want to believe in something. Chocolate contains phenylethylamine, a chemical substance that supposedly contributes to that giddy feeling when one is "in love." But scientists have found that there is even more phenylethylamine in sauerkraut! And I've never noticed any of my female friends, after a heart-wrenching breakup, say, "Hey, I'll skip burying myself in a gallon of Double Chocolate Fudge Dream Ice Cream and dive headfirst into a pint of sauerkraut." For a double dose of phenylethylamine just in case, see the Chocolate Sauerkraut Cake by Lorraine Langlois on page 108.

Chocolate causes acne. Yes, chocolate does cause acne when you smear it on your face and don't wash if off for a week. But if you eat it, according to several dermatological studies, chocolate does not cause acne. If you are eating chocolate while under stress and you break out, don't get rid of the chocolate, get rid of the stress.

Carob is a healthier alternative to chocolate. About five hundred years ago, the Indians of Central America revered the cocoa bean as a gift from the gods and used it as currency. Land, cows, even women were purchased with cocoa beans. Meanwhile, in the Middle East, carob pods were being thrown on the ground as cattle feed. Hmmm, something to think about.

But carob is a good alternative if any amount of caffeine, even the negligible amount in chocolate, cannot be tolerated, since carob contains no caffeine. Chocolate and carob are similar in makeup and processing. Carob is produced from the dried pulp of the carob pod. It contains its own sugar, whereas cocoa must have sugar added to it. This is where people may feel more comfortable with it as a "natural" product. Although chocolate is more than 33 percent fat (cocoa butter), carob confections and coatings are usually made with palm kernel oil, which is a saturated fat that raises cholesterol levels even more than cocoa butter. Also, FYI, while carob may not contain caffeine, it does contain tannin, an astringent substance used in tanning or dyeing leather. So it's all reduced to a matter of choice.

> *"Chocolate is forever and ever until I have to*
> *consume it through an IV."*
> —*diehard chocolate lover's motto*

A mythnomer: Women have a special relationship with chocolate. This is true. Scientific studies have proven it. That's why the chocolate manufacturer Hershey (HER-SHEE) is not known as Hishim. Men may come and go, but the love of chocolate is forever. It's always there when you crave it. The love is faithful and the satisfaction is guaranteed. In a survey, 50 percent of women said they would choose chocolate over sex. In the book *Why Women Need Chocolate* (Hyperion, 1995), Debra Waterhouse, M.P.H., R.D., has researched why the female biology triggers a need for chocolate and other foods, and how women can benefit physically and emotionally by responding to these cravings. She has found chocolate is the number-one food women crave. And she elaborates on why women actually need the combination of fat and sugar and why chocolate is essentially the perfect food for women to indulge in. She also explains how to satisfy these cravings in a healthy manner.

The Lighter Side of Chocolate: Fat-Reducing Tips

■ ■ ■

*"He desperately wanted something more filling
and satisfying than cabbage and cabbage soup.
The one thing he longed for more than
anything else was . . . CHOCOLATE."*
—*Roald Dahl*, Charlie and the Chocolate Factory

Like Eating a Mink Coat

Chocolate has fat. Okay? Now, I love this fat, because it's why chocolate melts in your mouth and contributes to it's luxurious velvetiness. I'm going to tell you the good news and the bad news about fat and chocolate:

The bad news: Unsweetened chocolate, used in baking, has 76 percent of its calories from fat. That is why it is known as bittersweet. Milk chocolate has 50 percent fat, and cocoa powder has 30 percent fat calories.

The good news: No-no becomes yes-yes with cocoa butter. Although cocoa butter is a no-no saturated fat, studies conducted at the University of Texas Southwestern Medical Center at Dallas have found that stearic acid, the type of saturated fat found in cocoa butter, does not—I repeat, does not—elevate blood cholesterol levels like other saturated fats. The stearic acid may actually help lower blood cholesterol levels (LDLs—low-density lipoproteins) without affecting HDLs (high-density lipoproteins), which are the good cholesterol that can help reduce the risk of cardiovascular disease.

Chocolate engineers are working on a reduced-fat chocolate that could be used in baking. We'll keep you posted. But it's like making a mink coat into polyester.

Until that miracle invention occurs, you can control the fat content of most of the other ingredients used in baking. Here are some guidelines for substitution:

- There are many fat-reduced brands of ingredients you can substitute in the recipes. For example, fat-reduced Oreo cookies, low-fat and fat-free sour cream, plain low-fat yogurt, low-fat mayonnaise, and low-fat cream cheese. There's even fat-reduced peanut butter. Hallelujah!
- Most buttermilk you purchase today is low-fat.
- For recipes using milk, use 1 percent milk or substitute skim milk, if you wish.
- Several of the recipes use sweetened condensed milk and/or evaporated milk, and there are reduced-fat versions of both that provide the same flavor and consistency.
- A Note About Butter: For those watching cholesterol, although butter is required in several recipes, at times the ingredients list will give the option of using margarine or a butter substitute. Be aware that you cannot always substitute margarine for butter. Margarine has more moisture and may affect the texture of your recipe. This is especially true of cookies, which will tend to spread if margarine is substituted when not specified.
- There are several recipes in the book that use cocoa powder as the chocolate ingredient, and cocoa powder has just 30 percent fat.

Chocolate and Dieting

As you probably already know, low in fat does not mean low in calories. But psychologists have suggested you allow yourself the indulgence of some chocolate while dieting. Going down the diet aisle of the grocery store is like surveying the Ben and Jerry's chocolate selection of the diet world, with products promising you slimness by drinking chocolate mocha malts and eating candy bars. Simply amazing. Maybe if we had real chocolate in small, satisfying, guilt-reduced or even guilt-free amounts, we could hop off the binge-y cord of yo-yo dieting.

Omit the Guilt

Do we have this fear we may never see chocolate again? That somehow it will break the law of gravity and float far from our reach? With all the political unrest in the world, could there ever be a chocolate embargo? Is that why when we have chocolate we have to eat it *all* . . . until it's all gone?

Let me assure you there will always be chocolate. It's up to you not to feed the fear factor by denying yourself that one truffle or small piece of chocolate cake.

Chocolate in its true form can be so satisfying and truly give women a feeling of well being. According to Debra Waterhouse (see page 18), if we satisfy the chocolate cravings without denial and without guilt, we will not trigger binge eating. By properly taking care of our bodies and minds, we can have our chocolate cake and eat it too.

Busting the Sugar Blues: Using Natural Sweeteners and Unrefined Sugars

■ ■ ■

When you use it in baking, sugar is not just for sweetening. When used in cake baking, for example, the sugar slows down the development of gluten in flour in the batter and inhibits the setting of the protein in the flour, allowing the cake to rise to full volume. That is why it may take some experimenting if you wish to reduce the sugar, or try using low-calorie sugar substitutes. Sugar substitutes are usually made with aspartame or saccharin, which do not always heat well. The sugar substitutes also seem to impart a different flavor. But let me not discourage you from experimenting and becoming the first on your block to create a Chocolate Sweet 'n Low Cake.

Concerned parents and individuals who wish to curtail the consumption of white sugar can use the following guidelines for the use of sugar alternatives such as honey, fructose, and naturally processed sugar.

We have tested selected recipes using these guidelines, but not all of them. You may wish to combine the use of sugar alternatives with low-fat ingredients to healthify the chocolate creations in this book.

Using Honey

Honey is produced by bees from the nectar of flowers. According to the National Honey Board in Longmont, Colorado, there are about three hundred honey flavors. Surprised? I know I was. Busy bees.

To use honey as a sugar substitute here are some guidelines:

- Infants under the age of one year should not be fed honey.
- Honey is more intense in sweetness than granulated sugar. Therefore, use only 1 cup honey for every 1¼ cups granulated sugar and reduce proportionately if necessary.
- Reduce the amount of liquid in the recipe by ¼ cup for each cup of honey used. Don't include vanilla or other flavorings used in small quantity in this reduction, however.
- Add ½ teaspoon baking soda for each cup of honey used. This will help with the rising process. You may need to experiment with this.
- Reduce the oven temperature by 25 degrees when baking with honey to prevent over-browning.

For a delicious recipe using honey as a sweetener, try Sally-Mary Cashman's "Heavenly Devil's Food Surprise Cake" on page 163. For honey-flavored whipped cream and frosting recipes, see "Topping It All Off," on page 297.

Sugar as a Natural Blond

Sugar is born to be blond. Referred to as unrefined sugar, turbinado sugar from natural cane comes packaged in a widely distributed brand known as Sugar in the Raw, which can be found in the natural or dietetic foods sections of your grocery store or health food store. Turbinado sugar contains the same amount of sucrose as refined white granulated sugar, but it is cleaned more than raw sugar while still retaining up to 5 percent of the natural molasses that gives it its blond color and enhanced flavor. In comparison, commercial brown sugar is refined and has molasses added to it for flavor and color, but it has less sucrose than plain refined sugar.

If it is your preference to use turbinado sugar in your baking, keep in mind that it is not as fine in texture as granulated white sugar, so we recommend that you process it to a finer texture in the food processor or blender before measuring and using it in baking. The sugar may be substituted without modification for granulated sugar. Recipes calling for brown sugar may require less of the turbinado in substitution.

Fructose

Another sugar substitute is fructose, also available in the dietetic section of your grocery store or health food store. Fructose is a natural sweetener derived in a granulated form (it looks like sugar) from honey, fruit, and berries. It is sweeter than refined granulated sugar. Fructose may be used as an alternative to granulated sugar as an ingredient in baking with these guidelines:

- Use approximately ⅓ less fructose than the specified amount of granulated sugar in a recipe (the exact amount will depend on your taste and the desired sweetness).
- Reduce the oven temperature by 25 degrees.
- Baking time may increase by 5 to 10 minutes. Check the item after the specified baking time and give it another 5 to 10 minutes if it isn't quite done.

Fructose may be used for and consumed by people with diabetes, but you should check with your physician first.

For those of you with friends or family members who cannot tolerate too much sugar, there is a recipe on page 205, Brenda's Sugar-Free Dirt Cake, developed by Brenda Webb of Clarksville, Arkansas, for her husband, who is a diabetic. You can use the alternative ingredients in this delicious cake as a guideline for effectively reducing the sugar quantity in other recipes in that chapter as well as throughout the book.

Effective Methods for Melting Chocolate

■ ■ ■

I've already found every way to scorch chocolate—now you can avoid them. Because chocolate scorches easily, direct heat is not recommended unless the chocolate is combined with another ingredient in the recipe. I prefer the microwave to melt chocolate because it is fast and there is no possibility of moisture hitting the chocolate. This is also the method recommended by chocolate professionals.

Microwave Method

Place the desired amount of chocolate into a microwave-safe bowl. Heat the chocolate on high power* for 20 seconds, stirring afterward to disperse the heat. If necessary, heat for another 10 seconds, stirring again afterward.

Double-Boiler Method

If you don't have a double boiler, use a heatproof bowl that fits well over a large saucepan. Fill the bottom of the double boiler or saucepan with water so that it comes close to the bottom of the bowl or top double boiler without actually touching it. Place over

---

*Microwaves have a wide range of wattages, so to be on the safe side and to familiarize yourself with this method, you may want to try it slowly (for a microwave) at medium (or 50 percent power) at 1-minute intervals.

moderate heat and bring the water to a simmer, *not* a boil. When the water is simmering, add the desired amount of chocolate to the double boiler or bowl and stir until melted. Do not let the water boil, because any moisture, even a drop, can cause the melted chocolate to stiffen, or "seize." If this happens, remove the chocolate from the heat, add 1 tablespoon shortening or oil, and stir. Return to the heat and continue adding shortening or oil 1 tablespoon at a time to restore the chocolate to a melted state.

Oven Method

Preheat the oven to 250 degrees. Put the chocolate in a shallow baking dish or a standard loaf pan (9 × 5 × 3 inches) and place in the oven. Heat the chocolate, stirring frequently (every 3 to 5 minutes), until completely melted. Watch carefully to avoid scorching.

Bread, Muffins, Coffee Cakes, and Chocolate

■ ■ ■

*"A jug of milk, a loaf of
chocolate bread and thou."*

—Omar I Am a Chocolate Lover

*read and Chocolate** is a wonderful Italian movie. It's also a
wonderful combination of foods that is relished by Europeans but is not as well celebrated here—something we hope
to change in this chapter.

Tips for Success

The recipes here are all quick breads that require no yeast. The
following tips will ensure your success making breads, muffins, and
coffee cakes:

- Don't overbeat the batter. This kind of batter needs a light
  touch, which is best achieved with a wooden spoon or a fork.

Bread and Chocolate (1978), Franco Brusati, director. "Nino Manfredi is marvelous as a
Chaplinesque everyman, an optimistic lower class worker who treks to Switzerland to make
his fortune yet remains the eternal outsider. Memorable sequence in a chicken coop." ★★★½,
from *Leonard Maltin's TV Movies and Videos Guide*.

- Mix the dry ingredients with the wet ingredients by making a well in the center of the dry ingredients and pouring the wet ingredients into the well. Then mix the batter for about 20 seconds for muffins and maybe a little longer for breads. Lumps are OK. Overmixing the batter creates "tunnels," which are handy for getting through mountains, but not muffins. Overmixing muffin batter can also toughen the texture, making it rubbery.
- For breads, coffee cakes, and muffins, mix all the dry ingredients together first to evenly distribute the baking soda and/or baking powder.
- Be sure to use baking powder that was made in this century. Baking powder that is past its expiration date produces flat, leaden muffins. And don't use baking soda that has been sitting in your refrigerator open for several months.
- Always line your muffin pans with paper cups or generously and thoroughly grease each cup.
- Let muffins cool in the pan for 1 to 2 minutes, unless otherwise instructed, then remove them immediately. If the muffins or breads remain in the pan too long, they can get soggy from the steam. Yuck.

Freezing

Leftover breads and muffins may be stored in an airtight container. And, yes you can freeze them: wrap them first in a layer of wax paper and then in aluminum foil. Make sure you label the package and mark the date so you are not left wondering what's inside the metallic UFO stuck between the ice cream bars and the ground round.

Coffee cakes do not freeze as well and should be eaten within one or two days of preparation. Use the "it will go stale" routine to encourage your guests to "help" you out in consuming it all in one sitting.

Oven Note

You'll see this "Oven Note" repeated in a lot of chapters, but it's important, so get used to it: Use an oven thermometer to accurately gauge your oven's temperature, because most ovens are not calibrated correctly (they can run "cold" or "hot"). Always check for doneness about 5 minutes before the end of the suggested baking time, just to make sure you don't burn your bread, muffins, or coffee cake.

The Perfect Marriage Muffins

Jo Ann Mullen · Honolulu, Hawaii

■ ■ ■

"Good Morning Sunshine, Good Morning Chocolate.
Chocolate in the morning, starts the day off right.
—*Good Morning Chocolate* by Margaret A. Wise Brownie

Choc Talk: If you can't have a perfect marriage between two people, you might as well have it in muffins. Chocolate, cherry, and coconut marry beautifully in this recipe. Volunteer to bring these muffins to the next brunch or office breakfast meeting—they are easy, pretty, and delicious.

"My husband prefers chocolate, but I love coconut, and we both love cherries. This is a perfect marriage of all three flavors and our favorite baked treat. They are easy to take on picnics."
—Jo Ann Mullen

Yield: *24 muffins* **Preparation Time:** *10 minutes* **Baking Time:** *12 to 15 minutes* **Bakeware Required:** *Two 12-cup muffin pans, well greased or lined with paper baking cups*

3 ounces semisweet chocolate	*½ cup walnuts, pecans, or*
⅔ cup unsalted butter	*almonds, coarsely chopped**
1⅓ cups all-purpose flour	*½ cup sweetened flaked coconut*
2 cups granulated sugar	*1 teaspoon almond extract*
1 teaspoon baking powder	*24 maraschino cherries,*
4 large eggs, lightly beaten	*stemmed but not drained*

Preheat the oven to 350 degrees.

1. Melt the chocolate (for effective methods and instructions, see page 27). Set aside to cool completely.

*For extra nutty flavor, spread the nuts on a cookie sheet and toast them in a preheated 350 degree oven for 10 to 15 minutes. Stir the nuts occasionally to toast them evenly and prevent buring. Or, toast the nuts in the microwave (they will not change color but they will taste toasted). Place 1 cup nuts on a paper plate and microwave uncovered on high power for 3 to 4 minutes, rotating the plate a half turn after 2 minutes.

2. Melt the butter. Set aside to cool.

3. In a mixing bowl, sift together the flour, sugar, and baking powder. Make a well in the flour mixture and place the eggs and cooled melted butter in the well. Stir until just blended.

4. Transfer two thirds of the batter to another bowl and add the melted chocolate and nuts, stirring to combine the mixture. Fill the prepared muffin pans half full with the batter.

5. Mix the coconut and almond extract into the remaining batter. Spoon this mixture evenly on top of the chocolate batter in each of the muffin pans.

6. Place a maraschino cherry in the center of each muffin pan, and press lightly into the batter. Bake for 12 to 15 minutes, or until the coconut is just golden. Do not overbake. Let the muffins cool in the pan for 1 to 2 minutes, then carefully remove and place on a wire rack to cool.

The I-Man's Double-Chocolate Muffins

Chocolate, Coffee, and "Imus in the Morning"

Chocolate Heaven Creation

■ ■ ■

***C**hoc Talk:* Many, many mornings, I would test chocolate recipes and listen to "Imus in the Morning," a nationally syndicated radio show out of New York. I learned I could actually laugh in the morning on only two cups of coffee. And that was before I saw myself in the mirror. On "Imus in the Morning" there is always a lighter side to the news, thanks to Charles McCord, who laughs like Renfield from the Bela Lugosi version of *Dracula*. Chocolate and laughter go together. Thanks, Imus, for jump-starting my mornings and letting me be the first to name a chocolate muffin after you. You deserve it.

Yield: *16 muffins* **Preparation Time:** *15 minutes* **Baking Time:** *15 to 20 minutes* **Bakeware Required:** *Two 8-cup muffin pans, well greased or lined with paper baking cups*

5 ounces semisweet chocolate	*2 large eggs*
2 ounces unsweetened chocolate	*1 teaspoon vanilla extract*
⅓ cup unsalted butter	*1½ cups all-purpose flour*
¾ cup sour cream	*1 teaspoon baking soda*
⅔ cup firmly packed light	*¼ teaspoon salt*
* brown sugar*	*6 ounces semisweet or milk*
¼ cup light corn syrup	* chocolate chips*

Preheat the oven to 375 degrees.

1. Melt the semisweet and unsweetened chocolate with the butter (for effective methods and instructions, see page 27). Set aside to cool completely.

2. Add the sour cream, brown sugar, corn syrup, eggs, and vanilla to the cooled chocolate and butter and mix well.

3. In a separate bowl, combine the flour, baking soda, and salt. Make a well in the flour mixture and pour the chocolate mixture into the well. Stir until just blended. The batter will be lumpy. Stir in the chocolate chips. (If using variations below you may wish to omit the chocolate chips.)

4. Pour the batter evenly into the prepared muffin pans, filling three fourths full. Bake for 15 to 20 minutes, or until a toothpick inserted in the center of a muffin comes out clean. Let the muffins cool in the pan for 3 minutes, then carefully remove and place on a wire rack to cool.

Variations: Laughter in the morning sparked my creative engines. So here are some other muffin ideas:

I-Man's Surprise Kiss: Place a Hershey's Chocolate Kiss or Hug in the middle of each muffin before baking.

I-Man's a Peanut: Place a Reese's miniature peanut butter cup in the center of each muffin before baking.

I-Man Goes Nuts: Add 1 cup chopped pecans or walnuts or salted sunflower seeds to the muffin batter.

It's a Rocky Road I-Man: Now, don't get grossed out, but miniature marshmallows and peanuts are delicious in these muffins (1 cup miniature marshmallows and ½ cup salted roasted peanuts). When we made these muffins, we had kids asking if they could "please, pretty please" have breakfast with us. And we don't even know these kids.

Lizbeth's Low-Fat 'Nilla-'Nana Chocolate Chip Muffins

Elizabeth Howard

■ ■ ■

Chocolate Heaven Assistant Chocolatier

hoc Talk: Elizabeth wanted to make muffins using low-fat vanilla yogurt and applesauce. She developed these banana-vanilla chocolate chip muffins. Elizabeth's mom, Jean, shared with us her secret for moist cakes—adding baby food. It really works! I just had to calm my poor, excited mother when she saw her child-less daughter had baby food jars in the cabinet. (See Recipe Note for variation.)

"Silly Lilly making muffins but they weren't quite right.
Her friend Lizbeth soon came over and showed her the light.
Add some 'nilla and some 'nanas and they will be yummy.
Add a lot o' chocolate chips, I'll put them in my tummy."
—Elizabeth Howard (nursery rhyme inspired after eating leftover jars of baby food)

Yield: *16 muffins* **Preparation Time:** *10 minutes* **Baking Time:** *10 to 15 minutes* **Bakeware Required:** *Two 8-cup muffin pans, well greased or lined with paper muffin cups*

1 cup granulated sugar	10 ounces semisweet chocolate
1 large egg	chips
2 ripe bananas, mashed	2 cups all-purpose flour
⅓ cup applesauce (sweetened or	1 teaspoon baking powder
unsweetened)	1 teaspoon baking soda
One 8-ounce container vanilla-	½ teaspoon salt
flavored low-fat yogurt	

Preheat the oven to 375 degrees.

1. In a large bowl, combine the sugar and the egg and blend well. Add the mashed bananas, applesauce, and yogurt and stir to combine. Stir in the chocolate chips.

2. In a separate bowl, combine the flour, baking powder, baking soda, and salt. Make a well in the center of the flour mixture and pour the wet ingredients into the well. Stir until just blended. The batter will be lumpy.

3. Pour the batter evenly into the prepared muffin pans. Bake for 10 to 15 minutes, or until a toothpick inserted in the center of a muffin comes out clean. This is a light-colored muffin so be careful not to overbake. Let the muffins cool in the pan for 2 to 3 minutes, then carefully remove and place on a wire rack to cool.

Recipe Note: Substitute two 4-ounce jars of banana baby food (such as Gerber) for the applesauce and use just 1 ripe banana. Or try other baby food fruits such as pineapple, apple, or plum.

Willodean's Cream Cheese Chocolate Coffee Cake

Willodean Hopkins · North Little Rock, Arkansas

■ ■ ■

***C**hoc Talk:* Coffee cakes are perfect for those days when you have the time to sit around and shoot the breeze. This is a traditional coffee cake filled with cream cheese, topped with brown sugar, and sprinkled with nuts. But chocolate is the secret ingredient.

Yield: *10 to 12 servings* **Preparation Time:** *20 minutes* **Baking Time:** *25 to 30 minutes* **Bakeware Required:** *Two 9-inch round cake pans, greased*

CAKE

12 ounces semisweet chocolate chips
3 tablespoons unsalted butter
2 cups all-purpose flour
1 teaspoon baking powder
1 teaspoon baking soda
¼ teaspoon salt
1 cup solid vegetable shortening
1 cup granulated sugar
3 large eggs
1 cup sour cream
1 teaspoon vanilla extract

FILLING

One 8-ounce package cream cheese, softened
3 tablespoons unsalted butter

1½ teaspoons all-purpose flour
¼ cup granulated sugar
½ teaspoon vanilla extract

TOPPING

½ cup firmly packed light brown sugar
½ cup granulated sugar
1 teaspoon ground cinnamon
½ teaspoon ground nutmeg

GARNISH

1 cup chopped walnuts or pecans

Preheat the oven to 350 degrees.

To Make the Cake

1. Melt the chocolate chips with the butter (for effective methods and instructions, see page 27). Set aside to cool, but do not let the mixture harden.

2. In a large bowl, combine the flour, baking powder, baking soda, and salt.

3. In a separate bowl, cream the shortening and sugar together. Add the eggs one at a time, beating well after each addition. Add the melted chocolate mixture, sour cream, and vanilla and blend thoroughly.

4. Add the flour mixture to the wet ingredients and stir until just blended. Set aside.

To Make the Filling

1. In a medium bowl, combine the cream cheese, butter, flour, sugar, and vanilla and mix well. (Optional: Stir in ½ cup chocolate chips or mini chocolate chips. See Recipe Note.) Set aside.

To Make the Topping

1. In a small bowl, mix the brown sugar, granulated sugar, cinnamon, and nutmeg. Set aside.

Putting It All Together

1. Pour only one quarter of the cake batter evenly into each of the two pans. Spread half the cream cheese filling evenly on top of the batter in each pan. Sprinkle one quarter of the topping mixture over the filling layer in each pan.

2. Top the filling layer with the remaining cake batter. Sprinkle with more of the topping. You may have more topping left over.

3. Garnish each cake evenly with the chopped nuts. Bake for 25 to 30 minutes, or until a toothpick inserted in the center of each cake comes out clean. Let the cakes cool partially. Serve warm from the pan with a big pot of coffee and lots of friends, or just one best friend who shares your passion for chocolate.

Recipe Note: For an even more chocolaty taste, which I am never opposed to, add ½ cup semisweet chocolate chips (or mini semisweet chocolate chips) to the cream cheese filling.

Path the Heath Coffee Cake, Pleath

■ ■ ■

Choc Talk: "Thally thells theathells by the theathore and Thally altho thells Heath bars." When I was four years old, I had a terrible lis(th)p. Although it was cute in a four-year-old, my parents had the angst of envisioning me as a still lisping, socially inept, forty-year-old spinster living at home. So my father worked with me every night after work as he sipped his martini. He would have me repeat over and over the "Sally sells seashells" routine. I thought it was more interesting if she sold Heath bars, my favorite candy bar. In honor of the fact that now I enunciate pretty well, thanks to speech therapy with my dad, I bring to you the "Path the Heath Coffee Cake, Pleath." (Sometimes I slip back into a lis(th)p when I write.)

Yield: *8 to 10 servings* **Preparation Time:** *15 minutes* **Baking Time:** *30 to 40 minutes* **Bakeware Required:** *9 × 12-inch baking pan, greased*

COFFEE CAKE
¼ cup unsalted butter, softened
½ cup firmly packed light brown sugar
½ cup granulated sugar
1 large egg
1 teaspoon vanilla extract
1½ cups all-purpose flour
½ cup unsweetened cocoa

1 teaspoon baking soda
1 cup buttermilk
*1½ cups chopped Heath English Toffee Bars**

TOPPING
½ cup chopped pecans
*½ cup chopped Heath English Toffee Bars**

*The two cups total for this recipe equals approximately four to five 1.55-ounce candy bars, chopped, or you can use the new Heath Sensations, which are already broken into pieces.

Preheat the oven to 350 degrees.

To Make the Coffee Cake

1. In a large bowl, cream the butter, brown sugar, and granulated sugar together. Add the egg and mix well. Add the vanilla and mix well.

2. In a separate bowl, sift together the flour, cocoa, and baking soda.

3. Stir the dry ingredients into the creamed mixture in thirds, alternating with the buttermilk. Stir in the chopped Heath bars.

4. Pour the batter into the prepared pan and set aside.

To Make the Topping

1. In a medium bowl, stir the chopped pecans and chopped Heath bars together until well blended.

Putting It All Together

1. Sprinkle the topping over the batter in the pan. Bake for 30 to 40 minutes, or until a toothpick inserted in the center of the cake comes out clean. Let the cake cool slightly in the pan. Serve warm from the pan.

Recipe Note: It is best to chop the Heath bars in a food processor or blender, but be careful not to pulverize them. The fabulous Heath people knew what all of us Heath lovers were doing crushing up their candy bar, so they came out with a new product, available in candy sections, called Heath Sensations—chocolate-covered bits-o-Heath. This works just as well.

Hoosier Chocolate Bread

Jean Willour · Bristol, Indiana

■ ■ ■

Family and Friends Chocolate Lover Category

hoc Talk: Jean is Elizabeth Howard's mom. Not only did Jean provide us with Elizabeth, a dedicated chocolate lover who works at Chocolate Heaven, but she also gave us this fabulous bread recipe. This is a family favorite and is now one of our favorites.

Approximate Yield: *2 loaves (16 servings)* **Preparation Time:** *5 minutes* **Baking Time:** *50 to 55 minutes* **Bakeware Required:** *Two 9 × 5 × 3-inch loaf pans, well greased*

½ cup unsweetened cocoa plus 2 tablespoons for dusting pans

2 cups all-purpose flour

1⅓ cups granulated sugar

1½ teaspoons baking soda

1 teaspoon vanilla extract

1½ cups buttermilk

1 cup mayonnaise

12 ounces semisweet chocolate chips

1 cup pecans, chopped

GARNISHES

10 to 15 pecan halves

2 to 3 tablespoons confectioners' sugar

Preheat the oven to 350 degrees.

1. Place 1 tablespoon unsweetened cocoa in each well-greased loaf pan. Shake each pan and tilt it until it is coated with the cocoa (on the bottom and all the way up the sides). Shake out the excess cocoa. (If you are using nonstick pans, you may only need to lightly grease and dust the pans, if at all.)

2. Combine the flour, ½ cup cocoa, sugar, baking soda, vanilla, buttermilk, and mayonnaise in a large bowl and blend well. Add the chocolate chips and chopped pecans and mix thoroughly.

3. Pour the batter evenly into the loaf pans and arrange the pecan halves on top of the batter for each loaf. Bake for 50 to 55 minutes, or until a toothpick inserted in the center of each loaf

comes out clean. Do not overbake. Let the loaves cool completely on a wire rack before turning them out of the pans. If necessary, use a knife to separate the bread from the pans' sides. When they are cool, sprinkle with confectioners' sugar and serve.

Presentation Note: This makes a great holiday gift bread.

Recipe Notes: The baked bread freezes well. You can eat one and freeze one, although most of the time the second bread never makes it to the freezer. • The recipe can be easily cut in half to make one loaf. • Make mini loaves by dividing the batter among four 5¾ × 3¼ × 2¼-inch mini loaf pans; reduce the baking time to 30 to 40 minutes.

Chunky Choco-Nut Bread

Sandra Bradley · Ward, Arkansas

■ ■ ■

***C**hoc Talk:* Sandra's recipe is a super fusion of a chocolate chip cookie and nut bread.

"My husband requested something different—he was tired of nut bread, so I decided to turn a chocolate chip cookie into bread. It worked perfectly on the first try. He loved it!" —Sandra Bradley

Yield: *8 to 10 servings* **Preparation Time:** *5 to 10 minutes* **Baking Time:** *50 minutes* **Bakeware Required:** *Two 9 × 5 × 3-inch loaf pans or four 5¾ × 3¼ × 2¼-inch mini loaf pans, greased and dusted with unsweetened cocoa or all-purpose flour*

1 cup firmly packed light brown sugar	*1½ cups all-purpose flour*
½ cup unsalted butter or margarine	*1 teaspoon baking soda*
1 large egg	*1 teaspoon baking powder*
l cup sour cream	*2½ cups milk chocolate chunks* or chips, divided*
1 teaspoon vanilla extract	*1¼ cups coarsely chopped pecans, divided*

Preheat the oven to 350 degrees.

1. In a large mixing bowl, cream the sugar and butter together. Add the egg, sour cream, and vanilla, beating well after each addition.

2. In a separate bowl, combine the flour, baking soda, and baking powder. Gradually add the dry ingredients to the creamed mixture and stir to combine.

3. Gently fold into the batter 2 cups of the milk chocolate chunks and 1 cup of the chopped pecans.

---

*Use your favorite chocolate candy bar (approximately three to four 5-ounce bars) and chop with a sharp knife so the chunks are big.

4. Spoon the batter into the prepared pans. Bake for 50 minutes, or until a toothpick inserted in the center of the loaves comes out clean. (If you are using mini loaf pans, reduce the baking time to 20 to 30 minutes.) Let the loaves cool in the pans on a wire rack for 10 to 15 minutes.

5. Meanwhile, melt the remaining ½ cup milk chocolate chunks (for effective methods and instructions, see page 27). Carefully remove the cooled loaves from the pans and drizzle the melted chocolate over the top. Sprinkle with the remaining chopped pecans.

Chocolate Zuke Bread

Leslie Knowles · Kent, Washington

■ ■ ■

*C*hoc Talk: Zucchini for breakfast has never been more appealing. Don't tell anyone the bread is made with zucchini until *after* they've eaten a few slices. Many people seem to have this "thing" about eating vegetables in the morning unless they're buried in an omelette. What they don't know won't hurt them.

Yield: *16 servings* **Preparation Time:** *10 to 15 minutes* **Baking Time:** *50 minutes* **Bakeware Required:** *Two 9 × 5 × 3-inch loaf pans or four 5¾ × 3¼ × 2¼-inch mini loaf pans, well greased and floured or dusted with unsweetened cocoa*

continued

4 ounces (1 bar) Baker's
German's sweetened
chocolate
1 cup vegetable oil
3 large eggs
2 cups granulated sugar
3 teaspoons vanilla extract
2 cups shredded zucchini
3 cups all-purpose flour, sifted

1 teaspoon salt
1 to 3 teaspoons ground
cinnamon, depending on how
much you like it
1 teaspoon baking soda
1/4 teaspoon baking powder
1 cup semisweet chocolate
chips*

Preheat the oven to 350 degrees.

1. Melt the chocolate with the oil (for effective methods and instructions, see page 27). Set aside to cool completely.

2. In a large bowl, beat the eggs until foamy. Add the sugar, vanilla, and shredded zucchini and mix well. Add the melted chocolate-oil mixture and stir to combine.

3. In a separate bowl, sift together the flour, salt, cinnamon, baking soda, and baking powder.

4. With a wooden spoon, stir the flour mixture into the wet ingredients until well blended. Stir in the chocolate chips.

5. Divide the mixture evenly between the prepared loaf pans. Bake for 50 minutes, or until a toothpick inserted into each loaf comes out clean. (If you are using mini loaf pans, reduce the baking time to 30 to 40 minutes.) Do not overbake. Let the loaves cool on a wire rack for 15 minutes before removing from the pans.

Recipe Note: For a delicious gift, make this bread in mini loaf pans.

---

*Feel free to add an extra 1/2 cup semisweet chocolate chips to the recipe if you *really* love chocolate.

Cookies and Chocolate

...

*C*lose your eyes and think of your favorite chocolate cookie. Well, it's somewhere in this chapter. If not, then send it to me right away. In this chapter there is an incredible variety of chocolate cookies created by contestants from all over the country. Testing them was like taking a chocolate cookie tour of the United States.

Most of these cookies are great for dunking in a big glass of milk (skim milk for those who are weight or fat conscious). And there's even one contestant who suggests serving her cookie with a big glass of orange juice ("Raisin Wild Oats Will Make Your Date Nuts" Cookies by Gladys Gibbs on page 62).

Tips for Making Great Chocolate Cookies

- If you want a tender, chewy cookie, then treat the dough with tenderness. Tough cookies are usually the result of overmixing. Creaming the butter and sugar is done to beat air into the batter, but even this process should not be overdone. Beat the butter-sugar mixture just until it is light and fluffy. Mix in the eggs thoroughly, then "stir" in the dry ingredients.
- When the term "stir" is used in the recipe instructions, it usually means by hand or at very *low* speed with an electric mixer. Why? Because you only want to incorporate the ingredients into the mixture. When you overwork or overmix

the flour, the gluten starts activating, which can make the dough gluey. There's a little chemistry for you.

- It is best to have all your ingredients at room temperature, even your eggs. If you're like me, the urge to make cookies can occur during a moment of madness at 11:30 P.M. while watching *Late Night with David Letterman.* Who has time to wait for room temperature? Get a large bowl, fill it with warm water (not too hot), and place the eggs and your other ingredients (in watertight containers) in the bowl. You can also place ingredients except the eggs in the microwave on defrost power for a few seconds.
- Always add chocolate chips and nuts last (also any other ingredient that you want to have remain intact), unless otherwise instructed. And gently stir them in.
- As we stated in the preceding chapter, remember to use baking soda and baking powder manufactured in this century and preferably before the expiration date printed on the box, or you will have cookies that resemble crepes (a very flat, very French pancake). Sometimes I have had trouble reading the date printed on baking powder cans. Here is a simple test you can use instead: Place ½ teaspoon baking powder in ⅓ cup hot water. If it bubbles, the baking powder is still active and ready for use. If not, it's time to shop for baking powder.
- Most of the recipes call for unsalted butter, which is a sweet butter without salt added to it (as a preservative). Butter makes a crispier cookie than margarine does, and it also burns more quickly—so watch carefully. When margarine is

used in a recipe it is primarily to make a softer and chewier cookie.

- Use fresh eggs. The fresher the eggs, the more air they can sustain during the beating process, which makes for a more tender cookie.
- Why is brown sugar such a pain? Well, now, let's not blame brown sugar for our failure to store it properly in an airtight container. If your brown sugar is rock hard, don't throw it out. There is a remedy. Place the brown sugar in a dish and cover it with a dampened dish towel or paper towel. Put the covered bowl in the microwave and zap it for 2 to 3 minutes, or longer, until it softens. You can also use a regular oven, but don't use a dish towel or paper towel; just place the bowl in an ovenproof dish and sprinkle a little water on it. In the future, place a slice of white bread in the brown sugar bag or box to prevent the sugar from hardening.
- For tips on honey, corn syrup, fructose, and other sweeteners, see "Busting the Sugar Blues" on page 23.

Getting Burned

Here are some tips to help you avoid baking disasters:
- I'm going to repeat this every chapter: Use an oven thermometer to accurately gauge your oven's temperature.
- Use light, reflective cookie sheets, or at least remember, if you are using dark cookie sheets (such as the nonstick variety), that you will need to reduce the baking time and possibly even the baking temperature because they will brown the cookies more quickly.
- Try lining your cookie sheets with parchment paper.
- Try greasing the cookie sheets with something other than butter (i.e., vegetable shortening or nonstick cooking spray), since it does tend to burn.
- Place the cookie sheets in the middle or the upper third of the oven.
- Don't take the dogs for a walk and expect the cookies to be fine on their own. Also check them *before* the dinger dings on your timer.
- You may have hot spots in your oven. Don't worry—a lot of ovens have them. Turn the cookie sheets around halfway

through the baking time if you notice that one row is browning before the others.

- Cookies do not broil. I knew someone once who thought the cookies would cook more quickly if he put them under the broiler. That theory went up in smoke.

A Rare Phenomenon—Cookie Leftovers

If you actually have leftovers, an experience I seldom have, place the cookies in an airtight container. If you forget and leave the cookies out overnight, place them in the microwave on high power for 20 seconds or so and they will soften.

Chocolate Meringue Puffs

Lois McAtee · Oceanside, California
■ ■ ■

Choc Talk: These puffs are perfect with a cup of cappuccino or Earl Grey, but not for dunking. They disintegrate the minute they hit something warm—like an open mouth.

"This recipe has been in my family for forty years. The puffs are best served the day they are made. They're a fragile, melt-in-the-mouth type cookie. Enjoy!" —Lois McAtee

Yield: *2 to 3 dozen cookies* Preparation Time: *10 minutes* Baking Time: *10 minutes* Bakeware Required: *Cookie sheets, lined with wax paper*

1 cup semisweet chocolate chips	½ cup granulated sugar
2 large egg whites	½ teaspoon vanilla extract
⅛ teaspoon salt	¾ cup coarsely chopped
½ teaspoon white vinegar	walnuts

Preheat the oven to 350 degrees.

1. Melt the chocolate chips (for effective methods and instructions, see page 27). Set aside to cool completely.

2. In a large bowl, beat the egg whites with the salt and vinegar until they become foamy. (For further instructions and tips on beating egg whites, see page 184). Gradually add the sugar 1 tablespoon at a time, beating well after each addition. Beat until stiff peaks form.

3. Beat in the vanilla.

4. Gently, fold in by hand the melted chocolate and walnuts into the mixture.

5. Drop the batter by rounded teaspoons onto the prepared cookie sheets approximately 1 inch apart. Make sure the cookies are small.

6. Bake for 10 minutes, or until the cookies are firm just on top. Immediately remove the wax paper with the cookies to a cooling rack and allow the cookies to cool for 5 minues. Then carefully remove the cookies from the wax paper to finish cooling. You may reuse the wax paper or reline the cookie sheet with a fresh piece.

Recipe Note: These aren't the best cookies to store in the cookie jar for a week. That's why they're called puffs. Puff—now you see them. Poof—now you don't. If you do have them around for a day or so and they harden, heat them in the microwave on high power for 20 seconds.

Martin's Short Chocolate Pecan Cookie

Martin Polanco · San Leandro, California

■ ■ ■

Professional Chocolate Lover Category

***C**hoc Talk:* This cocoa-colored shortbread cookie is delicate, light, and crumbly—the kind of cookie you hate to drop on the floor because you'll be forever crushing the crumbs underfoot even after sweeping and sweeping.

"I like short dough, but I also like chocolate. I thought, 'Wouldn't it be great if I could make a chocolate short dough cookie?' And since nothing goes better with chocolate than nuts, I simply put it all together, and the rest, as they is say, is history."
—Martin Polanco

Yield: *3 dozen cookies* **Preparation Time:** *10 minutes* **Chilling Time:** *30 minutes* **Baking Time:** *8 to 10 minutes* **Bakeware Required:** *Cookie sheets, lightly greased*

8 ounces semisweet chocolate	*1½ cups pecans, chopped*
1 cup unsalted butter, softened	*2 cups all-purpose flour*
½ cup granulated sugar	*1½ teaspoons baking powder*
1 large egg	

Preheat the oven to 350 degrees.

1. Melt the chocolate (for effective methods and instructions, see page 27). Set aside to cool completely.

2. In a large bowl, mix together the butter, sugar, and melted chocolate. Add the egg and mix thoroughly. Stir in the pecans.

3. In a separate bowl, mix the flour and baking powder together. Add the flour mixture to the chocolate mixture and stir until the dry ingredients have been absorbed.

4. Cover the dough with plastic wrap and refrigerate for 30 minutes to allow it to become firm.

5. With a small scoop or teaspoon, form the dough into balls and place them approximately 1 inch apart on the prepared cookie sheets. Gently press down on the dough with the palm of your hand to flatten it a little.

6. Bake for 8 to 10 minutes, or until done. Do not overbake. Let the cookies cool on the cookie sheets for 10 minutes, then carefully remove to a wire rack to cool.

Recipe Note: This is a great cookie on its own, or serve it with one of the chocolate mousses on pages 187–192. Also, *real* chocolate lovers can add 1 cup semisweet chocolate mini morsels to the shortbread dough just before baking.

PMS Cookies

Patti Slattery · Redmond, Utah
■ ■ ■
Professional Chocolate Lover Category

***C**hoc Talk:* Patti thinks these cookies work nearly as well as ibuprofen when she's experiencing PMS. Some men think this syndrome is just an excuse for women to eat cookies with mega doses of chocolate. For a very good reason, those men live alone and eat store-bought, rock-hard, cardboard cutouts called cookies.

Yield: *2 dozen cookies (double the batch if you care to share)*
Preparation Time: *10 minutes* **Baking Time:** *8 to 10 minutes* **Bakeware Required:** *Cookie sheets, lightly greased*

2 ounces unsweetened chocolate	*½ cup white chocolate broken*
½ cup unsalted butter, softened	*into chunks∗*
1 cup granulated sugar	*1¼ cups semisweet chocolate*
2 large eggs	*chips (see option in Recipe*
2 teaspoons vanilla extract	*Notes)*
1½ cups all-purpose flour	*¼ cup milk chocolate chips*
½ teaspoon baking soda	

Preheat the oven to 350 degrees.

1. Melt the unsweetened chocolate (for effective methods and instructions, see page 27). Set aside to cool completely.

2. In a large bowl, cream the butter and sugar. Add the melted chocolate to the mixture. Then add the eggs and vanilla and beat the mixture until smooth.

3. In a separate bowl, combine the flour and baking soda. Blend in the flour mixture thoroughly. Stir in the white chocolate, semisweet chips, and milk chocolate chips to the mixture.

4. Drop the dough by rounded teaspoons onto the cookie sheets about 1 inch apart and bake for 8 to 10 minutes, or until done. Be careful not to overbake. Let the cookies cool on the cookie sheets

∗Use Ghirardelli white chocolate chips. If you just can't find white chocolate, substitute more milk chocolate and/or semisweet chips.

for 10 minutes and remove them from the cookie sheets to wire racks to finish cooling.

Presentation Note: Eat them by the handfuls without stopping while watching *All My Children* or *General Hospital* (capture them on video if you can't call in sick) curled up on the couch in your fluffy robe with a copy of *Cosmopolitan* opened to the quiz of the month.

Recipe Notes: These can freeze to keep on hand for an emergency. • In Patti's original recipe, she melts the 1¼ cups semisweet chocolate chips with the unsweetened chocolate. This will make a deep chocolate cookie.

Horse Show Chocolate Chip Cookies

Best Cookie Created by a Barn Crew Special Award

Smokey Lynne Bare · Westerville, Ohio
■ ■ ■

*C*hoc Talk: This cookie was a favorite among our chocophiles. Moist and delicious, it is also a *big* cookie—Smokey recommends using a ¼ cup measure to form the dough. This is convenient for those who promise to "eat just one."

"This recipe originated with an Amish family who would take the cookies to local draft horse sales where I did the braiding on the sale horses. My barn crew each added their favorite ingredient. The cookies travel well to the horse shows and stay fresh when stored in old coffee cans." —Smokey Lynne Bare

Yield: *A little short of 4 dozen. Enough to fill three 2-pound coffee cans.* **Preparation Time:** *10 minutes* **Baking Time:** *10 to 12 minutes* **Bakeware Required:** *Cookie sheets, well greased*

continued

1 cup margarine

1 cup butter-flavored solid vegetable shortening

2 cups firmly packed light brown sugar

2 cups granulated sugar

4 large eggs, beaten

2 cups rolled oats* (such as Old Fashioned Quaker Oats)

2 teaspoons vanilla extract

4 cups all-purpose flour, sifted

2 teaspoons baking powder

2 teaspoons baking soda

2 cups corn flakes or Rice Krispies

12 ounces semisweet chocolate chips

1 cup sweetened flaked coconut

1 cup pecans, chopped

Preheat the oven to 350 degrees.

1. In a large mixing bowl, cream the margarine with the shortening. Add the sugars and cream the mixture again. Add the eggs, rolled oats, and vanilla. Mix well.

2. In a separate bowl, mix together the flour, baking powder, and baking soda. Add to the creamed mixture and stir well.

3. With a large spoon, gently stir in the corn flakes or Rice Krispies, chocolate chips, coconut, and pecans.

4. For each cookie, scoop up ¼ cup of dough and place it on a cookie sheet, spacing the cookies at least 2 inches apart. Bake for 10 to 12 minutes, or until done. Let the cookies cool on the cookie sheets for 5 minutes, then carefully remove to a wire rack to cool.

Presentation Note: Horse Show Chocolate Chip Cookies look best in coffee cans, but only those that held coffee cowboys would drink, like Maxwell House or Folgers. Coffee cans with a French or Italian name will not work.

Recipe Notes: If you're not heading for a horse show, you can reduce the recipe by half. • And you can cut the size of the cookie down, but that's like eating only half of the *big* cookie; what's the point?

*Rolled oats, unlike quick-cooking oats, will keep their shape and texture, adding more crunch to the cookie. For a nuttier and a little oatier taste, try lightly toasting the oats before dumping them in the batter. Spread them out on a large cookie sheet and place them in a preheated 325 degree oven for 10 to 15 minutes, stirring frequently (for even toasting and to prevent burning). Everyone will want to know your secret.

Alaskan Chocolate Chip Cookies

Laura Richardson · Bountiful, Utah

■ ■ ■

hoc Talk: Vanilla pudding is what makes these cookies white (what a good idea). Not only are they very pretty, but they taste as good as they look.

Yield: *3 dozen cookies* **Preparation Time:** *10 minutes* **Baking Time:** *8 to 10 minutes* **Bakeware Required:** *Cookie sheets, well greased*

One 3.4-ounce package vanilla instant pudding mix	*2 teaspoons vanilla extract*
2 cups cold milk	*2 large eggs*
1 cup unsalted butter, softened	*2¼ cups all-purpose flour*
⅓ cup granulated sugar	*1 teaspoon baking powder*
¾ cup firmly packed light brown sugar	*12 ounces semisweet chocolate chips*

Preheat the oven to 350 degrees.

1. In a medium bowl, prepare the vanilla pudding by combining the pudding mix and cold milk together, mixing well. Set aside to let the pudding set until firm. (This should take about 5 minutes.)

2. In a large bowl, cream together the butter, granulated sugar, and brown sugar. Add one cup of the prepared vanilla pudding and the eggs. Mix thoroughly after each addition.

3. In another bowl, mix the flour and baking powder together. Blend the flour mixture into the wet ingredients until combined. Stir the chocolate chips into the mixture with a spoon.

4. Drop the dough by rounded teaspoons onto the prepared cookie sheets about 1 inch apart and bake for 8 to 10 minutes, or until done. Let the cookies cool on the cookie sheets for 10 minutes, then carefully remove to a wire rack to cool.

Tony and Tina's Wedding Cookie

Stephanie Drehs · Lockport, New York
▪ ▪ ▪

***C**hoc Talk:* Black pepper in a cookie? It gave me pause, but the guys painting my house thought the cookies were delicious, so there you have it from the experts. If you crash a wedding with these cookies, you'll be welcomed like a member of the family.

"This is one of the traditional wedding cookies made for Italian weddings." —Stephanie Drehs

Yield: *5 dozen cookies* **Preparation Time:** *15 minutes* **Baking Time:** *8 to 10 minutes* **Bakeware Required:** *Cookie sheets*

4½ cups all-purpose flour
2 cups granulated sugar
½ teaspoon salt
3 tablespoons baking powder
½ cup unsweetened cocoa
½ teaspoon black pepper
1 teaspoon ground cloves
1½ teaspoons ground cinnamon
¾ cup margarine

1 cup milk
¾ cup finely chopped blanched almonds, toasted*

ICING
4 cups confectioners' sugar
2 teaspoons vanilla extract
2 tablespoons milk (or more to achieve desired spreading consistency)

Preheat the oven to 400 degrees.

1. In a large bowl, sift together the flour, sugar, salt, baking powder, cocoa, black pepper, cloves, and cinnamon.

*For extra nutty flavor, spread the nuts on a cookie sheet and toast them in a preheated 350 degree oven for 10 to 15 minutes. Stir the nuts occasionally to toast them evenly and prevent burning. Or, toast the nuts in the microwave (they will not change color but will taste toasted). Place 1 cup nuts on a paper plate and microwave uncovered on high power for 3 to 4 minutes, rotating the plate a half turn after 2 minutes.

2. Cut the margarine in small pieces and place in the flour mixture. Using a pastry cutter or 2 knives in a scissor style, work the pieces of margarine into the flour until the mixture resembles small peas.

3. Add the milk and almonds to the flour mixture and mix together until well blended.

4. Roll the dough into balls the size of a small walnut. Place on the cookie sheets 1 inch apart and bake for 8 to 10 minutes, or until done. Let the cookies cool slightly on the cookie sheets while you make the icing.

To Make the Icing

1. In a large bowl, combine the icing ingredients and mix well. If necessary, add more milk to achieve a spreading consistency.

2. Roll the cookies in the frosting while they are still warm.

Presentation Idea: Beautiful for the holidays or for a festive gathering.

Recipe Note: If you're not catering a wedding, cut the recipe in half. Or freeze half the dough and make only half the icing.

Hunka Maca Chunka Chocolate Chip Cookies

Diana M. Padilla Hanau · West Palm Beach, Florida

■ ■ ■

hoc Talk: Munching on macadamia nuts reminds me of luxurious tropical evenings in Hawaii, and I've never even been there. Nothing can be substituted for macadamias. Diana matches their chunky goodness with *chunks* of chocolate.

Yield: *2 dozen cookies* **Preparation Time:** *10 minutes* **Baking Time:** *8 to 10 minutes* **Bakeware Required:** *Cookie sheets, lined with parchment paper*

2 cups unbleached or white all-purpose flour	1 cup unsalted butter, softened
1 teaspoon baking soda	1 large egg
1 teaspoon baking powder	1 teaspoon caramel flavoring*
½ teaspoon sea salt (See Recipe Notes)	10 ounces semisweet chocolate bars, coarsely chopped
¾ cup firmly packed light brown sugar	1 cup macadamia nuts, coarsely chopped

Preheat the oven to 350 degrees.

1. In a large bowl, combine the flour, baking soda, baking powder, and salt.

2. In another bowl, beat the brown sugar and butter together until creamy. Add the egg and caramel flavoring to the mixture and beat until well blended.

3. Add the flour mixture gradually to the sugar and butter mixture, then stir in the chopped chocolate and macadamia nuts with a wooden spoon.

*Any caramel ice cream topping will do, or try the homemade caramel sauce recipe on page 276.

4. Drop the dough by rounded tablespoons onto the prepared cookie sheets. Bake for 8 to 10 minutes, or until done. Let the cookies cool for 5 minutes on the cookie sheets, then carefully remove to a wire rack to cool.

Recipe Notes: This recipe calls for some interesting ingredients you may not have on hand in the cupboard such as sea salt, which is an unrefined coarse salt. It is great for cooking, and for coating the rim of margarita glasses when you are imbibing. You can substitute an equal amount of table salt if that is easier. Please make substitutions with what you do have and try this recipe in its pure form when you have the time and the ingredients. • Diana recommends Tobler chocolate bars, but use your favorite semisweet chocolate brand.

"Raisin Wild Oats Will Make Your Date Nuts" Cookies

Gladys Gibbs · Brush Creek, Tennessee

■ ■ ■

Choc Talk: "I like this one—it's sort of fruity and nutrition-y and chewy. I invented the word nutrition-y, which you are welcome to use."—Elizabeth Howard, Chocolate Heaven Assistant Chocolatier. Elizabeth, you wordsmith. This cookie has lots of delicious and, dare I say, health-y ingredients.

"Over a period of time, by trial and error, I created this recipe. I enjoy serving these cookies. They make a great snack served with milk or orange juice." —Gladys Gibbs

Yield: *4 dozen cookies* **Preparation Time:** *15 minutes* **Baking Time:** *8 to 10 minutes* **Bakeware Required:** *2 large cookie sheets, lightly greased*

½ cup solid vegetable shortening	*¾ teaspoon baking soda*
	¾ teaspoon baking powder
¼ cup applesauce	*½ teaspoon salt*
1 cup firmly packed light brown sugar	*¾ teaspoon ground cinnamon*
	½ teaspoon ground ginger
¼ cup granulated sugar	*¼ teaspoon ground cloves*
2 large eggs	*1½ cups (9 ounces) semisweet*
½ cup buttermilk	*chocolate chips*
1⅓ cups all-purpose flour	*1¼ cups quick-cooking oats∗*
1 tablespoon plus 1 teaspoon instant coffee granules or powder	*½ cup raisins*
	½ cup finely chopped dates
	½ cup slivered almonds

∗Quick-cooking oats are thinner than old-fashioned (rolled) oats and will blend into the batter and be less noticeable. For a nuttier and oatier taste, you may want to try lightly toasting the oats before dumping them in the batter. Spread them out on a large cookie sheet and place in a preheated 325 degree oven for 10 to 15 minutes, stirring frequently for even toasting and to prevent burning.

Preheat the oven to 400 degrees.

1. In a large bowl, cream together the shortening, applesauce, sugars, and eggs. Stir in the buttermilk.

2. In a separate bowl, sift together the flour, instant coffee, baking soda, baking powder, salt, and spices. Stir the dry ingredients into the creamed mixture.

3. Stir in the chocolate chips, oats, raisins, dates, and almonds.

4. Drop the batter by rounded tablespoons onto the prepared cookie sheets, about 2 inches apart. Bake for 8 to 10 minutes, or until done. Let the cookies cool on the cookie sheets for 5 minutes, then carefully remove to a wire rack to cool.

Recipe Note: These cookies freeze well. When we tried the recipe again at Chocolate Heaven, we increased the spices we liked and added nutmeg, one of our favorite spices.

Chocolate-Glazed Shortbread

Lynne Schaefer · Novato, California

■ ■ ■

Choc Talk: Two of my loves come together in this cookie: shortbread and chocolate. Shortbread lovers will also want to try Martin's Short Chocolate Pecan Cookie (page 52) and Millionaire's Shortbread (page 83), which is a traditional shortbread topped with chocolate.

"The shortbread cookie has always been a favorite of mine. One day I added another favorite, chocolate, to create chocolate shortbread. Then I topped it with a mint glaze." —Lynne Schaefer

Yield: *2 dozen cookies* **Preparation Time:** *15 minutes* **Baking Time:** *40 to 45 minutes* **Bakeware Required:** *10½ × 15½ × 1-inch jelly roll pan or cookie sheet with sides, lined with foil*

continued

1¾ *cups all-purpose flour*
¾ *cup cornstarch*
½ *cup granulated sugar*
1 cup unsalted butter
4 ounces semisweet chocolate
1 teaspoon vanilla extract

MINT GLAZE
4 ounces sweet dark chocolate
(such as Baker's German's
chocolate)
1 teaspoon peppermint extract

Preheat the oven to 325 degrees.

1. In a large bowl, combine the flour, cornstarch, and sugar and set aside.

2. Melt the butter and chocolate together (for effective methods and instructions, see page 27). Let the mixture cool for about 5 minutes, then stir in the vanilla.

3. Add the melted chocolate to the flour mixture, stirring until the dough holds together in a ball.

4. With the back of a large spoon, spread the dough evenly in the prepared pan and bake 40 to 45 minutes, or until done.

5. Let the shortbread cool until it is just warm. Cut the shortbread into 48 rectangles and leave in the pan until completely cool.

To Make the Mint Glaze

1. Melt the chocolate (for effective methods and instructions, see page 27) and let cool for 5 minutes.

2. Gradually stir in the peppermint extract.

3. With a spatula, spread the glaze completely over the cut shortbread rectangles. Allow the glaze to cool and harden.

4. Lift the foil to remove the shortbread from the pan and break the rectangles apart.

Recipe Note: Place one glazed cookie face down on top of another to create a cookie sandwich.

Chewy Chocolate Chip Cookies

Karen Mills-Price · Riddle, Oregon

■ ■ ■

*C*hoc Talk: This is just a different version of an old favorite. The addition of the coconut contributes to the chew-i-ness.

Yield: *3 dozen cookies* Preparation Time: *20 minutes* Baking Time: *8 to 10 minutes* Bakeware Required: *Cookie sheets, lightly greased*

2½ cups all-purpose flour
½ cup whole wheat flour (if not available, use all-purpose)
1 teaspoon baking soda
1 teaspoon salt
1 tablespoon baking powder
1 cup butter or margarine, softened
½ cup granulated sugar

¾ cup firmly packed brown sugar
¼ cup honey
1 teaspoon vanilla extract
1 teaspoon lemon juice
2 large eggs
12 ounces semisweet chocolate chips
¾ cup sweetened flaked coconut

Preheat the oven to 350 degrees.

1. In a medium bowl, combine the flours, baking soda, salt, and baking powder and set aside.

2. In a large bowl, using an electric mixer, cream together the butter, sugars, honey, vanilla, and lemon juice until light and fluffy. Add the eggs one at a time, mixing well after each addition.

3. Stir the flour mixture into the creamed mixture and beat at medium speed for 1 minute.

4. Stir in the chocolate chips and coconut by hand until well blended.

5. Drop the dough by rounded tablespoons onto the prepared cookie sheets approximately 2 inches apart and slightly flatten each mound so that it is about 2½ inches across. Bake for 8 to 10 minutes, or until done. Be careful not to overbake. Let the cookies cool on the cookie sheets for 5 minutes, then carefully remove to a wire rack to cool.

continued

Variations: Here are some creative variations you can use with this chocolate chip cookie recipe and with Hunka Maca Chunka Chocolate Cookies by Diana Hanau on page 60.

Peanutty Chocolate Chip Cookies: Add 1 cup smooth peanut butter to the creamed mixture and reduce the amount of flour to 1½ cups and the butter or margarine to ½ cup. Stir in 1 cup roasted peanuts for a nutty crunch.

Sunshine Chocolate Chip Cookies (contributed by Marlys Ward, Mankato, Minnesota):   Add 1 teaspoon orange extract, 1 tablespoon grated orange peel, and 1 cup salted sunflower seeds. (If using Chewy Chocolate Chip Cookies as the base recipe, omit the lemon juice.)

Spicy Chocolate Chip Cookies: Spice the cookie by adding ½ teaspoon cinnamon, ¼ teaspoon nutmeg, and ⅛ to ¼ teaspoon allspice.

Chocolate Chip Dunk: Dunk each cookie halfway in melted chocolate (see the Taking a Chocolate Dip recipe on page 223).

Brownies—Simple to Sublime

...

I was the world's worst brownie baker. No matter what recipe I tried, what chocolate I used, what prayer I said, my brownies were disasters destined for the garbage disposal. I was doomed to be forever a victim of this brownie block, bitter toward all who said, "Care for a brownie? I just made them."

Fortunately, The Great American Chocolate National Recipe Contest™ proved excellent therapy for my brownie-making dysfunction. The contestants in this chapter helped to build my brownie-baking confidence and unleash the chocolate creativity blocked for so long. Now I can say, "Which brownie would you like? 'Butter 'Em Up Brownies,' 'The Brownie of Seville,' or 'Shy-Town Cream Cheese Brownies' (pages 72, 74, and 76)? I just made them all by myself, thank you very much."

Keep the following tips in mind and you'll make great brownies every time.

Tips for Making Better Brownies

- Brownies with a cakier texture usually have more eggs.
- Make sure the melted chocolate is completely cool before mixing it with other ingredients. This will help create a light, moist brownie.
- Fudgier, moister brownies may not pass the clean toothpick rule for doneness. If you want your brownie firmer and crisp-

ier, bake it longer than required. But to keep brownies light and moist, which most brownie enthusiasts seem to prefer, check them a few minutes before the end of the suggested baking time.

- Certain ingredients like raisins, cream cheese, or fruit make brownies moister.
- Use sugar. After years of analyzing why I made the lousiest brownies, I found that for some reason I kept forgetting to add the sugar. That can kill a brownie all right.

To Top It All Off

A great ice cream store here in Boston offers terrific brownie toppings. Put them atop warm brownies so they melt slightly. These toppings are festive looking, and if you eat them with ice cream, you may find yourself bursting into song: "I'm in heaven, in Chocolate Heaven . . ." Try these topping ideas:

Raisinets

Peanut M&M's or, if you must, plain M&M's (even the red ones)

Butterscotch morsels

Peanut butter morsels

Mini peanut butter cups

Cadbury's Caramello bars, chopped

Oven Note

Use an oven thermometer to accurately gauge your oven's temperature because most ovens are not calibrated correctly (they can run "cold" or "hot").

Quick Brudgies

Patti Lebens · Columbus, Ohio

■ ■ ■

***C**hoc Talk:* A brudgie is a divine cross between a chocolate brownie and chocolate fudge. Culinary genetics never cease to amaze me.

"My mother-in-law gave me this recipe thirty years ago. It was her mother's recipe. I've made it many times over the years, and now my daughters are making it. It's one of our favorite recipes!"
—Patti Lebens

Yield: *12 servings* **Preparation Time:** *10 minutes* **Baking Time:** *20 to 25 minutes* **Bakeware Required:** *9 × 13-inch baking pan, well greased*

1 cup margarine	*1½ cups all-purpose flour*
¾ cup unsweetened cocoa	*1 teaspoon salt*
2 cups granulated sugar	*½ cup chopped walnuts or*
4 large eggs	*pecans*
1 teaspoon vanilla extract	

Preheat the oven to 350 degrees.

1. Melt the margarine completely in a medium saucepan over moderate heat. Add the cocoa to the melted margarine and stir until smooth. Add the sugar and mix well. Remove the saucepan from the heat.

2. In a small bowl, beat the eggs and stir in a small amount of the chocolate mixture. Stir the egg mixture into the saucepan and beat until well mixed. Add the vanilla.

3. In a separate bowl, combine the flour, salt, and nuts. Add the dry mixture to the chocolate mixture in the saucepan and stir together.

4. Spread the batter in the prepared pan and bake for 20 to 25 minutes, or until a toothpick inserted in the center comes out clean but slightly moist (brudgies are fudgy). Let the brudgies cool in the pan on a wire rack for 20 minutes, then cut into squares.

Fudge Walnut Brownie Pie with Homemade Hot Fudge Sauce

Regina Albright · Memphis, Tennessee

■ ■ ■

***C**hoc Talk:* This was a definite hit at one of our chocolate parties. Regina Albright's hot fudge sauce is one to keep close by just in case a gallon of ice cream magically appears in your freezer and simply cries for hot fudge.

"Chocolate is my family's sinful passion. I had this recipe at a restaurant and tried to get as close to it as I could. After many tries, I finally came up with this great dessert." —Regina Albright

Yield: *8 to 10 servings* **Preparation Time:** *20 minutes* **Baking Time:** *25 to 35 minutes* **Bakeware Required:** *9-inch pie pan, greased*

BROWNIE PIE

2 ounces unsweetened chocolate

1 cup granulated sugar

½ cup unsalted butter, softened

2 large eggs

2 tablespoons milk

1 teaspoon vanilla extract

⅓ cup all-purpose flour

½ cup chopped walnuts

HOT FUDGE SAUCE

⅓ cup unsalted butter

2 ounces unsweetened chocolate

¾ cup granulated sugar

1 cup heavy cream

2 teaspoons vanilla extract

TOPPINGS

1 quart vanilla ice cream

Chopped or broken walnuts

To Make the Brownie Pie

Preheat the oven to 350 degrees.

1. Melt the chocolate (for effective methods and instructions, see page 27). Set aside to cool completely.

2. In a small bowl, combine the sugar, butter, and eggs. Using an electric mixer, beat the mixture at high speed until it is very fluffy, about 5 minutes.

3. Using low speed, blend in the milk, vanilla, and flour. Then blend in the chocolate. Stir in the chopped walnuts with a spoon.

4. Pour the mixture into the prepared pie pan and bake for 35 minutes, or until it is puffed in the center and a toothpick inserted into the center comes out almost clean. (The brownie pie will rise during baking and sink slightly as it cools.) Let the pie cool completely in the pan on a wire rack while you make the sauce.

To Make the Hot Fudge Sauce

1. In a medium saucepan over low heat, melt the butter and chocolate together.

2. Blend in the sugar and cream. Continue cooking the mixture over low heat, stirring frequently, for about 5 minutes.

3. Remove the mixture from the heat and stir in the vanilla.

To Assemble and Serve

1. When the brownie pie is completely cool, cut it into wedges. Top each brownie wedge with a scoop of vanilla ice cream and ladle some hot fudge sauce over the ice cream. Sprinkle with walnuts.

Recipe Notes: You can cover and store the leftover hot fudge sauce in the refrigerator or freezer. Reheat in a saucepan over low heat. • If you really want to be incredibly decadent, place some fresh whipped cream on this entire chocolate creation, then sprinkle with the walnuts. Ahhhh.

Butter 'Em Up Brownies
Cookies and Mint-Layered Brownies

Caryn S. Burnett • Yuba City, California

■ ■ ■

hoc Talk: I was burning up the fax wires sending this rich chocolate brownie recipe to members of the tasting panel, who requested it just in time to impress those attending the obligatory company picnics. I had never tasted the new Hershey's Cookies 'n' Mint candy bar. It's a great idea. Of course, I had to eat two or three candy bars without sharing, just to make sure.

"I introduced one of our favorite new candy bars (Hershey's Cookies 'n' Mint) to this simple brownie recipe. I call them Butter 'Em Up Brownies because they would serve as a great treat for the boss, a disgruntled neighbor, a friend you need a favor from, etc. Although this can serve up to ten people, my husband says he thinks it serves two just fine. Serve with cold milk, of course!"
—Caryn S. Burnett

Yield: *10 servings or 1 boss*

Preparation Time: *15 minutes* **Baking Time:** *35 minutes* **Bakeware Required:** *9 × 13-inch baking pan, lightly greased*

8 ounces unsweetened chocolate	*1½ cups all-purpose flour*
1 cup unsalted butter	*Twelve 1.55-ounce Hershey's*
3 large eggs	*Cookies 'n' Mint chocolate*
1½ cups granulated sugar	*candy bars∗*
1 tablespoon vanilla extract	

Preheat the oven to 350 degrees.

1. Melt the unsweetened chocolate and butter together (for effective methods and instructions, see page 27). Set aside to cool completely.

∗You may wish to substitute other candy bars for a variation on this recipe. Try plain Hershey bars if you are not a mint fan. Be creative.

2. In a large bowl, beat the eggs, sugar, and vanilla with an electric mixer at high speed until well blended. Beat in the chocolate mixture on low speed until well mixed.

3. Add the flour to the mixture and stir until just combined.

4. Spread half the batter in the prepared pan. Place 6 candy bars on top, breaking as necessary to cover the batter evenly. Pour the remainder of the batter on top of the candy bars. Reserve the other 6 bars.

5. Bake the brownies for 35 minutes, or until a toothpick inserted in the center comes out almost clean (remember, there are melted candy bars in the middle).

6. Remove the pan from the oven and immediately place the remaining candy bars on top of the hot brownies. Break as necessary to cover the surface evenly. Allow the candy bars to melt on the hot brownies (place the pan back in the warm oven to help melt the candy bars if necessary) and then spread the melted chocolate smooth with a small spatula. Allow the brownies to cool completely in the pan on a wire rack before cutting into squares.

The Brownie of Seville

Mary Ann Lee · Marco Island, Florida

■ ■ ■

***C**hoc Talk:* With its subtle orange flavor, this is a sophisticated brownie, yet it is easy to make. The Grand Marnier and orange zest give it an extra surge that pushes the envelope of brownie making. Serve it on your best Wedgwood with a snifter of Grand Marnier for a fabulous after-the-opera snack. Or plunk it on a napkin with a big glass of milk and enjoy it during half-time on a football-filled Sunday afternoon.

Yield: *16 servings* **Preparation Time:** *20 minutes* **Baking Time:** *30 to 40 minutes* **Bakeware Required:** *8 × 8-inch baking pan*

BROWNIES

1 cup chopped walnuts (break whole walnuts into large pieces)

2 tablespoons unsalted butter, melted

2 ounces unsweetened chocolate

4 ounces semisweet chocolate

½ cup unsalted butter

1 teaspoon vanilla extract

1 tablespoon grated orange zest*

1 cup granulated sugar

2 large eggs

¼ cup sifted all-purpose flour

ICING

2 ounces unsweetened chocolate

6 ounces semisweet chocolate

2 tablespoons unsalted butter

2 tablespoons Grand Marnier or other orange-flavored liqueur or orange juice

GARNISH

3 tablespoons confectioners' sugar

To Make the Brownies

Preheat the oven to 400 degrees.

1. Spread the walnuts on a cookie sheet and place in the oven for about 10 minutes, stirring periodically to toast evenly. The flavor is wonderful and really enhances the brownie.

*Using a sharp paring knife or a zester, carefully scrape very thin slices of just the orange part of the peel. Do not use any of the white part, which is bitter.

Reduce the oven temperature to 325 degrees.

2. Line the baking pan with foil, pressing it gently into the corners. Do not puncture the foil. Thoroughly grease the foil with the melted butter; wipe away any excess butter.

3. Melt the unsweetened and semisweet chocolate with the ½ cup butter (for effective methods and instructions, see page 27). Stir the melted chocolate and butter together until smooth. Set aside to cool completely.

4. Pour the chocolate-butter mixture into a medium bowl. Stir in the vanilla, orange zest, and sugar. Add the eggs one at a time, stirring after each addition. Add the flour and stir briskly for about 1 minute, until the mixture is smooth and shiny and comes away from the sides of the bowl. Stir in the toasted nuts.

5. Place the batter in the prepared pan and smooth the top. Bake for 30 to 40 minutes, or until a toothpick inserted gently into the middle comes out clean and dry. Let the brownie cool completely in the pan on a wire rack.

To Make the Icing

1. Melt the unsweetened and semisweet chocolates with the butter (for effective methods and instructions, see page 27). Let cool slightly and stir in the Grand Marnier.

2. Turn the cooled brownie out onto a flat serving platter and carefully remove the foil. Leave the brownie upside down—do not turn it over. Spread the icing over the top of the brownie. Do not let the chocolate drip down the sides. Refrigerate until partially firm. Dust with confectioners' sugar by placing the sugar in a sieve or small wire strainer and gently sprinkling the sugar over the top. Cut with a sharp knife into 16 squares.

Shy-Town Cream Cheese Brownies

Jennifer Ross Shapiro · Chicago, Illinois

■ ■ ■

Choc Talk: We made this very rich, moist brownie two different ways: First, we swirled the cream cheese filling to create a marbleized effect. In the second method, we spooned the brownie batter over the cream cheese filling and created a layered effect. Either way, it looked great and tasted even better.

Yield: *16 servings* **Preparation Time:** *15 minutes* **Baking Time:** *30 to 40 minutes* **Bakeware Required:** *8 × 8-inch baking pan, greased and floured*

BROWNIES
4 ounces unsweetened chocolate
½ cup unsalted butter, softened
1⅓ cups granulated sugar
1 tablespoon vanilla extract
3 large eggs
¾ cup all-purpose flour

FILLING
One 8-ounce package cream cheese, softened

5 tablespoons granulated sugar
1 large egg
1¼ teaspoons all-purpose flour
1 teaspoon vanilla extract
6 ounces semisweet chocolate chips (optional)
1 cup pecans, chopped (optional)

To Make the Brownies

Preheat the oven to 350 degrees.

1. Melt the chocolate and butter together (for effective methods and instructions, see page 27). Stir until combined. Set aside to cool completely.

2. In a large bowl, combine the sugar and vanilla. Add the melted chocolate-butter mixture and blend well. Add the eggs and mix well. Add the flour and blend thoroughly. Set the mixture aside.

To Make the Filling

1. In a large bowl, using an electric mixer, or preferably in a food processor, combine all the ingredients, except the optional chocolate chips and pecans. Mix or process until thoroughly combined. Stir in the chocolate chips and nuts, if using.

To Assemble the Brownies

1. Spoon half the brownie batter into the prepared pan, then spoon all of the cream cheese batter evenly over it. Add the remaining brownie batter, dropping it by large spoonfuls on top of the cream cheese layer.*

2. Bake for 30 to 40 minutes, or until a toothpick inserted in the center of the brownies comes out clean but moist. The brownies may be somewhat moist because of the cream cheese. Bake until the desired doneness is reached but do not overbake! Cool the brownies in the pan on a wire rack for about 2 hours before cutting into squares.

Recipe Notes: Since we're not shy, we added chocolate chips to the cream cheese filling. A broken-up chocolate bar also works well if you want to just lay the pieces over the cream cheese filling. • And since we're slightly nuts, we added some pecans to the cream cheese for a bit of crunch.

*If you wish to achieve a marbleized effect with the cream cheese filling, use a knife to swirl the cream cheese mixture throughout the batter.

San Francisco Fudge Foggies

Susan Downard · Athens, Ohio

■ ■ ■

***C**hoc Talk:* I left my heart . . . in a San Francisco Fudge Foggie. Simply rich with chocolate. You cut them in small squares like fudge, yet Foggies are easy to prepare, very much like a brownie. When your boyfriend hasn't called in two days, we highly recommend you make this dense chocolate treat, eat a few squares, and Fogget him.

"My sister gave this recipe to me. Another friend had given it to her. Everyone who takes one bite of a San Francisco Fudge Foggie wants the recipe. This is a favorite in my office, where someone asks me to make a batch and bring it in just about every other month. Die-hard chocoholics can't get enough of these."
—Susan Downard

Yield: *15 servings* **Preparation Time:** *15 minutes* **Baking Time:** *20 to 30 minutes* **Chilling Time:** *6 hours total* **Bakeware Required:** *9 × 13-inch baking pan, double lined with foil, with a 2-inch border around the pan. Lightly grease the foil.*

1 pound bittersweet (such as Baker's German's Chocolate), coarsely chopped	*4 large eggs*
	1½ cups granulated sugar
	½ cup all-purpose flour
1 cup unsalted butter, cut into tablespoons	*1 cup chopped walnuts or pecans (optional)*
⅓ cup strong brewed coffee	

Preheat the oven to 375 degrees.

1. Melt the chocolate, butter, and coffee in a double boiler over hot, but not boiling, water. Stir until smooth. Set aside to cool for 10 minutes, stirring occasionally.

2. In a large bowl, with an electric mixer at high speed, beat the eggs for 30 seconds, or until foamy. Gradually add the sugar while continuing to beat on High for 2 minutes, until the mixture is light and fluffy.

3. Reduce the speed to Low and beat in the chocolate mixture just until blended. Stir the flour into the creamed mixture with a wooden spoon, just enough to combine well.

4. Spread evenly in the prepared pan. Bake for 20 to 30 minutes, or until the brownie is firm around the edges. Let the foggies cool in the pan on a wire rack for approximately 10 minutes, then carefully remove them by lifting the foil border. Place the foggies, still on the foil, on a wire rack for 30 minutes.

5. Cover the foggies tightly with more aluminum foil and refrigerate for at least 6 hours before cutting and serving.

Recipe Note: "Because of the amount of chocolate and sugar in this recipe, refrigerator storage is recommended. The original recipe calls for 2 cups of chopped nuts stirred into the batter. I never put nuts in the recipe because, as far as I'm concerned, the nuts would compromise the purity of the chocolate."—Susan Downard.

I liked 1 cup chopped walnuts in this recipe, but Susan has a point, so you decide.

Chocolate-Covered Memory

■ ■ ■

"In spite of my fury I smiled, remembering. . . . I knew serving clients chocolate nurtured them emotionally. I'd read an article that said people crave chocolate, gorge on it in fact, when they have been let go by a lover, boss, or spouse.

"I used chocolate in three forms, which was what you needed when times were tough. . . . The brownies came out looking like a chocolate lunar surface. I knew I was supposed to let them cool, but who can do that? I cut out a corner and popped it into my mouth."

—from *Dying for Chocolate: A Culinary Mystery,* by Diane Mott Davidson

Belly Up to the Chocolate Bar

∎∎∎

Lazy People Make Beautiful Chocolate Bars

Unlike brownies and cakes, bars may not pass the clean toothpick test for doneness because of the gooey-ingredient factor. If you see that the sides of the bar or the topping is brown, the bar is probably done. Besides, you can always return it to the oven if it is not.

Invite friends over to join you in a chocolate bacchanalia some evening while you watch the latest gotta-see-it made-for-TV sob fest. Tell them you'll provide the ingredients (you already have most of them) if they'll make the chocolate bars. Then sit back, eat, watch, sob, and enjoy.

Your Own Personal Chocolate Bar

Be creative! Many of these recipes provide basic guidelines, so you can substitute equivalent amounts of a similar ingredient and personalize your chocolate bar. Maybe I've missed your favorite chocolate bar in this contest. Well, you didn't send it to me. But in the back of the book is an address, and if you feel so inclined, write the recipe down and send it to us at Chocolate Heaven.

Great Moments in Chocolate History— Birth of the Bar
■ ■ ■

There once was a mother of four who was actually tired one day. The kids whined and begged her to make chocolate chip cookies. Too exhausted to say no, she agreed. But by the time she had mixed the dough, the very thought of baking batch after batch of cookies every 10 minutes was overwhelming. How could she take a bath and read a chapter in her Danielle Steel novel while the kids were on a whine sabbatical waiting for their treats? She dumped the cookie dough into a 9 × 13-inch pan, baked it for 30 minutes, enjoyed a hot bath, finished a riveting chapter, cut the bars into squares, and everyone was happy. The chocolate bar was born!

Millionaire's Shortbread

Jean Hughes · York, Pennsylvania

■ ■ ■

Family and Friends Chocolate Lover Category

***C**hoc Talk:* Based on a traditional recipe, this shortbread bar is so superbly satisfying you just want to live by "bread" alone. Jean is Scottish and knows what she's doing. Her son Craig, a computer genius, is currently working on chocolate virtual reality. I found this rich, chocolate-covered shortbread satisfying to munch on right after paying taxes.

Yield: *30 servings* **Preparation Time:** *15 minutes* **Baking Time:** *1 hour*
Bakeware Required: *9 × 9-inch baking pan, well greased*

SHORTBREAD
1 cup unsalted butter
¾ cup granulated sugar
2 cups all-purpose flour
1 cup cornstarch

FILLING
½ cup unsalted butter
1 tablespoon firmly packed light brown sugar
7 ounces (half of a 14-ounce can) sweetened condensed milk

TOPPING
Three to four 1.6-ounce premium chocolate candy bars (such as Cadbury's Milk Chocolate or Hershey's Symphony) or one to two 5-ounce bars (Please feel free to use more candy bars if you really need to feel rich.)

To Make the Shortbread

Preheat the oven to 350 degrees.

1. In a large bowl, cream the butter and sugar together.

2. Add the flour and cornstarch to the mixture and knead for a few minutes by hand.

3. Spread the batter in the prepared pan and press down firmly with a spatula or the palm of your hand.

continued

4. Bake for 1 hour, or until the shortbread is golden brown. Let the shortbread cool in the pan on a wire rack while you make the filling.

To Make the Filling

1. In a medium saucepan, heat the butter, brown sugar, and sweetened condensed milk over low heat until the butter is melted and the mixture is bubbling. Simmer for 5 minutes, stirring constantly, until the mixture turns golden brown in color.

2. Remove from the heat and let cool slightly. Spread the filling over the cooled shortbread.

To Make the Topping

1. Melt the chocolate bars (for effective methods and instructions, see page 27). Spread the melted chocolate over the cooled filling. Let the assembled shortbread cool in the pan for 20 minutes. Cut into 2-inch bars and serve during a tax audit or any other special occasion.

Recipe Notes: To add even more chocolate flair to this shortbread bar, add 1 cup semisweet mini morsels to the batter before baking. • If you're a shortbread lover, also try Martin Polenco's Martin's Short Chocolate Pecan Cookie (page 52) and Lynne Schaefer's Chocolate-Glazed Shortbread (page 63).

Chocolate Gooey Bars

Mary David · Kaplan, Louisiana

■ ■ ■

C*hoc Talk:* Creativity was blasting on all cylinders at Chocolate Heaven when we tried Chocolate Gooey Bars. We modified the crust in this recipe so that it would not conflict with the gooeyness (a chocolate technical term) of the filling. Check out the options in the Recipe Note or get the kids (use your own or borrow some) involved in making the bars with their own variations.

Yield: *48 bars* **Preparation Time:** *10 minutes* **Baking Time:** *20 to 25 minutes* **Bakeware Required:** *10 × 15-inch jelly roll pan or 9 × 13-inch baking pan*

CRUST
½ cup unsalted butter
1½ cups graham cracker crumbs

FILLING
1½ cups miniature marshmallows

16 ounces semisweet chocolate chips
2 cups Cheerios
One 14-ounce can sweetened condensed milk

Preheat the oven to 350 degrees.

1. Put the butter in the pan and place in the oven. Allow it to melt completely.

2. Stir in the graham cracker crumbs and combine well with the melted butter. Spread the mixture to cover the pan completely and pat firmly into place. (If using a 9 × 13-inch pan, you may need less crust mixture to cover the bottom. Freeze the extra for future use.)

3. Sprinkle the marshmallows, chocolate chips, and cereal over the graham cracker crust. Drizzle the sweetened condensed milk evenly over the top.

continued

4. Bake for 20 to 25 minutes, or until the cereal is golden brown. While the bars are warm, run a knife around the sides of the pan to loosen the edges. Let cool in the pan on a wire rack for 1 hour, then cut into 2-inch bars.

Recipe Note: You can use this as a basic Gooey Bars recipe and substitute equivalent amounts of other gooey and chocolaty ingredients, such as Cocoa Krispies or Rice Krispies, for the cereal ingredient. We also made the bars with three to four 1.55-ounce chopped Hershey's Cookies 'n' Mint candy bars instead of chocolate chips.

Fee-Phy Fillo Bars

Nita Folsom · Menifee Valley, California
■ ■ ■

C hoc Talk: A funny thing happened on the way to making this recipe. When I realized it used fillo (also spelled phyllo and pronounced either "fee" or "phi") dough, I felt like a fumbling fillo freshman fraught with fury. I fretted and fumed, ever fearful of fillo's fragility, which further frustrated the fruition of this fantastic food. Fortunately, this fretted-over fillo foible was false (it's almost foolproof). Fortified, I flew to the freezer and foraged past forgotten frozen fudge and fricassee to find friendly fillo. Now I'm a flourishing fan of Nita Folsom from Menifee forever.

"Having eighteen grandchildren and always trying to come up with something different for goodies, I concocted this recipe for them because it is flexible. I make a double batch, and for those who do not like nuts, I use creamy peanut butter. For those who love nuts, I add an extra ¼ cup chopped nuts. For those who like coconut, I add ¼ cup coconut. You can also add ⅛ teaspoon cinnamon to the original recipe for a different flavor." —Nita Folsom

Yield: *12 servings* **Preparation Time:** *15 to 20 minutes* **Baking Time:** *20 minutes* **Bakeware Required:** *Cookie sheet, lightly greased*

FILLING	FILLO DOUGH WRAPPING
2 cups bran flakes	*6 fillo leaves*
½ cup low-fat cottage cheese	*¼ cup margarine or butter,*
¼ cup chunky peanut butter	*melted*
⅛ cup granulated sugar	
1 cup semisweet chocolate chips	

Preheat the oven to 375 degrees.

1. In a medium bowl, mix together the bran flakes, cottage cheese, peanut butter, and sugar. Stir in the chocolate chips.

2. Cut each fillo leaf in half crosswise and brush lightly with the melted margarine. Put ¼ cup of the filling mixture toward the end of the leaf and roll the fillo around it a couple of times. Then fold over each end and continue rolling to make a bar that looks like an egg roll.

3. Place the bars on the prepared cookie sheet, seam side down. Lightly coat the top of each roll with the melted margarine. Bake for 20 minutes. Remove from the oven and allow the bars to cool on the cookie sheet for 3 to 4 minutes. These are best served warm.

Deee-luxe Layered Choco-Oat Bars

Nina Schondelmeier · West Hartford, Connecticut

■ ■ ■

hoc Talk: As you bite into this bar, you encounter a complex, deluxe combo of oatmeal cookie, chocolate, and graham cracker crust. Here at Chocolate Heaven, we kept on layering the chocolate blankets and added an optional chocolate cover.

"I tasted a bar similar to this in Farmington, Connecticut, which I bought at a country store across from my obstetrician's office. I was very pregnant and very hungry and it tasted very good."
—Nina Schondelmeier

Yield: *30 bars* **Preparation Time:** *15 to 20 minutes* **Baking Time:** *40 minutes total* **Bakeware Required:** *9 × 11-inch baking pan*

CRUST
⅓ cup unsalted butter or margarine, melted
1½ cups graham cracker crumbs

FILLING
12 ounces semisweet chocolate chips
1 cup butter or margarine, melted
2 cups firmly packed light brown sugar
1 tablespoon hot water

2 large eggs, lightly beaten
2 teaspoons vanilla extract
2 cups all-purpose flour
¼ teaspoon baking soda
1 teaspoon baking powder
1 teaspoon salt
1¼ cups Quick Quaker Oats
1 cup chopped walnuts＊

CHOCOLATE TOPPING (OPTIONAL)
6 ounces semisweet chocolate chips

＊For extra nutty flavor, spread the nuts on a cookie sheet and toast them in a preheated 350 degree oven for 10 to 15 minutes. Stir the nuts occasionally to toast them evenly and prevent burning. Or, toast the nuts in the microwave (they will not change color but will taste toasted). Place 1 cup nuts on a paper plate and microwave uncovered on high power for 3 to 4 minutes, rotating the plate a half turn after 2 minutes.

To Make the Crust

Preheat the oven to 350 degrees.

1. Put the ⅓ cup melted butter in the bottom of the pan. Sprinkle the graham cracker crumbs on top and pat down firmly, covering the bottom of the pan and going ½ inch up the sides. Bake in the oven for 10 minutes.

To Make the Filling Layers

1. Immediately sprinkle chocolate chips on top of the crumb crust after removing it from the oven. Let them melt, then spread the melted chocolate evenly over the entire crust.

2. In a large bowl, mix the 1 cup melted butter with the brown sugar and add the water. Add the eggs and vanilla. Mix well.

3. In a separate bowl, sift together the flour, baking soda, baking powder, and salt. Stir the flour mixture into the creamed butter mixture. Add the oatmeal and mix well. Stir the walnuts into the batter.

4. Spread the batter in the pan over the melted chocolate chips and bake for 30 minutes, or until the sides of the bar pull away from the pan.

To Make the Topping

1. As soon as the bar is out of the oven, immediately sprinkle the chocolate chips evenly on top and allow them to melt. Spread the melted chocolate over the bar. Allow the bar to cool in the pan on a wire rack for at least 1 hour before cutting into squares.

Recipe Note: The added chocolate topping is purely optional. We enjoyed creating the concept. Also, for a true oatmeal cookie taste, you may want to substitute ½ cup raisins for ½ cup of the walnuts.

Double-Mud Bars

Audrey Thibodeau · **Mesa, Arizona**
■ ■ ■
Professional Chocolate Lover Category

***C**hoc Talk:* There's mud in your eye and mud in chocolate pie, but here's mud in a bar that obliterates "No, thank you" from the English (French, Italian, or any) language.

Yield: *18 bars* **Preparation Time:** *15 minutes* **Chilling Time:** *30 minutes to 1 hour* **Baking Time:** *30 minutes* **Bakeware Required:** *9 × 13-inch baking pan, lightly greased*

"Adapted from my tried-and-true brownie recipe, Double-Mud Bars have been a popular treat with my family for many years. Grandchildren especially love their rich chocolate goodness."
—Audrey Thibodeau

2 ounces unsweetened chocolate
1 cup unsalted butter or margarine
2 large eggs
2 cups firmly packed light brown sugar
2 teaspoons vanilla extract
1 cup plus 2 tablespoons all-purpose flour

½ teaspoon baking soda
½ teaspoon salt
24 ounces semisweet chocolate chips, divided
1 cup chopped pecans, toasted*
(optional)

Preheat the oven to 375 degrees.

1. Melt the unsweetened chocolate and butter together (for effective methods and instructions, see page 27). Set aside to cool completely.

---

*For extra nutty flavor, spread the nuts on a cookie sheet and toast them in a preheated 350 degree oven for 10 to 15 minutes. Stir the nuts occasionally to toast them evenly and prevent burning. Or, toast the nuts in the microwave (they will not change color but will taste toasted). Place 1 cup nuts on a paper plate and microwave uncovered on high power for 3 to 4 minutes, rotating the plate a half turn after 2 minutes.

2. In a large bowl, using an electric mixer, beat the eggs lightly. Slowly add the brown sugar to the eggs, continuing to mix at low speed until just combined. Do not overbeat. Add the vanilla and cooled chocolate mixture and blend well.

3. In a separate bowl, combine the flour, baking soda, and salt. Slowly add the flour mixture to the egg mixture and beat at low speed until well mixed. Stir in 1½ cups of the semisweet chocolate chips and the pecans.

4. Spread the mixture in the prepared pan. Bake for 30 minutes, or until a toothpick inserted in the center comes out clean. Do not overbake.

5. Remove the pan to a wire rack and immediately sprinkle the remainder of the chocolate chips over the top. When the chips start to melt, spread them evenly over the bar. If necessary, place the bar back in the hot oven to melt the chocolate chips completely. Refrigerate for 30 minutes to 1 hour to set the chocolate before cutting into squares.

Cool-Whipped Chocolate Peanut Butter Bars

Catherine Winter · San Rafael, California

■ ■ ■

***C**hoc Talk:* This peanut butter and chocolate fantasy is quickly assembled layer by luscious layer. The peanut butter–cream cheese layer is lightened by the addition of whipped cream. Easily whipped up for parties, the bars are considered "awesome," "wicked," and "cool" by kids under the age of eighty-five.

Yield: *10 to 15 servings* **Preparation Time:** *20 minutes* **Baking Time:** *20 minutes* **Chilling Time:** *3 to 5 hours* **Bakeware Required:** *9 × 13-inch baking pan*

CRUST	SECOND FILLING LAYER
1 cup all-purpose flour	*Two 3.9-ounce packages instant*
¾ cup margarine	*chocolate pudding mix*
1 cup chopped peanuts	*3 cups milk*
FIRST FILLING LAYER	**TOPPING**
Two 8-ounce packages cream	*One 8-ounce container Cool*
cheese, softened	*Whip*
¾ cup creamy peanut butter	*½ cup chopped peanuts*
1 cup confectioners' sugar	
One 8-ounce container Cool	
Whip	

To Make the Crust

Preheat the oven to 350 degrees.

1. In a large bowl, combine all the crust ingredients and mix well. Press the mixture into the pan, entirely covering the bottom of the pan and slightly up the sides. Bake for 20 minutes, then remove from the oven and set aside on a wire rack to cool completely.

To Make the First Filling Layer

1. In a large bowl, mix together the cream cheese, peanut butter, and confectioners' sugar.

2. Fold in the Cool Whip, then spread the mixture over the bottom of the cooled crust.

To Make the Second Filling Layer

1. In a large bowl, combine the pudding mix and milk. Whip the mixture for 1 minute. Let the mixture sit for 5 minutes or until firm. (You may need to refrigerate the pudding for an additional 5 minutes if it is not firm.) Then spread it on top of the first layer.

To Make the Topping

1. Spread the Cool Whip on top of the second filling. Sprinkle the chopped nuts on top.

2. Refrigerate for 3 to 5 hours before cutting into squares.

Presentation Note: For a fancier presentation, make your own freshly whipped cream or even try one of the simple flavored whipped cream recipes on page 304. Optional garnish: Drizzle 2 ounces melted semisweet chocolate in a decorative design over the whipped cream topping. For tips on decorating, see page 306.

The Chocolate Cake Walk

■ ■ ■

"Because someone will adore me when my ribs show clearly
and I'm thin even when I sit down
Someone will admire my gorgeous arms and legs
when I'm only one hundred pounds

"Last night I dreamed I ate a chocolate cake, and when I
woke up I was sure it was true, so I weighed myself just to
make sure and drank a diet Coke

"I want to be skinny (Oh I am so hungry) Chow-chow-chow!"
—*Excerpts from the song "Fatso," music and lyrics by Jonatha Brooke,*
performed by The Story, Angel in the House, *© 1993 Elektra Entertainment.*
Reprinted with permission.

You are going to meet a variety of cakes in this chapter, contributed by contestants from all over the country—from quick dump-and-bake cakes (always a favorite) to more elaborate party cakes. In this Chocolate Cake Walk, you will tour through good old-fashioned chocolate cakes, multi-layered tortes, and even a splendid seven-layer white and dark chocolate creation.

From Scratch or a Box?

If you have some flour, eggs, and cocoa or chocolate, you can find a cake to bake in this chapter. There is even a cake (Cheap Chocolate Cake, page 102) that uses sour milk. So keep that milk that's edging past its expiration date. If you don't have flour, we have flourless cakes like the Fallen Cake on page 130, which resembles a chocolate soufflé. So there's no excuse not to bake a cake.

I am a great fan of box cakes. If you don't have the time to make a cake from scratch (you have kids to take care of, work to do, and a life that's pulling at you from a b-zillion directions), box cakes are a quick and easy dessert. The contestants who are on the bake-and-go came up with some very creative and very quick modifications to the basic box cake.

Tips for Making Successful Cakes

- Grease the pan with something other than butter, like short-ening or nonstick cooking spray. Butter has a tendency not to coat the pans thoroughly, and the flour may not adhere to it consistently.
- For chocolate cakes, it is best to line the bottom of the greased pans with wax paper or parchment paper. To cut the paper evenly, place the cake pan on a piece of wax paper or parchment and trace the bottom of the pan with pen or pen-cil. Cut the round out and place it in the bottom of the pan, then thoroughly grease the paper.
- To dust the pans, place a few tablespoons of flour in the pans and shake and tilt them to cover the bottoms and sides. Invert to discard the excess flour.
- Have the ingredients at room temperature. Place the ingre-dients in watertight containers and set them in a large bowl of warm water if you're getting them from the refrigerator and you're in a time crunch. This method is especially rec-ommended for eggs.
- Some of the cake recipes, especially for flourless cakes, re-quire beaten egg whites. For a detailed description of beating egg whites effectively, see page 184.
- Are you fresh out of cake flour? You can substitute all-purpose flour, using ⅞ cup for every 1 cup of cake flour needed. Cake flour will make a lighter cake.
- Buttermilk is a great low-fat cake-baking ingredient. Al-though my wonderful in-laws (the Buies) love the farm-fresh goodness and drink it straight, I prefer buttermilk in a cake

or in a dip. There are gobs of recipes in this book that use buttermilk, so don't throw the rest out after you've used the required amount for a recipe.

- Before preheating the oven, make sure the racks are placed in the center. To prevent your cakes from turning out lopsided, check that the racks are set evenly and that your cake pans aren't warped.
- If you wish to learn more about the art of cake baking from a real master, I suggest you read *The Cake Bible* by Rose Levy Beranbaum (William Morrow, 1988). An incredible resource for any cake-making problem or question, it will assist you and inspire you to bake more challenging and beautiful cakes.

Oven Note

It is best to have an oven thermometer to accurately gauge the temperature, as most ovens are not calibrated correctly (they can run "cold" or "hot"). Always check for the doneness of the recipe prior to the suggested baking time, just to make sure. To check the doneness of a cake, unless it is a soufflé-like cake, you can insert a toothpick or cake tester in the center to see if it comes out clean.

Frosting Tips

- If you want to experiment with different toppings for your chocolate cake, turn to the chapter on frostings (page 297).
- If your cakes come out a little rough on top, carefully cut and even the tops before frosting.
- To make and fill more layers from a two-layer cake, cut each layer in half with either a tightly held piece of dental floss or a cake leveler, which can be found at most kitchen stores. It looks like (and probably is) piano wire strung tightly in an adjustable mechanism that will help you run the wire evenly through the cake. A large, thin, sharp knife will also work.
- Once the pans are removed from the oven, let them cool on wire racks so that the bottoms cool quickly. Unmold the cakes

when instructed in the recipes, but do not let them sit too long in the pans or they will become soggy.

- Once the cakes are unmolded, let them continue to cool on the wire racks.
- Frost the cakes only when they are completely cool or the frosting will melt.
- Dust the cake free of crumbs before frosting.
- Have fun with frosting. Practice with piping, starting off with a simple piping bag. My first piping equipment looked like it belonged in the operating room at the local hospital. So I've learned to do my own thing and have slowly—and I mean slowly—progressed. I recommend cake-decorating classes because you can learn some professional tricks that will make it much easier. There are also cake-decorating videos you can purchase, which may be worth the investment.

Rapid Garnishes

- Finely chopped nuts (you may toast them, too) make a quick garnish on the top and sides of a frosted cake.
- Make a flake cake by sprinkling coconut on the frosting. You can also toast the coconut to a golden color (which is not only pretty but delicious) by spreading it on a cookie sheet and baking it in a 350 degree oven for 10 minutes, or until it turns somewhat golden; stir occasionally for even toasting.
- For flaky color, tint white coconut with a few drops of food coloring diluted in ½ teaspoon of water. Sprinkle this over 1 cup coconut and toss with a fork to coat. Then sprinkle over a frosted cake.
- For a colorful garnish, use jimmies or other cake sprinkles.
- Use broken bits of colorful hard candy (like butterscotch or brightly colored fruit candy) and sprinkle them on the frosted cake in a decorative fashion. A sophisticated version is to use candied ginger (located in the spice section of the grocery store).
- There are some white chocolate frostings on page 301 that you can tint with food coloring for a festive look. Or, see Teri Lindquist's Heaven on Earth Mint Frosting on page 302 and modify it with your favorite flavor and color.

Cakes Take Shape

You can use heart-shaped cake pans or other special molds for holiday cake presentations. If all the batter doesn't fit, bake the extra in muffin tins. The secret to success with unusual shapes is to make sure they are thoroughly greased. The most effective method is to use a nonstick cooking spray.

Okay, it's Valentine's Day and the store has run out of heart-shaped cake pans and you had your heart set on making a Valentine cake for your honey. Here's a quick trick. Divide the cake batter between an 8 × 8-inch square pan and an 8-inch round pan. When the cakes are unmolded and cool, cut the round cake in half crosswise (into 2 half moons). On a cake plate or other presentation platter, place the square cake so that it looks like a diamond. Place one half moon against one side of the diamond and the other half moon against the other side of the diamond. Do you see a heart forming? Then frost it with chocolate frosting or tinted pink frosting (there are white chocolate frostings and plain icing recipe references on page 301).

Cupcakes

Most of the recipes in this chapter can be baked in muffin pans to make cupcakes. Use paper liners and fill the individual cups two thirds full for cupcakes. Cupcakes cook more quickly than cakes, averaging about 12 to 15 minutes, so watch them.

You can also bake cupcakes in flat-bottomed ice cream cones. Fill the cones more than two thirds full, carefully place them on a cookie sheet, and bake until the cupcakes rise. Let them cool before frosting, then decorate with colorful candies.

"I never met a chocolate cake I didn't like."—Willma Rogers, while eating a piece of chocolate cake

The Fastest Chocolate Chip Cake in the World

Stacia Taylor · Overland Park, Kansas

■ ■ ■

Choc Talk: This is the fastest cake in the West (or the world, for that matter). It's all mixed in the pan, so there are few dishes to clean up. It tastes wonderful and is perfect when you need a quick dessert.

Yield: *12 to 16 servings* **Preparation Time:** *5 minutes* **Baking Time:** *35 to 40 minutes* **Bakeware Required:** *9 × 13-inch baking pan, well greased*

¼ cup vegetable oil	*2 large eggs*
One 18.25-ounce chocolate cake mix	*One 3.9-ounce package instant chocolate pudding mix*
1¼ cups water	*1 cup semisweet chocolate chips*

Preheat the oven to 350 degrees.

1. Pour the oil into the pan to coat the bottom.

2. Put all the remaining ingredients into the pan in the order listed.

3. Mix the ingredients thoroughly with a fork.

4. Spread the batter evenly in the pan and bake for 35 to 40 minutes, or until a toothpick inserted in the center of the cake comes out clean. Allow the cake to completely cool before unmolding. Or, serve warm from the pan with toppings as suggested in the Recipe Note.

Recipe Note: This is delicious served warm with Cool Whip or fresh whipped cream. For other topping ideas, see page 297.

Aunt Fannie's Chocolate Cake

Natalie Levy · New York, New York

■ ■ ■

hoc Talk: This is a very easy basic cake to throw together. The Hershey's chocolate syrup gives the cake a chocolaty-brown color and moist texture.

Yield: *12 servings* Preparation Time: *10 minutes* Baking Time: *45 to 55 minutes* Bakeware Required: *9 × 13-inch baking pan, greased*

1 cup margarine, softened	*1 teaspoon vanilla extract*
1 cup granulated sugar	*1 cup plus 2 tablespoons sifted*
4 large eggs	*all-purpose flour*
One 5-½-ounce can Hershey's	*1 teaspoon baking powder*
chocolate syrup	

Preheat the oven to 350 degrees.

1. In a large bowl, cream together the margarine and sugar. Add the eggs one at a time, beating after each addition. Mix in the chocolate syrup and vanilla.

2. In a separate bowl, combine the flour and baking powder. Stir into the creamed mixture.

3. Pour the batter into the prepared pan and bake for 45 to 55 minutes, or until a toothpick inserted into the center of the cake comes out clean. Let the cake cool in the pan on a wire rack for 15 minutes, then remove from the pan, allow the cake to cool completely, and frost if desired.

Recipe Note: This cake is "Heaven on Earth" with Teri Lindquist's green mint frosting and glaze on page 302. Great for St. Patrick's Day! (Or see other frosting suggestions on page 300.)

Cheap Chocolate Cake

Vivian MacKenzie · Fitzgerald, Georgia

■ ■ ■

Choc Talk: This cake may be cheap, but it's rich in chocolate and moistness. You can serve it at the most elegant parties— just use a French name when someone asks you for the recipe (call it "Faux Gateau").

"When a very dear friend gave this recipe to me, my husband had been hospitalized for seven weeks and would not be able to work for a year. We lived on a farm and made a good living, but when my husband was injured, we had to sell most of our animals to pay the large hospital bill. With the help of our four children, my husband did as much of the household duties as he could, and thrifty planning and cooking brought us to the end of that anxious time free of any debts.... We seldom even frost the cake. Sometimes we sprinkle some confectioners' sugar on it, but mostly the cake is eaten warm, right out of the oven, with a glass of cold milk." —Vivian MacKenzie

Yield: *10 to 12 servings* **Preparation Time:** *5 to 10 minutes* **Baking Time:** *45 minutes* **Bakeware Required:** *9 × 9-inch baking pan (glass is preferred but not necessary), greased*

1½ cups sifted all-purpose flour	*1 cup cold water*
1 cup granulated sugar	*⅓ cup oil*
½ teaspoon salt	*1 tablespoon cider vinegar*
1 teaspoon baking soda	*1 teaspoon vanilla extract*
3 well-rounded tablespoons	
* unsweetened cocoa*	

Preheat the oven to 350 degrees.

1. In a large bowl, sift together the flour, sugar, salt, baking soda, and cocoa and set aside.

2. In a separate bowl, combine the remaining ingredients and mix well. Add the dry ingredients to this mixture and stir them

together with a wooden spoon or a wire whisk until just blended smooth.

3. Pour the batter into the prepared pan. Bake for 45 minutes, or until a toothpick inserted in the center of the cake comes out clean. Place the pan on a wire rack and allow the cake to cool for 10 to 15 minutes. Carefully remove the cake from the pan and place the cake on the wire rack to cool completely before frosting.

Recipe Note: Although this cake is delicious plain, we have some fun topping ideas and frostings you may wish to try on it, starting on page 297.

Ginny's "Better Than Sex" Cake

Ginny Willour · Palo Alto, California

■ ■ ■

Family and Friends Chocolate Lover Category

hoc Talk: The cake is simply, sinfully rich, a perfect aphro-disiac to prepare for the opposite sex. This recipe was sub-mitted by Ginny's father, Chuck Willour. Ginny discovered the cake as an undergraduate at the University of Michigan, and it quickly became a Willour family favorite.

"The ultimate chocolate cake, this recipe evidently is an Ann Arbor legacy that is passed down year after year to scores of young women attending the University of Michigan, who delight in shocking their dads (by announcing the title) just before serving them the richest chocolate dessert they will ever eat."
—Chuck Willour

Yield: *12 servings* **Preparation Time:** *20 minutes* **Baking Time:** *25 minutes* **Bakeware Required:** *9 × 12-inch baking pan, greased and floured*

CAKE

5 tablespoons unsweetened cocoa

1 large egg yolk

1½ cups milk, divided

½ cup unsalted butter, softened

2 cups granulated sugar

1 teaspoon vanilla extract

2 large eggs

2 cups all-purpose flour

2 teaspoons baking powder

¼ teaspoon baking soda

½ teaspoon salt

TOPPING

One-half 14-ounce can (7 ounces) sweetened condensed milk

6 ounces caramel ice cream topping

2–4 Heath English Toffee Bars,* crushed

One 8-ounce container Cool Whip

*If you can't find Heath bars, use Skor bars (made by Hershey), which provide the chocolate toffee crunch required in this recipe.

To Make the Cake

Preheat the oven to 350 degrees.

1. In a small saucepan, mix the cocoa, egg yolk, and 1 cup of the milk. Cook the mixture over low heat, stirring, until smooth and thickened. Set aside to cool completely.

2. In a large bowl, cream the butter and add the sugar a little at a time, beating until the mixture is fluffy. Add the vanilla and eggs one at a time, beating well after each addition. Blend in the cooled cocoa mixture.

3. In a separate bowl, sift together the flour, baking powder, baking soda, and salt, then gradually add the dry ingredients to the creamed mixture, alternating with the remaining ½ cup milk and beginning and ending with the dry ingredients. Stir the batter until smooth.

4. Pour the mixture into the prepared pan. Bake for 25 minutes, or until a toothpick inserted in the center of the cake comes out clean. Cool in the pan on a wire rack for 5 minutes.

5. Make several slits in the top of the cooled cake, making sure not to cut through to the bottom.

To Make the Topping

1. In a small saucepan, heat the condensed milk and caramel topping, stirring, until smooth and completely blended. Slowly pour the warm caramel mixture over the top of the cake, letting it sink into the slits, then sprinkle the crushed Heath bar chunks liberally across the entire cake while it is still warm.

2. When the cake is completely cool, top it with the Cool Whip. Serve from the pan.

Presentation Idea: Make this cake in a large heart-shaped cake pan. You may have extra batter, which you can use at another time or bake into cupcakes.

Recipe Note: You may wish to substitute the caramel Heath bar topping with the Coconut Pecan Frosting on page 303.

Hot Chocolate Sundae Cake

Marilyn Mueller · Fayetteville, Arkansas

■ ■ ■

hoc Talk: Now you won't have to choose between a hot choc-olate sundae and chocolate cake. This unusual cake has the chocolate sauce cooked right with the batter. Go all the way and serve the cake with ice cream, fresh whipped cream, and chopped nuts. Or go bananas and top it with sliced ripe bananas and all the other makings for your very own Banana Split Chocolate Sundae Cake.

Yield: *9 servings* **Preparation Time:** *20 minutes* **Baking Time:** *40 minutes* **Bakeware Required:** *8 × 8-inch baking pan, well greased*

CAKE
1 cup semisweet chocolate chips
¾ cup granulated sugar
3 tablespoons margarine
⅓ cup milk
¼ cup crème de cacao liqueur
1¼ cups all-purpose flour
¼ cup unsweetened cocoa
3 teaspoons baking powder

CHOCOLATE SAUCE
¼ cup granulated sugar
¼ cup firmly packed light brown sugar
¼ cup unsweetened cocoa
1½ cups hot water
¼ cup crème de cacao liqueur

To Make the Cake

Preheat the oven to 350 degrees.

1. Spread the chocolate chips evenly on the bottom of the pre-pared pan.

2. In a large bowl, cream together the sugar and margarine. Add the milk and the crème de cacao.

3. In a separate bowl, combine the flour, cocoa, and baking powder.

4. Stir the dry ingredients into the creamed mixture and mix well. Place the batter by spoonfuls over the chocolate chips.

To Make the Chocolate Sauce

1. In a medium saucepan, heat the granulated sugar, brown sugar, cocoa, water, and crème de cacao until the mixture comes to a simmer.

2. Pour the chocolate sauce over the batter and bake the cake for 40 minutes, or until done. Serve the cake hot and garnish as suggested in the Choc Talk.

Recipe Note: You will wonder how the soupy concoction could possibly turn into a cake, but it does. Trust me.

Chocolate Sauerkraut Cake

Lorraine Langlois · Newark, Ohio

■ ■ ■

Choc Talk: Beer and sauerkraut ... in a chocolate cake? Are we kidding? Well, no. The beer and sauerkraut work together to create a moist and surprisingly delicious cake. Our chocolate tasters had no idea what the ingredients were. Have a Polish sausage dinner with a bottle of your favorite German beer, and serve this cake for dessert.

"We moved in 1961 from Rhode Island to Ohio and discovered the area had originally been settled by Germans, who used sauerkraut for many purposes. I was served this cake by a friend and fell in love with it. It is popular around here and has turned out to be a favorite with my chocolate-loving family." —Lorraine Langlois

Yield: *12 to 14 servings* **Preparation Time:** *15 minutes* **Baking Time:** *30 to 45 minutes* **Bakeware Required:** *9 × 13-inch baking pan, well greased*

CAKE

½ cup unsalted butter, softened
1½ cups granulated sugar
3 large eggs
1 teaspoon vanilla extract
2 cups all-purpose flour
¼ teaspoon salt
1 teaspoon baking powder
½ cup unsweetened cocoa
1 cup beer (I use Stroh's), opened 1 hour before using
One half 14½-ounce can (approximately 7 ounces) sauerkraut, rinsed, drained, and chopped very fine

SOUR CREAM CHOCO ICING

6 ounces semisweet chocolate chips
4 tablespoons unsalted butter or margarine
½ cup sour cream
2 to 3 cups confectioners' sugar

To Make the Cake

Preheat the oven to 350 degrees.

1. In a large bowl, cream the butter and sugar together. Add the eggs one at a time, beating well after each addition. Add the vanilla and mix well. Set the mixture aside.

2. In a separate bowl, sift together the flour, salt, baking powder, and cocoa. Add the dry ingredients to the creamed mixture, alternating with the beer (end with the dry ingredients) and mixing well after each addition.

3. Add the sauerkraut to the batter and stir to combine.

4. Pour the batter into the prepared pan. Bake for 30 to 40 minutes, or until a toothpick inserted in the center of the cake comes out clean. Do not overbake. Let the cake cool on a wire rack for 30 minutes, then carefully remove the cake from the pan. Allow the cake to cool completely before icing.

To Make the Icing

1. Melt the chocolate chips and butter together (for effective methods and instructions, see page 27). Set aside to cool slightly.

2. Place the melted chocolate and butter in a large bowl and blend in the sour cream.

3. Add 2 cups confectioners' sugar to the mixture and mix well. Add more confectioners' sugar as needed until the icing reaches the desired consistency.

Recipe Note: The sour cream choco icing is excellent, and I recommend you try it on other chocolate cakes in this chapter.

Gardner's Chocolate Zucchini Cake

Mavis Gardner · Oakland, California

■ ■ ■

***C**hoc Talk:* Fresh from the Gardner. Zucchini has a subtle flavor, which is enhanced by cloves and chocolate in this recipe. It also adds moistness, which makes this cake memorable.

Yield: *20 servings or 5 hungry men* **Preparation Time:** *15 minutes* **Baking Time:** *30 to 40 minutes* **Bakeware Required:** *9 × 11-inch baking pan, greased*

½ cup vegetable oil	*¼ cup unsweetened cocoa*
½ cup margarine, softened	*½ teaspoon baking powder*
1½ cups granulated sugar	*½ teaspoon baking soda*
2 large eggs	*½ teaspoon ground cloves*
1 teaspoon vanilla extract	*2 cups finely diced zucchini*
½ cup sour milk∗	*½ cup semisweet chocolate*
2½ cups all-purpose flour	*chips*

Preheat the oven to 350 degrees.

1. In a large bowl, beat the oil, margarine, and sugar together until creamy. Add the eggs, vanilla, and sour milk. Using an electric mixer, blend the mixture thoroughly.

2. In a separate bowl, sift together the flour, cocoa, baking powder, baking soda, and cloves. Add the dry ingredients to the creamed mixture and beat until well combined.

3. Gently stir the zucchini and chocolate chips into the batter.

4. Pour the batter into the prepared pan. Bake for 30 to 40 minutes, or until a toothpick inserted in the center of the cake comes out clean. Set the pan on a wire rack and cool for 10

∗To make sour milk, add ½ teaspoon cider vinegar or white vinegar to ½ cup milk and let stand for 5 minutes.

minutes. If you wish, carefully remove the cake from the pan or serve from the pan when completely cool.

Recipe Notes: Add one of the great chocolate glazes starting on page 299 for even more chocolate flavor. • If you love zucchini or have a bumper crop in the garden this year, see page 45 for Chocolate Zuke Bread and page 264 for Marion Karlin's Eat-Your-Vegetables Chocolate Cake.

Texas Sheet Cake

Eleanor Cook · Walker, Iowa

■ ■ ■

*C**hoc Talk:** Yummmmmmmm—a universal chocolate mantra meaning peace and harmony that perfectly describes this cake. Spread the frosting on other cakes in this chapter, or on a graham cracker or simply on your finger.

Yield: *12 servings* **Preparation Time:** *15 minutes* **Baking Time:** *30 to 40 minutes* **Bakeware Required:** *9 × 13-inch baking pan, greased and floured*

CAKE	CHOCOLATE FROSTING
2 cups granulated sugar	*⅔ cup semisweet chocolate*
2 cups all-purpose flour	*chips*
1 cup water	*3 tablespoons unsalted butter or*
1 cup margarine	*margarine, softened*
¼ cup unsweetened cocoa	*⅓ cup sour cream*
½ cup sour milk*	*¼ teaspoon vanilla extract*
2 large eggs	*2 to 2½ cups confectioners'*
1 teaspoon baking soda	*sugar*
1 teaspoon vanilla extract	
¼ teaspoon salt	

continued

*To make sour milk, add ½ teaspoon cider vinegar or white vinegar to ½ cup milk and letstand for 5 minutes.

To Make the Cake

Preheat the oven to 350 degrees.

1. In a large bowl, combine the sugar and flour and mix well.

2. Place the water, margarine, and cocoa in a medium microwave-safe bowl and microwave on high power for 1 minute, or until the margarine is melted and the mixture is hot.

3. Add the hot margarine-cocoa mixture to the sugar and flour mixture and beat together. Add the sour milk mixture to the batter and mix well. Then add the eggs, baking soda, vanilla, and salt and mix the batter until smooth.

4. Pour the batter into the prepared pan. Bake for 30 to 40 minutes, or until a toothpick inserted in the center of the cake comes out clean.

To Make the Frosting

1. Melt the chocolate chips (for effective methods and instructions, see page 27). Set aside to cool.

2. In a large bowl, cream the butter with the sour cream and vanilla. Add the melted chocolate, then add the confectioners' sugar to reach the desired consistency. Spread the frosting over the cooled cake.

Recipe Note: You can also use this recipe to make a layer cake. Use two 8-inch round cake pans, greased and floured, and reduce the baking time by 5 to 10 minutes. Or you can make 12 to 16 cupcakes, baking them for 15 to 20 minutes.

Sour Cream Chocolate Cake

Helen Bogucki · Grand Rapids, Michigan

■ ■ ■

***C**hoc Talk:* I think one of the greatest and most versatile culinary inventions is sour cream. It can perk up a potato, dress up a dip, and add creamy moistness to a cake like this one. Try it with sour cream frosting.

"My brother was always hungry for chocolate cake, and every weekend I would bake this cake for him. He never had enough of it." —Helen Bogucki

Yield: *8 servings* **Preparation Time:** *15 minutes* **Baking Time:** *25 to 30 minutes* **Bakeware Required:** *Two 8-inch round cake pans, well greased*

½ cup unsalted butter	*¼ teaspoon salt*
1 cup granulated sugar	*½ cup unsweetened cocoa*
2 large eggs, well beaten	*2 cups sour cream*
1¾ cups all-purpose flour	*½ cup milk*
1½ teaspoons baking powder	*1 teaspoon vanilla extract*

Preheat the oven to 350 degrees.

1. In a medium bowl, cream together the butter and sugar. Add the eggs and mix well.

2. In a large bowl, sift the flour, baking powder, salt, and cocoa together three times. Gradually add the sour cream and milk to the flour mixture, stirring well after each addition. Add the vanilla, then the creamed mixture. Mix well.

3. Divide the batter between the prepared pans. Bake for 25 to 30 minutes, or until a toothpick inserted in the center of the cakes comes out clean. Let the cakes cool on a wire rack for 10 to 15 minutes, then carefully remove from the pans. Let them cool completely on the wire rack before frosting with the recommended frosting (see Recipe Note) or another frosting or glaze suggested on pages 299–300.

continued

Recipe Note: For the perfect frosting for this cake, see the recipe for sour cream icing by Lorraine Langlois on page 108 and don't let the fact it was created for her Sauerkraut Cake turn you off. The frosting is terrific (and so is the cake).

Après Ski Chocolate Cake

Sharron Daily · Colorado Springs, Colorado

■ ■ ■

*C*hoc Talk: I have eaten this cake *avant* and *après* skiing, but you may choose to eat it *au lieu de* skiing (that's "instead of," for those of you who failed French 101). The cake is delicious and moist, and the glaze is wonderful.

"This cake recipe is from a friend I worked with thirty-six years ago in Cedar Rapids, Iowa. The frosting is from a friend in Marion, Iowa. The cake is very moist and the frosting can be eaten right away." —Sharron Daily

Yield: *15 servings* **Preparation Time:** *25 minutes* **Baking Time:** *45 to 50 minutes* **Bakeware Required:** *9 × 13-inch baking pan, well greased and floured*

CAKE	CHOCOLATE GLAZE
½ cup margarine, softened	*1 cup water*
2 cups granulated sugar	*1 cup granulated sugar*
2 large eggs	*3 tablespoons cornstarch*
2 teaspoons baking soda	*⅛ teaspoon salt*
⅛ teaspoon salt	*3 rounded tablespoons*
3 rounded tablespoons	*unsweetened cocoa*
unsweetened cocoa	*3 tablespoons unsalted butter*
2 cups all-purpose flour	*1 tablespoon vanilla extract*
1 cup hot water	

To Make the Cake

Preheat the oven to 350 degrees.

1. In a large bowl, cream the margarine and sugar together. Add the eggs one at a time, beating well after each addition.

2. In a separate bowl, combine the baking soda, salt, cocoa, and flour.

3. Add the dry ingredients to the creamed mixture, then add the hot water. Mix well.

4. Pour the batter into the prepared pan and bake for 45 to 50 minutes, or until a toothpick inserted in the center of the cake comes out clean. Allow the cake to cool on a wire rack for 30 minutes and then carefully remove from the pan. Or, you may serve the cake from the pan after glazing the top, if you prefer.

To Make the Chocolate Glaze

1. In a medium saucepan, combine the water, sugar, cornstarch, salt, and cocoa. Cook over moderate heat, stirring frequently, until the mixture thickens.

2. Remove the pan from the heat and stir in the butter and vanilla until they are well combined. Let the glaze cool, then spread it on the cooled cake.

Recipe Note: The chocolate glaze may also be used as a topping on ice cream.

Hazel Is Nuts—About Chocolate Torte

Kato Perlman · Madison, Wisconsin

■ ■ ■

C*hoc Talk:* Delicious hazelnut and orange flavors combine in this dense chocolate torte. Ground hazelnuts and bread crumbs take the place of flour and create an intriguing texture and a cake that cuts well. Garnish the glossy chocolate glaze with whole hazelnuts and some candied orange peel.

Yield: *12 servings* **Preparation Time:** *20 minutes* **Baking Time:** *40 to 50 minutes* **Bakeware Required:** *9-inch springform pan, greased and floured*

TORTE
¾ cup semisweet chocolate chips
*8 ounces hazelnuts**
⅓ cup plain bread crumbs
1½ teaspoons baking powder
½ cup unsalted butter, softened
1 cup sugar, divided
6 large eggs, separated

2 tablespoons Grand Marnier or orange juice
2 teaspoons grated orange zest†

CHOCOLATE GLAZE
5 ounces semisweet chocolate
3 tablespoons unsalted butter
1 to 2 tablespoons water

GARNISH
1 cup heavy cream, whipped

To Make the Torte

Preheat the oven to 350 degrees.

1. Melt the chocolate chips (for effective methods and instructions, see page 27). Set aside to cool completely.

*Slightly toast the hazelnuts for a more intense flavor. Spread them on a cookie sheet and place in a preheated 375 degree oven. Let them toast for 10 to 15 minutes, stirring frequently to toast evenly and prevent burning. It is not necessary to remove the skins before grinding but if you are saving a few whole hazelnuts for garnish, you can rub off the skins easily after toasting. You may also substitute blanched almonds for the hazelnuts if you cannot find them.

†Using a sharp paring knife or a zester, carefully scrape very thin slices of just the orange part of the peel. Avoid the white part, which is bitter. Chop the grated orange peel fine.

2. In a food processor, grind the hazelnuts and bread crumbs to a fine powder. Add the baking powder and mix well. Set aside.

3. In a large bowl, cream the butter with ¾ cup of the sugar, then add the egg yolks one at a time, mixing well after each addition. Stir in the melted chocolate, Grand Marnier or orange juice, and grated orange zest.

4. In a separate bowl, beat the egg whites until soft peaks form (for further instructions and tips on beating egg whites, see page 184). Add the remaining sugar and continue to beat until the egg whites form stiff peaks.

5. Gently fold one third of the beaten egg whites into the chocolate mixture, alternating in thirds with the hazelnut-crumb mixture until all the egg whites and bread crumbs are combined.

6. Pour the batter into the prepared pan. Bake for 40 to 50 minutes or until the top of the cake is firm. (The clean toothpick rule may not apply to this torte.) The inside of the cake should not be quite done. Remove the pan from the oven and carefully remove the sides of the pan. Allow the cake to cool completely on a wire rack before glazing.

To Make the Glaze

1. Melt the chocolate with the butter and water and mix until smooth (for effective methods and instructions, see page 27). Pour the glaze over the cooled cake. Serve garnished with whipped cream.

Recipe Notes: To enhance the orange flavor even further, substitute Grand Marnier or orange juice for the water in the chocolate glaze. • Hazelnuts are not always easy to find. I finally found some after sending four grocery clerks on a hazelnut hunt in my local supermarket. They came across the last two ½-pound containers stuck behind the eggplant. I have also made this recipe using toasted slivered or blanched almonds, and it works. Just be careful not to overgrind the nuts or you'll end up with almond or hazelnut butter.

Chocolate Mousse Torte
"I Torte I Saw a Pudding Cake"

Arlyn Blake · New York, New York

■ ■ ■
Professional Chocolate Lover Category

*C*hoc Talk: This torte does not rise very high, but it is very dense. Handle with care when removing it from the pans, as it is delicate. Arlyn is the author of her own cookbook, called the *I Love to Cook Book* (Essandess Special Editions, 1971).

"About thirty years ago, a lovely young Canadian woman, Ilsa Felheim, came into our overly competitive Long Island town as the wife of a new community figure. As luck would have it, shortly after she arrived there was a bake sale, and she melted all hearts and delighted all tummies with this quietly spectacular cake."
—Arlyn Blake

Yield: *8 servings* **Preparation Time:** *20 minutes* **Baking Time:** *20 minutes* **Bakeware Required:** *Two 8-inch round cake pans, lined with parchment paper with enough overhang to help unmold the cake, well greased and floured*

4 ounces unsweetened chocolate	*½ cup unsalted butter, softened*
1½ cups slivered almonds, or more as needed (see step 2)	*3 large eggs, separated*
1¼ cups superfine sugar, * *divided*	**OPTIONAL GARNISHES** *Confectioners' sugar* *Chocolate glaze (page 299)*

Preheat the oven to 325 degrees.

1. Melt the chocolate (for effective methods and instructions, see page 27). Set aside to cool completely.

*Superfine sugar is available at the grocery store, or just place 1½ cups granulated sugar in the food processor, grind the sugar to a finer consistency, then measure for the 1¼ cups needed in the recipe. Superfine sugar makes a finer-textured cake.

2. Place at least 1½ cups slivered almonds in a food processor and grind them to a fine texture. Use enough almonds to make 1 cup ground. Be careful not to overgrind the almonds into a paste.

3. In a large bowl, cream 1 cup of the superfine sugar with the butter.

4. Add the melted chocolate and ground almonds to the butter-sugar mixture, then beat in the egg yolks.

5. In a separate bowl, beat the egg whites until foamy. Add the remaining sugar 1 tablespoon at a time while continuing to beat until stiff peaks form (for further instruction and tips on beating egg whites, see page 184). Gently fold the beaten egg whites into the chocolate mixture one third at a time.

6. Place one third of the batter in each of the prepared pans, reserving the remaining batter for the mousse filling (see the Recipe Note for alternative instructions). Bake for 20 minutes, or until a toothpick inserted in the center comes out clean. Let the cakes cool on a wire rack for 5 minutes, then carefully remove from the pans. Place the cakes on the wire rack to completely cool.

7. When the cakes are completely cool, spread the reserved batter or alternative mousse filling over one layer and top with the other. If desired, sift confectioners' sugar over the cake, or spread on the chocolate glaze.

Recipe Note: This unusual recipe uses one third of the uncooked batter as the mousse filling. If this concerns you because of the uncooked eggs, see the mousse chapter (page 183) for alternative mousse fillings. For example, Lorraine Carr's mousse recipe on page 188 would be excellent and uses unflavored gelatin in place of the eggs. If you use an alternative mousse filling, divide all the batter among three 8-inch cake pans or use two 9-inch cake pans.

Festive Choco-Cherry Torte

Eleanor Froehlich · Rochester, Michigan

■ ■ ■

*C**hoc Talk:** This delicious cake rises beautifully and has a rich chocolate color. The cake is sliced into four layers, filled with a mascarpone-cherry filling, and garnished with whipped cream frosting. It is a very pretty torte and should go to a party to receive the adulation it deserves. For an Italian touch, serve it with spumoni ice cream.

"This torte was inspired by the traditional Italian ricotta-filled cake and coffee-flavored mascarpone 'pick-me-up-cake.'* English trifle was also an influence. I love the combination of chocolate/cherry and have carried that idea through in this creation."
—Eleanor Froehlich

Yield: *10 to 12 servings* **Preparation Time:** *30 minutes* **Baking Time:** *30 to 35 minutes* **Bakeware Required:** *Two 9-inch cake pans, greased and floured*

CAKE	
1½ cups granulated sugar	*¾ cup cherry syrup, reserved from can of cherries used in filling (if drained syrup does not equal ¾ cup, add water)*
1¾ cups all-purpose flour	
¾ Dutch-process cocoa†	
2 teaspoons baking soda	
1 teaspoon baking powder	*½ cup vegetable oil*
1 teaspoon salt	*2 teaspoons vanilla extract*
2 large eggs	
1 cup light sour cream	

---

*The Italian "pick-me-up" cake goes under the alias of *tiramisù*. See pages 193–196 for some wonderful tiramisù recipes that will not only pick you up but skyrocket you to the moon.

†This European-style cocoa has alkali in it and more cocoa butter, making a darker, richer cake. An example of a brand is Droste. If you can't find Dutch-process cocoa, use unsweetened cocoa such as Hershey's.

FILLING

16 ounces (1 pint) mascarpone cheese

¼ cup granulated sugar

3 tablespoons kirsch or other cherry-flavored liqueur

One 16-ounce can sweet black cherries, drained (reserve syrup), pitted, and cut into halves

½ cup semisweet mini chocolate chips (optional)＊

WHIPPED CREAM FROSTING

⅔ cup confectioners' sugar

¼ cup Dutch-process cocoa

2 cups heavy cream

1 teaspoon vanilla extract

GARNISH

Chocolate curls or semisweet mini chocolate chips

To Make the Cake

Preheat the oven to 350 degrees.

1. In a large bowl, combine the sugar, flour, cocoa, baking soda, baking powder, and salt. Add the eggs, sour cream, cherry syrup, oil, and vanilla. Beat the mixture using an electric mixer at medium speed for 2 minutes. The batter will be thin.

2. Pour the batter into the prepared pans and bake for 30 to 35 minutes, or until a toothpick inserted in the center comes out clean. Let the cakes cool on a wire rack for 10 minutes before removing them from the pans, then let them cool completely on the wire rack.

To Make the Filling

1. In a medium bowl, combine the mascarpone cheese, sugar, and kirsch. Beat the mixture until it is very smooth.

2. Blot the drained cherry halves with paper towels to absorb as much liquid as possible. Gently fold the cherries into the cheese mixture along with the mini chips, if using.

continued

＊The filling is so creamy, I recommend using the chips as a garnish instead.

To Make the Frosting

1. In a small bowl, combine the confectioners' sugar and cocoa. Add the whipping cream and vanilla. Beat the mixture until it is stiff.

To Assemble the Torte

1. Slice each cake layer in half horizontally (for instructions, see page 97). Place one slice on a serving plate and top with one third of the mascarpone filling. Alternate the cake layers and filling, ending with the last layer of cake on top.

2. Cover the top and sides of the torte with whipped cream frosting. Garnish with chocolate curls or mini chocolate chips. Refrigerate before serving and store any leftover torte in the refrigerator.

Recipe Notes: This cake can be frozen for up to 1 month. So make it in advance and have it ready to go when you are. • We found the extra whipped cream frosting delicious when stirred into coffee, which we drank in great quantities while making one thousand chocolate recipes. • This cake is great unfrosted as well, if you happen to accidentally use all the whipped cream in pots of coffee.

Eeee-Zeee Chocolate Cake

Vivian Cohen · Novato, California
■ ■ ■

*C**hoc Talk:** How can so few ingredients make such a fudg-ee cake? I always thought "E" was for effort, but this rich, flourless cake proves "E" stands for Easy and Everyone should Eat Everything. No frosting needed (see Recipe Notes).

"This recipe comes from my great-grandaunt from Czechoslovakia. My family cannot live without this cake!" —Vivian Cohen

Yield: *6 servings* **Preparation Time:** *10 to 15 minutes* **Baking Time:** *40 to 45 minutes* **Bakeware Required:** *9-inch springform pan, well greased and floured*

½ cup semisweet chocolate chips	*1 cup walnuts*
	4 large eggs, separated
4 tablespoons unsalted butter	*½ cup granulated sugar, divided*

Preheat the oven to 350 degrees.

1. Melt the chocolate chips with the butter (for effective methods and instructions, see page 27). Set aside to cool completely.

2. In a food processor or blender, grind the walnuts into very small pieces. Be careful not to grind them to a powder.

3. In a large bowl, beat the egg yolks. Gradually beat in ¼ cup sugar until the mixture is thick and lemon-colored. Add the chocolate-butter mixture and the ground walnuts to the egg yolk mixture.

4. In a separate bowl, beat the egg whites until foamy. Then, add the remaining ¼ cup sugar, 1 tablespoon at a time, while continuing to beat the egg whites until they form stiff peaks (for further instructions and tips on beating egg whites, see page 184). Gently fold the beaten egg whites into the egg yolk batter.

5. Pour the batter into the prepared pan. Bake for 40 to 45 minutes, or until a toothpick inserted in the center of the cake comes out clean. Place the pan on a wire cooling rack and allow to cool for 10 minutes before removing the sides of the pan. This is a delicate cake and should be served without removing the bottom of the pan.

Recipe Notes: Top each serving with whipped cream or ice cream. • This cake does not rise very high, but makes up for stature with its dense chocolatiness. This recipe can be easily doubled and baked in one 9-inch springform cake pan. If doubling the recipe, you may need to bake an additional 10 to 15 minutes, but still check it for doneness at 45 minutes.

Bittersweet Cake

Mary Ann Lee · Marco Island, Florida
■ ■ ■

*C**hoc Talk:** Light and chocolaty, this cake has a sophisticated, not-too-sweet flavor found in elegant chocolate cakes served at the finest restaurants. The frosting has an extra bite from bittersweet chocolate, adding that little edge sometimes needed in both love and chocolate to keep things interesting.

Yield: *10 to 12 servings* **Preparation Time:** *20 minutes* **Baking Time:** *30 minutes* **Bakeware Required:** *Three 8-inch layer pans, lined with wax paper or parchment paper and well greased*

CAKE	BITTERSWEET FROSTING
4 ounces unsweetened chocolate	*9 ounces unsweetened chocolate*
¼ cup solid vegetable shortening	*½ cup plus 2 tablespoons unsalted butter, softened*
2 cups sifted cake flour	*2¾ cups sifted confectioners' sugar*
¾ teaspoon salt	
2 cups granulated sugar	*¼ cup hot water*
2 large egg yolks	*3 large eggs*
1¾ cups milk, divided	*⅛ teaspoon salt*
1 teaspoon vanilla extract	*1½ teaspoons vanilla extract*
1 teaspoon baking soda	

To Make the Cake

Preheat the oven to 350 degrees.

1. Melt the chocolate with the shortening (for effective methods and instructions, see page 27). Set aside to cool completely.

2. In a large bowl, sift the flour with the salt.

3. Place the chocolate in a separate large bowl and add the sugar. Using an electric mixer at low speed, blend well. Mix in the egg yolks and 1 cup of the milk. Add the flour mixture and stir just until all the flour is dampened. Then, with the mixer at low speed, beat the batter for 1 minute, until smooth. Add the vanilla and ½ cup of the milk to the batter and mix well.

4. In a small bowl, dissolve the baking soda in the remaining ¼ cup milk. Using a spoon, stir this mixture quickly but thoroughly into the batter.

5. Divide the batter evenly among the prepared pans. Bake for 30 minutes, or until a toothpick inserted in the cake's center comes out clean. Let the cakes cool on wire racks for 10 minutes before carefully removing them from the pans. Peel the paper off the cakes and let them cool completely on the wire racks before frosting.

To Make the Frosting

1. Melt the chocolate with the butter (for effective methods and instructions, see page 27). Set aside to cool completely.

2. In a large bowl, combine the confectioners' sugar, water, and melted chocolate. Stir only to dampen the sugar. Add the eggs one at a time, beating well after each addition. Add the salt and vanilla and mix well.

3. Use the frosting as a filling between the cake layers and to frost the top and sides of the cake. Cover and refrigerate the cake after it is frosted. Remove the cake from the refrigerator and let it reach room temperature before serving.

Recipe Note: The bittersweet frosting contains uncooked egg whites. You can use an equivalent amount of egg substitute (which is pasteurized), if you wish. If you do, reduce the amount of confectioners' sugar and use only as much as you need to reach the desired consistency.

Double-Chocolate Mocha Supreme Cake

Ann Marshall · Hudson, Massachusetts

■ ■ ■

***C**hoc Talk:* This elegant cake rises well and has a good texture. It is a *real* "coffee cake," complete with brewed coffee, milk, and sugar. Have it for breakfast instead of a cup of coffee while you're commuting to work and reduce the risk of spills and stains. What a way to start the day.

"I love to create a cake that combines the flavors of coffee and chocolate in both the cake and the frosting—double the taste."
—Ann Marshall

Yield: *8 to 10 servings* **Preparation Time:** *25 minutes* **Baking Time:** *35 minutes total* **Bakeware Required:** *Two 8-inch round cake pans, greased and floured*

CAKE

½ cup hot brewed coffee
1 tablespoon unsalted butter
4 ounces unsweetened chocolate, chopped
½ cup unsalted butter, softened
1 cup granulated sugar
2 large eggs
1¾ cups all-purpose flour
¼ teaspoon salt
2 teaspoons baking powder
½ teaspoon ground cinnamon
½ cup milk
1 teaspoon vanilla extract

CHOCOLATE MOCHA FROSTING

4 ounces unsweetened chocolate, chopped
½ cup unsalted butter, softened
¼ cup hot brewed coffee
1 teaspoon vanilla extract
¼ to ½ teaspoon almond extract (optional)
1 pound confectioners' sugar

GARNISH

*1½ cups chopped walnuts, toasted**

*For extra nutty flavor, spread the nuts on a cookie sheet and toast them in a preheated 350 degree oven for 10 to 15 minutes. Stir the nuts occasionally to toast them evenly and prevent burning. Or, toast the nuts in the microwave (they will not change color but will taste toasted). Place 1 cup nuts on a paper plate and microwave uncovered for 3 to 4 minutes, rotating the plate a half turn after 2 minutes.

To Make the Cake

Preheat the oven to 350 degrees.

1. Place the coffee, 1 tablespoon butter, and chocolate in a double boiler. Bring the water to a boil. Reduce the heat and simmer until the chocolate melts. Set aside to cool completely.

2. In a large bowl, cream the ½ cup butter and gradually add the sugar. Add the eggs and beat the mixture well. Add the chocolate mixture and continue beating.

3. In a separate bowl, combine the flour, salt, baking powder, and cinnamon. Gradually add the dry ingredients to the creamed mixture, alternating with the milk and beating well after each addition (end with the dry ingredients). Using an electric mixer on low speed, beat the batter until smooth. Stir in the vanilla.

4. Divide the batter between the prepared pans and bake for 25 minutes, or until a toothpick inserted in the center of each cake comes out clean. Let the cakes cool on a wire rack for 10 to 15 minutes before carefully removing from the pans. Let them cool completely on the wire rack before frosting.

To Make the Frosting

1. Melt the chocolate (for effective methods and instructions, see page 27). Set aside to cool completely.

2. In a large bowl, cream the butter and add the melted chocolate, coffee, vanilla, and almond extract, if using, to taste. Stir the mixture together. Add as much of the confectioners' sugar as needed to reach the desired consistency then beat until light and fluffy.

3. Spread the frosting on the cooled cake between the layers and lightly on the sides. Spoon the remaining frosting on top of the cake, spreading just to the edge. Coat the sides of the cake with the toasted walnuts.

Wicked Good Chocolate Cake

Ellen Burr · Truro, Massachusetts

· · ·

hoc Talk: This is not an overly sweet cake, so kids may not like it, but the bittersweet chocolate flavor would please any Euro-palate. Rich, dark, moist, and wickedly good, this cake lets you experience the dark side of chocolate. Vicky Victor's Fallen Cake is another flourless cake that uses brandy in the recipe (see page 130).

"This 'fallen soufflé,' a favorite company dessert, is enhanced by traditional New England flavors and ingredients. I gather my own wild blueberries and use the freshest eggs available. Whether we're feasting on lobster or digging into a bowl of economical chowder, this finale makes any get-together a festive occasion. Of course, you may garnish this cake with raspberries or strawberries, but then it would be just decadent or sinful, not 'Wicked Good.'"
—Ellen Burr

Yield: *12 servings* **Preparation Time:** *20 minutes* **Baking Time:** *30 minutes* **Bakeware Required:** *9-inch springform pan, greased and dusted with 1 to 2 teaspoons unsweetened cocoa*

12 ounces bittersweet (such as Baker's German's Chocolate), broken up

½ cup unsalted butter, cut into small pieces

8 large eggs, separated

½ cup granulated sugar, divided

1 tablespoon* dark rum or 1 teaspoon rum extract

GARNISHES

Cinnamon-flavored whipped cream (see page 304)

Fresh blueberries

Diced crystallized ginger

*You may wish to increase the amount to taste.

Preheat the oven to 350 degrees.

1. Melt the chocolate and butter together (for effective methods and instructions, see page 27). Set aside to cool completely.

2. In a large bowl, using an electric mixer, beat the egg whites at high speed until soft peaks form. (For further instructions and tips on beating egg whites, see page 184). Gradually beat in ¼ cup of the sugar, 1 tablespoon at a time.

3. In a separate bowl, beat the egg yolks with the rum and the remaining ¼ cup sugar until the mixture is thick and lemon-colored. Fold the egg yolk mixture into the melted chocolate and butter. Gently fold this mixture into the beaten egg whites.

4. Pour the batter into the prepared pan and bake for 30 minutes, or until a toothpick inserted in the center of the cake comes out clean. Let the cake cool completely on a wire rack before carefully removing the sides of the springform pan. Transfer the cake to a serving platter.

5. Before serving, garnish with rosettes of whipped cream studded with blueberries and crystallized ginger. Serve at room temperature.

Presentation Note: Serve the cake with a raspberry or strawberry purée (see page 305).

Fallen Cake

Vicky Victor · London, Ohio

■ ■ ■

***C**hoc Talk:* I've fallen in love with this cake; it calls for *a lot* of eggs, but primarily egg whites, which give it buoyancy. And it's flourless—like a soufflé cake. While it's cooking, it may look like a horrible science experiment gone berserk, but don't worry. The about-to-explode cake falls back into shape. Be careful taking it out of the oven.

"My hairdresser's client gave me this recipe to try. I made it for my family, who enjoyed it and said, 'This is too rich, but can I have another small piece?'" —Vicky Victor

Yield: *10 to 12 servings* **Preparation Time:** *20 minutes* **Baking Time:** *1 hour 15 minutes* **Bakeware Required:** *9-inch springform pan*

10 ounces semisweet chocolate	*6 large eggs, separated*
2 ounces unsweetened chocolate, chopped	*6 additional large egg whites*
	⅓ cup rum, brandy, or cognac
1½ cups unsalted butter, chopped	*1 cup granulated sugar, divided*

Preheat the oven to 300 degrees.

1. Melt the chocolate chips, unsweetened chocolate, and butter together (for effective methods and instructions, see page 27). Transfer the melted chocolate and butter mixture to a large bowl and set aside to cool completely.

2. Add the 6 egg yolks, the rum, and ¾ cup of the sugar to the chocolate mixture. Stir until the mixture is smooth.

3. In another large bowl, beat the 12 egg whites until foamy. Add the remaining ¼ cup sugar, 1 tablespoon at a time, while continuing to beat the egg whites until they form soft peaks. (For further instructions and tips on beating egg whites, see page 184). Gently fold one third of the beaten egg whites into the batter, then fold in the remaining egg whites one third at a time until all are incorporated.

4. Pour the batter into the pan and bake for 1 hour 15 minutes. Let the cake cool on a wire rack for 15 minutes before carefully removing the sides of the springform pan. Transfer the cake to a serving platter and let cool completely.

Recipe Note: This cake is so moist, a frosting would be an insult. But it is sweet and would be well complemented by a raspberry purée (see page 305). Or simply sprinkle confectioners' sugar over the top. Since it does have a soufflé-like texture, I also recommend the Grand Marnier sauce on page 299 and the cherry whipped cream recipe that accompanies Diane Halferty's Hot Chocolate Soufflés on page 254.

Chocolate
Malted Milk Cake

Sophia Benfield · Valparaiso, Indiana

■ ■ ■

Choc Talk: I could eat this whole cake and never stop to consider whether anyone else would like a slice. But then I'm a
maltaholic, the worst kind of chocoholic. When I was a kid, I was
out of control around malted milk balls. Every time we went to
the candy store in Nisswa, Minnesota (out in the boonies, three
hours north of Minneapolis), my best friend and I would be loaded
with babysitting bucks. She would buy just a few lemon drops or
butterscotch candies, being sure to save her money for other
things. I would give the candy clerk all my money and ask, "How
many pounds of malted milk balls will this buy?" And I would smile
and smile, hoping that he'd add a few extra. When we were in the
car driving all the way back to Pequot Lakes, my frugal friend
would politely eat one or two candies while admiring the new moc-
casins she had just bought at the Totem Pole, then roll up her
white paper bag to save some for later, and while slowly sucking
her last lemon drop of the day, she would watch me shove even
more malted milk balls in my chipmunk face. "I am destined to be
a pig for the rest of my life," I'd say to myself, staring at my beat-
up Keds. "A *poor* and pitiful pig." And I went home with an empty
pocket and an empty white bag, while she went home with money
and candy. And thin, the girl was so thin.

Yield: *6 to 8 servings* **Preparation Time:** *20 minutes* **Baking Time:**
30 to 35 minutes **Bakeware Required:** *Two 8-inch square baking
pans, greased*

CAKE

2 ounces unsweetened
chocolate, chopped

1/2 cup unsalted butter or
margarine, softened

1 cup granulated sugar

2 large eggs

1/2 teaspoon salt

2 cups cake flour

1/4 cup chocolate malted milk
powder*

1/4 teaspoon baking soda

2 teaspoons baking powder

1 cup milk

MALTED MILK FROSTING

2 to 2 1/2 cups confectioners'
sugar

1/4 cup chocolate malted milk
powder*

1/4 cup unsalted butter, softened

1/2 teaspoon salt

1/4 cup strong brewed coffee

DECORATIVE GLAZE

1 ounce semisweet chocolate

1/2 teaspoon solid vegetable
shortening

To Make the Cake

Preheat the oven to 350 degrees.

1. Melt the chocolate (for effective methods and instructions, see page 27). Set aside to cool completely.

2. In a large bowl, cream the butter with the sugar until the mixture is light and fluffy. Add the eggs one at a time, beating well after each addition. Beat the salt and melted chocolate into the egg mixture.

3. In a separate bowl, sift together the cake flour, malted milk powder, baking soda, and baking powder. Gradually add the dry ingredients to the creamed mixture, alternating with the milk (end with the dry ingredients) and mixing well after each addition.

4. Using an electric mixer, beat the batter at low speed until well blended. Beat for 2 minutes at medium speed, scraping the sides of the bowl frequently.

5. Divide the batter between the prepared pans. Bake for 30 to 35 minutes, or until a toothpick inserted in the center of each cake comes out clean. Let the cakes cool on a wire rack for 10 minutes

*Chocolate malted milk powder is available in the baking section of most supermarkets, usually with the cocoa powders.

before removing them carefully from the pans. Let them cool completely on the wire rack before frosting.

To Make the Frosting

1. Sift the confectioners' sugar together with the malted milk powder.

2. In a large bowl, combine 1 cup of this mixture with the butter and salt and mix until creamy. Gradually add the rest of the sugar mixture, alternating with enough coffee to achieve a good spreading consistency.

3. Frost each layer of the cake with the frosting and position one layer on top of the other. Frost the outside of the cake completely.

To Make the Decorative Glaze

1. Melt the chocolate with the shortening (for effective methods and instructions, see page 27).

2. Drizzle the melted chocolate in a decorative fashion on top of the frosting. *Hint:* Place the melted chocolate in a small heavy-duty Ziploc plastic bag. Cut a very small piece off the bag's corner and squeeze gently, using it like a pastry bag to create designs.

Recipe Note: Buy a quart of Whoppers (malted milk balls in a wax milk-type container) and eat several straight from the milk spout. Reserve a few to crush and sprinkle on the cake as garnish.

Red Devil Cake
Dressed in Satin Beige

Peggy Bolmgren · Louisville, Ohio

■ ■ ■

*C*hoc Talk: Devilishly tempting, this is the chocolate cake for an occasion—all dressed in fluffs of satin. The gossamer-like frosting goes well with any dense or rich cake.

"I graduated from Timken Vocational High School in Canton, Ohio, in 1941. Our tearoom served delicious meals to the public, and the favorite cake was Red Devil's Cake with Satin Beige Frosting. I'm hoping that you will agree that 'it takes the cake'! Miss Groves, my instructor, would never let us give out her recipes, but now, since she is gone, I think she would be pleased to have her cake remembered as the favorite." —Peggy Bolmgren

Yield: *8 to 10 servings* Preparation Time: *20 to 25 minutes* Baking Time: *25 to 30 minutes* Bakeware Required: *Two 8-inch round cake pans, greased*

CAKE
2 ounces unsweetened chocolate, chopped
2 cups sifted cake flour
1¼ teaspoons baking soda
¼ teaspoon salt
½ cup butter or margarine
1 cup granulated sugar
2 large eggs
1 teaspoon vanilla extract
¾ cup sour milk* or buttermilk
⅓ cup boiling water

SATIN BEIGE FROSTING
½ cup firmly packed dark brown sugar
2 tablespoons water
¼ cup dark corn syrup
2 large egg whites
1½ teaspoons vanilla extract

continued

*To make sour milk, add ¾ teaspoon cider vinegar or white vinegar to ¾ cup milk and let stand for 5 minutes.

To Make the Cake

Preheat the oven to 350 degrees.

1. Melt the chocolate (for effective methods and instructions, see page 27). Set aside to cool completely.

2. In a medium bowl, combine the flour, baking soda, and salt.

3. In a large bowl, using an electric mixer, cream the butter until it is light and lemon-colored. Gradually add the sugar, beating after each addition until the mixture is light and fluffy. Add the eggs to the creamed mixture one at a time, beating well after each addition. Then stir in the melted chocolate.

4. In a small bowl, stir the vanilla into the sour milk.

5. Gradually add the dry ingredients to the chocolate mixture, alternating with the vanilla milk and beating well after each addition. Add the boiling water and beat until the mixture is smooth.

6. Divide the batter between the prepared pans and bake for 25 to 30 minutes, or until a toothpick inserted in the center of each cake comes out clean. Let the cakes cool on a wire rack for 10 minutes before removing them carefully from the pans. Let them cool completely on the wire rack before frosting.

To Make the Satin Beige Frosting

1. Place the brown sugar, water, and corn syrup in a small saucepan and mix thoroughly. Cover the pan and place over moderate heat for several minutes to dissolve the sugar.

2. Remove the cover and continue boiling, stirring occasionally until the mixture reaches a consistency that allows a thread approximately 6 inches long to be spun (by holding a tablespoon of the hot syrup above the pan and letting it drip back into the pan). If you want to use a candy thermometer for accuracy, the temperature should reach 234 degrees Fahrenheit.

3. In a large bowl, beat the egg whites until stiff peaks form (for further instruction and tips on beating egg whites, see page 184). Quickly pour the hot syrup over the stiffly beaten egg whites and beat the mixture until well combined. Add the vanilla and continue beating until stiff peaks form.

4. Frost both layers of the cooled cake, place one layer on top of the other, and completely frost the outside of the cake. If using a chocolate glaze, drizzle some near the sides (on the serving platter) and on top of the cake for presentation. Let the cake stand for 2 hours before cutting to allow the red color to develop.

Recipe Note: Use one of the recommended chocolate glazes on page 299 to decorate the cake.

Double-Chocolate Tornado Cake

Josephine Piro · Easton, Pennsylvania

■ ■ ■

***C**hoc Talk:* Tornado Cake will swoop you into its dark, chocolaty vortex. There's no escape. I grew up in Kansas and have been bombarded by real tornadoes and really bad Wizard of Oz jokes for most of my life ("How's Toto?"). This is one tornado that won't send me diving for cover.

"My chief taster and supporter is my husband, Tony (who loves food, especially anything chocolate), and he named this cake Double-Chocolate Tornado Cake. When you eat it, watch it disappear like a tornado!" —Josephine Piro

Yield: *12 servings* **Preparation Time:** *20 minutes* **Baking Time:** *30 to 35 minutes* **Bakeware Required:** *Two 9-inch round cake pans*

CAKE

2 cups all-purpose flour

2 teaspoons baking powder

2 teaspoons baking soda

³/₄ cup unsweetened cocoa

2 cups granulated sugar

4 large egg whites (or egg substitute equivalent to 2 whole eggs)

¹/₂ cup canola oil

2 cups cappuccino prepared from instant mix such as General Foods International Coffees or 2 cups hot brewed coffee

CHOCOLATE MOCHA FROSTING

3 cups unsifted confectioners' sugar

¹/₂ cup unsweetened cocoa

¹/₂ cup unsalted butter, softened, cut into small pieces

¹/₃ cup cappuccino or 1 tablespoon instant coffee dissolved in ¹/₃ cup boiling water or ¹/₃ cup hot strong brewed coffee

1 teaspoon vanilla extract

OPTIONAL GARNISH

Fresh raspberries

To Make the Cake

Preheat the oven to 350 degrees.

1. Grease the cake pans. Line the bottoms with wax paper or parchment paper (see page 96) and grease the paper well. Dust the lined and greased pans with flour, then shake out the excess flour.

2. In a large bowl, sift together the flour, baking powder, baking soda, cocoa, and sugar.

3. In a separate bowl, using an electric mixer at low speed, beat the egg whites with the oil until foamy.

4. Gradually stir the egg mixture into the flour mixture, alternating with the cappuccino and mixing well after each addition. (The batter should be a bit runny.)

5. Divide the batter between the prepared pans and bake for 30 to 35 minutes, or until a toothpick inserted in the center of each cake comes out clean. Let the cakes cool in the pans on a wire rack for 10 minutes, then invert onto the wire rack to cool completely. Carefully remove the wax paper from the cakes.

To Make the Frosting

1. In a large bowl, stir together the confectioners' sugar and cocoa. Add the butter, cappuccino, and vanilla. Beat the mixture with an electric mixer at low speed until well combined. Beat for 1 minute at medium speed. Chill for 20 to 30 minutes if necessary for the frosting to reach spreading consistency.

To Assemble

1. Trim the top of the cake layers with a long serrated knife, cutting off any raised areas. Place one layer on a serving plate. Spread 1 cup of the frosting evenly over it. Top with the remaining cake layer. Reserve some of the frosting for piping decorations if desired, then frost the sides and top of the cake with a thin layer of frosting.

2. Put the reserved frosting in a pastry bag with an open star tip. Pipe a border around the bottom and top edge of the cake. Refrigerate until ready to serve.

3. If desired, just before serving, garnish the cake with fresh raspberries.

Chocolate-Covered Memory

■ ■ ■

"Nobody makes chocolate wedding cakes."

"I'll find someone to make it."

"What will people think?"

"About a caterer who makes a chocolate wedding cake?"

"No, about a stubborn girl who wants a chocolate cake at her wedding when every other bride in the entire universe has a pure white cake."

"My friends will be happy because they love chocolate cake. Your friends will think that I'm not a virgin because the cake is brown. And they'll be happy because they'll have something to talk about."

"Don't talk dirty."

—The mother-daughter wedding duel in *Growing Up on the Chocolate Diet*, a memoir with recipes by Lora Brody.

Seven Sins Chocolate Torte

Lynda Sarkisian · Salem, South Carolina

■ ■ ■

***C**hoc Talk:* This seven-layered white/dark chocolate extravaganza is a little more complex to make but so worth the time and effort for a dessert that will absolutely *wow* a crowd. If cutting this towering *sin*sation proves a little intimidating, make two 3-layer tortes, topping them off with the white chocolate filling, and reap double the benefit.

Yield: *10 to 12 servings* **Preparation Time:** *1 hour* **Baking Time:** *45 to 50 minutes total* **Bakeware Required:** *Three 9-inch round cake pans, lined with wax paper or parchment paper (see page 96), greased, and floured*∗

MACAROON LAYERS

3/4 cup granulated sugar
1/2 teaspoon baking powder
3 large egg whites
3/4 cup sweetened flaked coconut
1/2 cup finely chopped pecans
1 cup vanilla cookie crumbs

CAKE LAYERS

1 cup solid vegetable shortening
2 cups granulated sugar
3 large eggs
1/2 cup unsweetened cocoa
2 teaspoons baking soda
1/2 teaspoon salt
1 cup milk
1 tablespoon white vinegar

1 teaspoon vanilla extract
2 1/2 cups all-purpose flour
1 cup hot water

WHITE CHOCOLATE FILLING

1 cup white chocolate chips
2 tablespoons Grand Marnier liqueur
1 cup half-and-half
One 8-ounce package cream cheese, softened
One 3.4-ounce package vanilla instant pudding mix
One 8-ounce container frozen whipped topping, thawed (or use fresh whipped cream)

continued

∗Two pans will be reused and will require preparation twice.

To Make the Macaroon Layers

Preheat the oven to 350 degrees.

1. In a small bowl, combine the sugar and baking power.

2. In a large mixing bowl, beat the egg whites to soft peaks. Gradually add the sugar mixture to the beaten egg whites, one tablespoon at a time, beating the mixture until stiff peaks form (for further instructions and tips on beating egg whites, see page 184).

3. In a medium bowl, combine the coconut, pecans, and cookie crumbs. Gently fold this mixture into the beaten egg whites. Divide the mixture between two of the prepared pans. Bake for 15 to 20 minutes, or until firm and lightly browned. Place the pans on wire racks and allow to cool for 10 minutes, then carefully remove them from the pans. Let the macaroon layers cool completely on the wire racks and then remove the wax paper.

To Make the Cake

1. In a large bowl, using an electric mixer at medium-high speed, cream the shortening and sugar together until light and fluffy. Add the eggs, and mix well.

2. In a medium bowl, combine the cocoa, baking soda, and salt. Beat this mixture into the creamed sugar and eggs until the batter is smooth and creamy.

3. In a small bowl, mix together the milk, vinegar, and vanilla. Add this mixture to the batter, alternating with the flour (end with the flour), and combine well, scraping the side of the bowl occasionally.

4. Add the hot water and beat again, blending all the ingredients well. Divide the batter among three prepared pans. Bake for 30 to 35 minutes, or until firm to the touch.

To Make the White Chocolate Filling

1. Combine the white chocolate chips, liqueur, and half-and-half in the top of a double boiler. Cook and stir over simmering water until the chocolate is melted and smooth. Remove from the heat and set aside to cool completely.

2. In a large bowl, using an electric mixer at medium-high speed, beat the cream cheese until light and fluffy. Reduce the speed to low and gradually add the pudding mix and cooled white chocolate mixture. Increase the speed if necessary, and beat until smooth and creamy. Fold in the whipped topping (or fresh whipped cream), blending all the ingredients well.

To Assemble the Torte

1. Place a chocolate cake layer on a serving plate and spread with white chocolate filling.

2. Top with a macaroon layer and spread with another layer of filling.

3. Continue layering the cakes and filling, alternating white chocolate and macaroon layers.

4. Frost the top and sides of the torte with any remaining filling. Refrigerate at least 1 hour before serving.

Chocolate Checkerboard Cake

Chocolate Heaven Creation

■ ■ ■

hoc Talk: Checkmate with this cake. This is very easy to make, but looks complex. This chocolate cake is a FUN idea, especially when you're designated the dessert maker for a school or social event.

Yield: *One 3-layer cake to serve about 6 people or 1 avid chess player* **Preparation Time:** *20 minutes* **Baking Time:** *25 minutes* **Bakeware Required:** *See Recipe Note*

3 ounces semisweet chocolate, chopped

Two 18.25-ounce (approximately) boxes of yellow or white cake mix

Ingredients required to prepare the cake mixes

Preheat the oven to 350 degrees.

1. Grease and flour the cake pans from Chicago Metallic's Checkerboard Cake Set (see Recipe Note). Line the bottom of each pan with parchment paper or greased and floured aluminum foil so that the cake can be easily removed from the pan. Place the divider ring in one of the pans, holding down the center and pressing gently on each of the three legs until you hear a click.

2. Melt the chocolate (for effective methods and instruction, see page 27). Set aside to cool.

3. Prepare the two packages of cake batter in separate bowls according to the instructions printed on the boxes. Stir the melted chocolate into only one of the bowls of batter.

4. Pour the chocolate batter carefully (we use a large spoon or ladle) into the outer ring and the center of the divided pan, filling it halfway up the sides of the pan and the divider. If you accidentally spill the chocolate batter into the empty middle ring, just wipe it clean with a paper towel.

5. Carefully pour or spoon the light-colored batter into the middle ring, halfway up the sides of the divider.

6. To remove the divider, press on the center and release each leg from the side of the pan, then gently lift the divider straight up from the pan. Rinse the divider ring and dry thoroughly.

7. Repeat the procedure for the next pan, but this time, fill the outer ring and the center with the light-colored batter. Fill the middle ring with the chocolate batter. Remove the divider as in step 6, rinse, and dry thoroughly.

8. For the final pan, repeat the process described in steps 4 and 5, for the first pan. Remove the divider. If you have leftover batter, use it for cupcakes.

9. Place the pans in the center of the preheated oven. Halfway through the baking time, rotate the pans 180 degrees for even baking. Bake for 25 minutes, or until a toothpick inserted in the centers comes out clean. Let the cakes cool in the pans on wire racks for 10 minutes. Loosen the sides with a spatula or knife and invert the cakes onto greased wire racks and allow them to cool completely.

10. Frost each cake layer with your frosting of choice (see page 300), using only a thin layer of frosting so as not to overwhelm the checkerboard effect. Layer the three cakes so the outside chocolate layer is on the top and bottom with the light-colored outside layer in the middle.

Recipe Note: To make this cake, you will need to use Chicago Metallic's Checkerboard Cake Set (available at specialty cooking stores like Williams-Sonoma). The set contains three cake pans and one divider, which will separate the different color batters.

Chocolate Bundt or Tube Cakes

■ ■ ■

*C*akes can be totally tubular. And, as in baseball, when you want to score, Bundt. Baked either in a standard 10-inch angel food tube pan (with removable bottom) or a fluted Bundt pan, these cakes are perfect party desserts. You usually have a hole in the center begging for berries, flowers, or fresh whipped cream. Featured in this chapter are box-cake Bundts, pound cakes you make yourself, and more from-scratch cakes baked in tubes or Bundts. So depending on your schedule and the occasion, there are cakes you can party with and casual cakes you can take camping.

Box-Cake Bundts

In this busy, busy time we all live in, you can have chocolate and elegance without any hassle. Box cakes are the best invention since instant pudding. And the innovation doesn't stop. This chapter starts off with quick 'n' easy box-cake recipes. Each contestant developed his or her own version.

Tips for Successful Bundt and Tube Cakes

- The cake pans are usually described as standard 10-inch. They hold 3 quarts, which also means 12 cups.

- Make sure the pan is thoroughly greased and floured. Non-stick cooking spray is effective.
- Before unmolding, separate the cake from the center tube and as much as possible from the edges of the pan.
- If you don't want to use a homemade glaze, warm your favorite canned frosting in the microwave or on the stove in a saucepan. The frosting will be thin enough for a glaze (add a little butter or solid shortening if you want it thinner).

What's the real reason these cakes are popular? They are basically upside down, which means you can gouge out cake samples for yourself while they're cooling and then turn them over to unmold them, and no one will ever know! Except the person getting the slice that resembles Swiss cheese.

Alliteration Lover and Wicked Chocolate Cake Lover Special Award

Wilson's Wickedly Wonderful Cake

Margaret Wilson · New Britain, Connecticut

■ ■ ■

Choc Talk: Now you're talking wicked and wonderful: wicked because you can't stop eating it; wonderful because you shouldn't stop eating it. This is a great recipe for dressing up a box cake (you can barely taste the box in it). The cake is incredibly light, which is why you need to anchor it with a chocolate glaze so it doesn't float to the ceiling.

"My partner tried to convince me to submit a chocolate meatloaf recipe, thinking it would be a sure winner, but instead I chose my family's very favorite chocolate cake recipe. This cake is requested at every birthday party for my son, daughter, and mother. The original cake recipe was handed to me by my friend Cyndi, and adaptations have been made over the years to make it more 'wickedly wonderful.'"* —Margaret Wilson

*Margaret had a mushroomy meatloaf selected for *The Great American Meatloaf Contest Cookbook,* titled "Four M Meatloaf (Margaret's Mushroom Muenster Meatloaf)."

Yield: *8 to 10 servings* **Preparation Time:** *15 minutes* **Baking Time:** *50 to 55 minutes* **Bakeware Required:** *10-inch (12-cup) Bundt pan, greased and floured*

CAKE

One 18.25-ounce package devil's
    food cake mix
One 3.4-ounce package instant
    vanilla pudding mix
3 large eggs
¾ cup vegetable oil
⅓ cup brandy or 2 teaspoons
    brandy or rum extract
2 heaping tablespoons instant
    coffee granules dissolved in 1
    tablespoon boiling water
2 cups sour cream

6 ounces semisweet chocolate
    chips

GLAZE

½ cup semisweet chocolate
    chips
2 tablespoons unsalted butter
1 tablespoon light corn syrup
1 teaspoon vanilla extract

GARNISH

Sliced fresh strawberries or
    fresh raspberries

To Make the Cake

Preheat the oven to 350 degrees.

1. In a large bowl, combine the cake mix, pudding mix, eggs, oil, brandy, coffee, and sour cream. Mix well until very smooth.

2. Add the chocolate chips and stir well to combine.

3. Pour the batter into the prepared pan and bake for 50 to 55 minutes, or until a toothpick inserted in the center of the cake comes out clean. Do not overbake. Let the cake cool on a wire rack for 10 to 15 minutes, then carefully turn it out of the pan. Let cool completely on the wire rack before glazing.

To Make the Glaze

1. In a saucepan, combine the chocolate chips, butter, and corn syrup. Stir over low heat until the chocolate chips are melted. Remove from the heat and stir in the vanilla.

2. Frost the cake with the glaze. Chill until set.

3. Just before serving, garnish the cake with strawberries or raspberries.

Camper's Chocolate Cake

Roberta Kelly · Meadow Vista, California

■ ■ ■

*C*hoc Talk: My idea of camping used to be staying at a hotel that didn't have twenty-four-hour room service—until I hiked the Grand Canyon. When it's 110 degrees at the bottom of the canyon, chocolate is but a mirage that keeps beckoning you: "Climb, climb to the top and there you will find chocolate." Next time, I'm taking this cake. Roberta's chocolate glaze is dee-luscious, and I recommend that you try it on other cakes.

"We camp four days a month from May to September with our children and six of our grandchildren. Each family takes a turn bringing dessert, but no one used to want the assignment for the fourth day, as by then no matter what you brought, it would be soggy or stale—until I developed this recipe. Our last outing we had temperatures around 105 degrees for the entire trip, and this cake was served on the last day and was still fresh and moist without refrigeration. You don't have to go camping to enjoy this cake. It easily can be made a day ahead of company and still taste wonderful." —Roberta Kelly

Yield: *12 servings* Preparation Time: *15 minutes* Baking Time: *50 to 60 minutes* Bakeware Required: *10-inch (12-cup) Bundt pan, greased and floured*

CAKE

One 18.25-ounce package devil's food cake mix
½ cup lukewarm water
½ cup vegetable oil
4 large eggs
One 3.9-ounce package instant chocolate pudding mix
8 ounces sour cream
12 ounces semisweet chocolate chips
1 cup miniature marshmallows
1 cup chopped walnuts

GLAZE

3 tablespoons unsalted butter
3 tablespoons light corn syrup
1 tablespoon water
1 cup semisweet chocolate chips

To Make the Cake

Preheat the oven to 350 degrees.

1. In a large bowl, combine the cake mix, water, oil, eggs, pudding mix, and sour cream and stir until the cake mix is moistened.

2. Add the chocolate chips, marshmallows, and walnuts and stir well to combine.

3. Pour the mixture into the prepared pan and bake for 50 to 60 minutes, or until a toothpick inserted in the center of the cake comes out clean. Do not overbake. Let the cake cool on a wire rack for 10 to 15 minutes, then carefully turn it out of the pan. Let cool completely on the wire rack before glazing.

To Make the Glaze

1. In a medium saucepan, combine the butter, corn syrup, and water. Stirring constantly, bring the mixture to a boil. Remove from the heat and stir in the chocolate chips until melted. Set aside to cool.

2. Just before serving, spread the glaze over the cake.

Recipe Notes: The cake will stay moist without refrigeration for up to 1 week. • Roberta recommends taking some canned frosting along on your camping trip. Heat the frosting in a saucepan over a cooking stove to give it more of a glaze consistency (non-campers can use the microwave).

Don't Take This Easy Pound Cake for Granted

Amy Grant · Nashville, Tennessee

■ ■ ■

Choc Talk: Amy Grant can sing and bake, probably at the same time. The mother of three kids and a top recording star and performer, she joined forces with a friend, Sloan Germann, for a duet in chocolate to create this quick, moist cake. This Bundt's a hit at her house. We received her recipe through e-mail and via a great guy, Dan Lee. I think a chocolate song is next on the agenda.

Yield: *8 to 10 servings* **Preparation Time:** *15 minutes* **Baking Time:** *1 hour* **Bakeware Required:** *10-inch (12-cup) Bundt pan, greased and floured*

One 18.25-ounce package Duncan Hines Yellow Butter Cake mix
One 3.9-ounce package chocolate instant pudding mix
8 ounces sour cream
½ cup vegetable oil
½ cup milk
4 large eggs
1 teaspoon vanilla extract
6 ounces semisweet chocolate chips
1 cup chopped pecans (optional)

Preheat the oven to 325 degrees.

1. In a large bowl, combine the cake mix, pudding mix, sour cream, oil, milk, eggs, and vanilla. Mix well.

2. Add the chocolate chips and pecans and stir well to combine.

3. Pour the batter into the prepared pan and bake for 1 hour, or until a toothpick inserted in the center of the cake comes out clean. Let the cake cool on a wire rack for 10 to 15 minutes, then carefully turn it out of the pan. Let it cool completely on the wire rack before serving.

Recipe Note: This cake is choco-licious by itself, or you can drizzle on the chocolate glaze from the Chocolate Mint Parfait Bundt Cake (page 155).

Barron de Chocolate Chip Cake

Mary Rose Barron · Arnold, Maryland

■ ■ ■

Choc Talk: A prince (or baron) among cakes. The cinnamon adds some zip, and the cake is deliciously stocked with chocolate chips.

"This particular cake has been my family's favorite for years. My husband usually requests it for his birthday, and whenever I offer to bring a dessert, this cake is always requested. The wonderful thing is that it can be eaten warm, cold, room temperature, and even right from the freezer. I have often baked one and frozen it for later use. I guess you could say that this cake has become my trademark. It also travels well. Try it and I know it will become one of your family's favorites too!" —Mary Rose Barron

Yield: *20 servings* **Preparation Time:** *15 minutes* **Baking Time:** *45 minutes* **Bakeware Required:** *10-inch (12-cup) Bundt pan, greased and floured*

½ cup unsalted butter or
   margarine
¾ cup granulated sugar
½ cup firmly packed brown
   sugar
2 large eggs, slightly beaten
2 cups all-purpose flour
1 teaspoon baking soda
1 teaspoon baking powder
1 cup sour cream

2 tablespoons milk
1½ teaspoons vanilla extract
1 tablespoon ground cinnamon
12 ounces semisweet chocolate
   chips

OPTIONAL GARNISHES
Chocolate glaze or Coconut
   Pecan Frosting (page 303)
Confectioners' sugar

continued

Preheat the oven to 350 degrees.

1. In a large bowl, cream the butter, sugars, and eggs with an electric mixer until the mixture is light and fluffy.

2. In a separate bowl, combine the flour, baking soda, and baking powder. Gradually add the flour mixture to the creamed mixture, beating well after each addition. Add the sour cream, milk, vanilla, and cinnamon to the batter and mix well.

3. Add the chocolate chips and, using a wooden spoon, stir until well combined.

4. Pour the batter into the prepared pan. Bake for 45 minutes, or until a toothpick inserted in the center of the cake comes out clean. Let the cake cool on a wire rack for 10 to 15 minutes, then carefully turn it out of the pan. Let cool completely on a wire rack before garnishing.

5. To really give the cake a baronial touch, frost it with Coconut Pecan Frosting (page 303) or use the chocolate glaze in the recipe for Camper's Chocolate Cake (page 150). Or simply dust with confectioners' sugar.

Chocolate Mint Parfait Bundt Cake

Eleanor Norris Adams · Linwood, New Jersey

■ ■ ■

***C**hoc Talk:* Great for St. Patrick's Day. Get Eleanor a federal grant to create more innovative cakes. In this one, there is a swirl of green inside the cake. The glaze is very good (and shiny) and could be used on other cakes as well.

Yield: *8 to 10 servings* **Preparation Time:** *20 minutes* **Baking Time:** *45 to 50 minutes* **Bakeware Required:** *10-inch (12-cup) Bundt pan or tube pan, greased and floured*

CAKE
4 ounces unsweetened chocolate, chopped
3 cups sifted cake flour
2 cups granulated sugar
½ teaspoon salt
1 teaspoon baking powder
1½ cups unsalted butter, softened
⅓ cup buttermilk
6 large eggs

1 teaspoon peppermint extract
5 drops green food coloring
1 teaspoon vanilla extract

GLAZE
2 ounces unsweetened chocolate
1 teaspoon unsalted butter
1 cup sifted confectioners' sugar
3 tablespoons warm water

To Make the Cake

Preheat the oven to 350 degrees.

1. Melt the chocolate (for effective methods and instructions, see page 27). Set aside to cool completely.

2. In a large bowl, combine the flour, sugar, salt, and baking powder. Add the butter, buttermilk, and only 3 eggs. Using an electric mixer at low speed, beat the mixture until the dry ingredients are just moistened. Increase the speed to high and add the remaining 3 eggs one at a time.

continued

3. Transfer about 1½ cups of the batter to another bowl (setting the rest aside) and add the mint extract and food coloring. Mix well.

4. To the remaining batter, add the cooled melted chocolate and the vanilla extract. Mix well.

5. Pour one third of the chocolate batter into the prepared pan. By teaspoonfuls, drop half the green mint batter onto the chocolate batter around the cake. Do not swirl it in; the baking will do the trick. Pour on another third of the chocolate batter, then drop the remaining mint batter by teaspoonfuls onto this layer. End the layering with the last third of the chocolate batter.

6. Bake for 45 to 50 minutes, or until a toothpick inserted in the center of the cake comes out clean. Let the cake cool on a wire rack for 10 to 15 minutes, then carefully turn it out of the pan. Let cool completely on a wire rack before glazing.

To Make the Glaze

1. Melt the chocolate and butter together (for effective methods and instructions, see page 27). Mix well.

2. Add ½ cup confectioners' sugar and 1 tablespoon of the water. Blend until smooth. Add the remaining sugar and water and beat until glossy.

3. Drizzle the glaze over the cooled cake. Refrigerate until the chocolate glaze is set.

Banana Bundt with Give-Them-the-Raspberries Chocolate Icing

Creative Combination in a Cake Special Award

Aline Ballentine · Wawarsing, New York

■ ■ ■

C*hoc Talk:* Overripe bananas are mashed and added to this cake, and the raspberry-chocolate icing is wild. For an arctic/tropical combo, serve this cake with ice cream and drizzle the whole thing with extra icing that's been heated slightly.

Yield: *8 to 10 servings* **Preparation Time:** *15 minutes* **Baking Time:** *45 to 50 minutes* **Bakeware Required:** *10-inch (12-cup) Bundt pan, well greased*

CAKE

3 ounces unsweetened chocolate, chopped
½ cup solid vegetable shortening
¼ cup margarine
1 cup granulated sugar
½ cup firmly packed light brown sugar
1 cup mashed bananas
¾ cup plain yogurt
2 large eggs
1 teaspoon vanilla extract
2 cups all-purpose flour, sifted
1 teaspoon baking powder
1 teaspoon baking soda
⅛ teaspoon salt

GIVE-THEM-THE-RASPBERRIES CHOCOLATE ICING

¼ cup milk
2 tablespoons margarine
⅛ teaspoon salt
1 cup semisweet chocolate chips
1 tablespoon raspberry liqueur (optional)
½ cup fresh or frozen raspberries, thawed and drained
1½ cups confectioners' sugar, sifted

GARNISHES

Whipped cream
Fresh raspberries

continued

To Make the Cake

Preheat the oven to 350 degrees.

1. Melt the chocolate (for effective methods and instructions, see page 27). Set aside to cool completely.

2. In a large bowl, cream the shortening, margarine, and sugars until fluffy. Add the bananas, yogurt, eggs, vanilla, and melted chocolate and mix well.

3. In a separate bowl, combine the flour, baking powder, baking soda, and salt. Add the flour mixture to the creamed mixture and mix thoroughly.

4. Pour the batter into the prepared pan and bake for 45 to 50 minutes, or until a toothpick inserted in the center of the cake comes out relatively clean. Let the cake cool for 10 minutes on a wire rack, then carefully turn it out of the pan. Let cool completely on the wire rack before frosting.

To Make the Icing

1. In a medium saucepan over moderate heat, combine the milk, margarine, and salt. Stir in the chocolate chips and continue stirring until they are melted.

2. Stir in the raspberry liqueur, if using, and the raspberries* and allow the mixture to simmer for about 3 minutes. Remove from the heat and gradually add as much of the confectioners' sugar as needed for taste and consistency. Beat the mixture with a spoon until thick.

3. Spread the icing over the top of the cake and garnish with whipped cream and/or fresh raspberries.

Recipe Note: Add ½ to 1 cup semisweet or milk chocolate chips to the batter to increase the chocolate quotient.

---

*If you would like a smoother icing, purée the raspberries in a blender or food processor, strain to remove the seeds, then stir the raspberry purée into the chocolate mixture.

Chocolate Kahlúa
Pound Cake Dream

Nikki Skelton · Quartz Hill, California

■ ■ ■

***C**hoc Talk:* This cake deserves a big "YUM." When I prepared it to serve at a speech I gave about chocolate, the cake was here and gone in a matter of minutes. After my presentation, there was a Q & A period. Several people from the audience had questions: "Is there any more Chocolate Kahlúa Pound Cake?" "Why didn't you make more Chocolate Kahlúa Pound Cake?"

Yield: *16 servings* **Preparation Time:** *20 minutes* **Baking Time:** *1 hour*
Bakeware Required: *10-inch (12-cup) Bundt pan, well greased*

CAKE	FROSTING
1 cup unsalted butter, softened	*3 tablespoons unsalted butter,*
2½ cups granulated sugar	*softened*
1 teaspoon vanilla extract	*3 tablespoons unsweetened*
6 large eggs	*cocoa*
1 cup unsweetened cocoa	*1 cup confectioner's sugar*
2⅓ cups cake flour∗	*1 to 2 teaspoons Kahlúa liqueur*
1 teaspoon baking powder	*2 tablespoons milk*
1 teaspoon salt	
1 cup buttermilk	

KAHLÚA GLAZE
*½ cup Kahlúa or other coffee-
flavored liqueur*
1 cup confectioner's sugar

continued

∗Cake flour makes a lighter cake, but you can substitute all-purpose flour, using ⅞ cup for every 1 cup cake flour.

To Make the Cake

Preheat the oven to 325 degrees.

1. In a large bowl, beat together the butter, sugar, and vanilla until light and fluffy. Add the eggs one at a time, beating well after each addition.

2. In a separate bowl, combine the cocoa, flour, baking powder, and salt. Gradually add the dry ingredients to the butter mixture, mixing well after each addition. Stir in the buttermilk until just combined.

3. Pour the batter into the prepared pan and bake for 50 to 60 minutes, or until a toothpick inserted in the center of the the cake comes out clean. If necessary, continue baking and check for doneness every 5 minutes. Let the cake cool on a wire rack for 15 minutes. Remove the cake from the pan, and while the cake is still warm, top with the Kahlúa glaze.

To Make the Kahlúa Glaze

1. In a large bowl, combine the Kahlúa and confectioners' sugar and beat until smooth.

2. While the unmolded cake is still warm, poke several holes (using a knife or toothpick) in the top of the cake. Pour the Kahlúa glaze over the cake. As it cools, the cake will absorb the Kahlúa glaze. When it has cooled completely, carefully turn the cake out of the pan and frost.

To Make the Frosting

1. In a small bowl, combine all the ingredients and mix well.

2. Spread the frosting over the cake and serve.

Choco-Loco
(A Frenzied but Saporous Adventure in Cakery)

Mary Alice Rodes · Doraville, Georgia

■ ■ ■

*C**hoc Talk:** The list of ingredients is suspenseful. Orange Jell-O mix and coffee yogurt? Together? Can this work? This recipe proves once again: Don't judge a cake by its ingredients. This one turns out very moist, with great texture. There's no need for a frosting; it's great on its own. Mary Alice also created an outstanding meatloaf for *The Great American Meatloaf Contest Cookbook.*

"This is a combination of several cakes and desserts that I have known and loved (vanilla wafer cake, dirt cake, Jell-O cake, Caribbean fudge pie, and tiramisù). A tasty substitution here and there plus a borrowed process or two completes the picture."
—Mary Alice Rodes

Yield: *12 servings* **Preparation Time:** *15 minutes* **Baking Time:** *1 hour 10 minutes* **Bakeware Required:** *10-inch tube pan, lined with parchment paper and greased*

One 9-ounce package Nabisco Famous Chocolate Wafers, finely crushed	1 teaspoon baking powder
	1 cup margarine, softened
	1 cup firmly packed light brown sugar
½ cup sweetened flaked coconut	
1 cup finely chopped pecans	3 large eggs
One 3-ounce package orange Jell-O mix	One 8-ounce container coffee-flavored yogurt
1 teaspoon ground cinnamon	1 teaspoon rum extract

continued

Preheat the oven to 325 degrees.

1. In a large bowl, combine the crushed wafers, flaked coconut, chopped pecans, orange Jell-O mix, cinnamon, and baking powder.

2. In a separate bowl, cream the margarine and brown sugar until smooth. Add the eggs and mix well. Add the yogurt and rum extract and blend well.

3. Add the dry mixture to the wet mixture 1 cup at a time, stirring well with a spoon after each addition.

4. Pour the batter into the prepared pan and bake for 1 hour, or until a toothpick inserted in the center of the cake comes out relatively clean. You may need to bake the cake an additional 5 to 10 minutes. Let the cake cool in the pan on a wire rack for 30 minutes. To remove the cake from the pan, work a small knife between the cake and the side of the pan and the center tube to loosen it. After turning it out of the pan, let cool completely on the wire rack before serving.

Recipe Note: As Mary Alice suggests, this is an excellent cake to serve with coffee or cocoa. *"In the winter, serve with espresso for adults and hot chocolate for the kids. In the summer, serve with iced coffee."* —Mary Alice Rodes

Heavenly Devil's Food Surprise Cake

Sally-Mary Cashman · Danbury, Connecticut

■ ■ ■

***C**hoc Talk:* The surprise in this rich, exceptional cake is that it's low-fat, low-sugar, and dare I say—healthy. Made with natural ingredients, moistened with zucchini, and sweetened with honey, this cake will satisfy the junkiest junk-food lover. Trust me. Those of you searching for something to satisfy the kids' sweet cravings will feel happy about giving them this cake.

"I love to cook and bake and also love reading about cooking and baking methods and recipes. I sometimes take ideas from different recipes and combine them into a new one I can consider my own. Since I'm also interested in healthy ingredients, I try to incorporate them into my creations, as I did with Heavenly Devil's Food Surprise Cake. This is one way to get my children to eat zucchini without knowing it and enjoy what they're eating."
—Sally-Mary Cashman

Yield: *12 servings* **Preparation Time:** *10 to 15 minutes (or 2 months in the summer if you are growing your own zucchini)* **Baking Time:** *40 to 50 minutes* **Bakeware Required:** *10-inch (12-cup) Bundt pan, well greased*

1¼ cups unbleached flour
1¼ cups whole wheat flour
2½ teaspoons baking powder
1½ teaspoons baking soda
½ cup unsweetened cocoa
1 teaspoon ground cinnamon
⅔ cup canola oil
1½ cups honey
2 teaspoons vanilla extract
3 large eggs
2 cups finely chopped zucchini
⅓ cup plain yogurt

¾ cup chopped pecans or walnuts
½ cup raisins

OPTIONAL ICING
1 cup heavy cream
¼ cup confectioners' sugar, sifted
1 teaspoon vanilla extract

OPTIONAL GARNISH
Semisweet chocolate shavings

continued

Preheat the oven to 350 degrees.

1. In a large bowl, combine the flours, baking powder, baking soda, cocoa, and cinnamon.

2. In a separate large bowl, beat the oil, honey, and vanilla until well blended. Add the eggs and beat well. Add the zucchini and yogurt and stir to combine.

3. Add the dry ingredients to the wet ingredients and mix well. Gently fold in the nuts and raisins.

4. Pour the batter into the prepared pan and bake for 40 to 50 minutes, or until a toothpick inserted in the center of the cake comes out clean. Let the cake cool on a wire rack for approximately 15 minutes, then carefully turn it out of the pan. Let cool completely on the wire rack before icing, if desired.

To Make the Icing

1. Whip the heavy cream in a chilled bowl. Gradually add the sugar and vanilla and continue whipping until soft peaks form.

2. Frost the cooled cake. With a vegetable peeler, make shavings from a semisweet chocolate bar and sprinkle the shavings on the frosted cake.

Recipe Note: The icing is optional because the cake is so moist on its own that you may not wish to adorn it further.

Her-She Bar Cake

Debbi Nelson · Colorado Springs, Colorado

■ ■ ■

*C**hoc Talk:** Although the recipe specifies seven Hershey bars, I recommend you get eight so that you can eat one while the others are melting. Actually, I recommend you get twelve Hershey bars so that you can melt a few to drizzle on the cake, grate one for garnish, and eat another while the cake is baking. The altitude directions are interesting (see Recipe Notes), and I hope to fly to Colorado Springs this winter and try them out.

"My mom has made this cake for special occasions for years, and I now do too. Since moving to Colorado, however, I have had to do a lot of experimenting to get it to come out right at this altitude. My family can attest to the fact that this is a great cake, no matter how you try to ruin it. One hint: if you bake it in a microwave, do not fill the pan past the DO NOT FILL PAST THIS LINE *mark! I did and the cake exploded into little pieces of candy, but it did make a great topping for ice cream!"* —Debbi Nelson

Yield: *12 servings* **Preparation Time:** *20 mintues* **Baking Time:** *1 hour 15 minutes* **Bakeware Required:** *10-inch (12-cup) Bundt pan or tube pan, lightly greased*

Seven 1.55-ounce Hershey milk chocolate bars
1 cup unsalted butter, softened
2 cups granulated sugar
4 large eggs
11 ounces (two 5½-ounce cans) Hershey's chocolate syrup
2½ cups all-purpose flour
¼ teaspoon salt

½ teaspoon (well-rounded) baking soda
1 cup buttermilk
2 teaspoons vanilla extract

GARNISH
1 Hershey bar, grated

continued

Preheat the oven to 350 degrees.

1. Melt the chocolate bars (for effective methods and instructions, see page 27). Set aside to cool completely.

2. In a large bowl, cream the butter and sugar together. Add the melted and cooled chocolate and mix well. Add the eggs and chocolate syrup and beat thoroughly.

3. In a separate bowl, combine the flour, salt, and baking soda. Gradually add the dry ingredients to the mixture, alternating with the buttermilk and mixing well after each addition. Mix until smooth and blend in the vanilla.

4. Pour the batter into the prepared pan and bake for 1 hour 15 minutes. (But check the cake after 1 hour of baking by inserting a toothpick into the center. The toothpick should come out slightly moist. If so, the cake is done. This is meant to be a dense, moist cake—do not overbake.) Let the cake cool on a wire rack for 30 minutes, then carefully turn it out of the pan. Let cool completely on the wire rack and garnish with the grated Hershey bar before serving.

Recipe Notes: This has the consistency of a pound cake and should be moist and dense. It can be served with simply a sprinkling of confectioners' sugar on top or with ice cream. Drizzle the cake with one of the chocolate sauces starting on page 297 or one of the glaze recipes on page 299. • If you are baking this cake at an altitude over 5,000 feet, reduce the sugar to 1½ cups and add an extra 2 tablespoons all-purpose flour and 3 tablespoons more buttermilk.

Chocolate Cheesecake Cha-Cha-Cha

■ ■ ■

*C*heese rhymes with please, as in "Another slice of cheesecake, please." Although I relish rich, creamy cheesecake, especially if someone else makes it, these recipes feed the fire in my chocolate-making (and eating) soul.

Light and Luscious Cheesecake Tips

- Make sure all the ingredients are at room temperature.
- To prevent lumps, cream the cheese with the eggs until smooth before adding the liquid ingredients.
- *Avoid cracking up.* Unlike traditional cakes, cheesecakes crack if too much air is beaten into the mixture. If you are using an electric mixer, beat the eggs and cheese at low speed. And you know that paddle that came with your electric mixer (the one that always jams the junk drawer when you yank it open)? This is a good time to put it to use. The paddle attachment prevents too much air from being beaten into the mixture.
- It is important to bake cheesecakes at a low temperature. So make sure you use your oven thermometer to measure the temperature accurately. The shrink-and-sink syndrome is common for cheesecakes and can be prevented by cooking them on low and allowing them to cool without an abrupt change in temperature. Before refrigerating, make sure they are completely cool.

- Like custards, cheesecakes continue to cook while they are cooling, so they may not pass the clean toothpick test fresh from the oven.

Other Tips

- As I searched for chocolate graham crackers for the crusts our contestants created, I often could not find traditional chocolate graham crackers to crush. So I used Chocolate Teddy Grahams. I hated crushing those little bears, but you do what you have to do to make a great cheesecake.
- When baking a cheesecake in a springform pan, be sure to place a cookie sheet on the rack below to catch the innards that sometimes ooze out from the bottom.
- Although most of the cheesecakes come with great topping or garnishing ideas, review the chapter starting on page 297 for other topping ideas. A delicious berry purée can be a great accompaniment.

Top-to-Bottom Chocolate Cheesecake

Kim Potember · Dayton, Maryland

■ ■ ■

C*hoc Talk:* This cheesecake is chocolate through and through, from the crust to the filling to the glaze.

Yield: *12 servings* **Preparation Time:** *20 minutes* **Chilling Time:** *2 hours 15 minutes total* **Baking Time:** *1 hour* **Bakeware Required:** *9-inch springform pan*

CRUST

1½ cups finely crushed chocolate wafer cookies (such as Nabisco Famous Chocolate Wafers) or chocolate sandwich cookies (such as Oreos) or Chocolate Teddy Grahams

6 tablespoons unsalted butter or margarine, melted

FILLING

4 ounces semisweet chocolate

1½ cups granulated sugar

2 tablespoons all-purpose flour

⅛ teaspoon salt

Three 8-ounce packages cream cheese, softened

4 large eggs

¼ cup milk

1 teaspoon vanilla extract

GLAZE

1 ounce semisweet chocolate, melted

1 teaspoon solid vegetable shortening

To Make the Crust

Preheat the oven to 325 degrees.

1. In a large bowl, combine the crushed chocolate wafers and melted butter and mix well. Press firmly on the bottom and 2 inches up the sides of the springform pan. Cover with plastic wrap or wax paper and place it in the freezer for at least 15 minutes.

continued

To Make the Filling

1. Melt the chocolate (for effective methods and instructions, see page 27). Set aside to cool completely.

2. In a small bowl, combine the sugar, flour, and salt.

3. In a large bowl, beat the cream cheese until creamy. Add the sugar mixture and mix well. Using an electric mixer, add the eggs one at a time, beating at low speed until well blended. Stir the melted chocolate, milk, and vanilla into the cream cheese mixture until combined.

4. Pour the filling into the crust and bake for 1 hour, or until the center appears set. Let the cheesecake cool in the pan on a wire rack for 20 minutes. Run a spatula along the inside of the pan to help separate the cheesecake from the pan. Cool the cheesecake for 30 minutes more *before* removing the sides of the pan. Cover and chill the cake at least 2 hours before glazing.

To Make the Glaze

1. Melt the chocolate with the shortening (for effective methods and instructions, see page 27). Drizzle the glaze over the top of the cooled cheesecake and chill until the chocolate is set.

Java Lava Cheesecake

Elizabeth Norris · Oakland, California

■ ■ ■

***C**hoc Talk:* All we can say is "Ooh, wow, mama, mama, Java Lava is a slice of cheesecake heaven." The cheesecake itself is light and custardlike. The java part is mild and will not keep you up at night. So go ahead, have another slice.

"This recipe was inspired by an arduous trek over two miles of newly hardened lava to see Kilauea's lava flow. My family and I hiked in pitch blackness, armed only with flashlights, to see the volcano's display of wrath and take spectacular pictures. The desert of black lava looked like dessert to me! So I created a very chocolaty cheesecake to commemorate the Kanai landscape; the hot caramel resembles lava. Like our adventurous hike, this rich chocolate cheesecake is not for the faint-hearted!"
—Elizabeth Norris

Yield: *10 to 12 servings* **Preparation Time:** *20 minutes* **Chilling Time:** *6 to 12 hours total* **Baking Time:** *40 to 50 minutes* **Bakeware Required:** *10-inch springform pan*

CRUST
1½ cups crushed chocolate graham crackers or Chocolate Teddy Grahams
½ cup unsalted macadamia nuts, coarsely chopped
2 tablespoons instant coffee granules
6 tablespoons unsalted butter or margarine, melted

FILLING
8 ounces semisweet chocolate
2 tablespoons instant coffee granules (plain or flavored)

⅓ cup boiling water
Three 8-ounce packages cream cheese, softened
2 cups granulated sugar
2 large eggs
1 cup sour cream

OPTIONAL TOPPING
One 16-ounce jar caramel ice cream topping, or see Recipe Note.

continued

To Make the Crust

1. In a medium bowl, mix all the crust ingredients together. Press firmly onto the bottom and slightly up the sides of the spring-form pan. Cover with plastic wrap or wax paper and place in the freezer for 15 minutes while making the filling.

Preheat the oven to 350 degrees.

To Make the Filling

1. Melt the chocolate (for effective methods and instructions, see page 27). Set aside to cool completely.

2. In a saucepan, dissolve the instant coffee in the boiling water and set aside.

3. In a large bowl, beat the cream cheese, sugar, and eggs on low speed with an electric mixer until smooth. Add the sour cream, chocolate, and coffee and continue beating on low until well blended. (Add the coffee by pouring down the side of the bowl to prevent splattering.)

4. Pour the filling into the crust and bake for 40 to 50 minutes. Do not overbake. The cheesecake will pull from the sides somewhat and the center will appear set. Cheesecake, like custard, will firm as it cools. Let the cake cool completely on a wire rack, cover, and refrigerate overnight in the pan.

5. When ready to serve, remove the sides of the springform pan. Warm the topping, if using, and drizzle it on each slice of cheesecake.

Recipe Note: Instead of the caramel ice cream topping, you can use the homemade caramel sauce in the white chocolate chapter (page 276).

Chocolate Goes Hawaiian

■ ■ ■

Until recently, chocolate was produced only outside the United States, with the best beans coming from the Ivory Coast, Ecuador, Brazil, and Ghana. But in the islands that give the world pineapple, macadamia nuts, Kona coffee, and Don Ho, cocoa beans are now being grown—in Hawaii's Keaau and Kona regions. The Hawaiian Cocoa Chocolate Company is the first totally American chocolate producer, although the chocolates are now available only commercially. Soon this premier chocolate will be available to you too, but for approximately sixty dollars a pound. Give me a box of that, a case of macadamia nuts, and a magnum of Dom Pérignon and I could be happy.

Black Tie Cheesecake

Kyle Nagurny · Harrisburg, Pennsylvania

■ ■ ■

Professional Chocolate Lover Category

Choc Talk: I once thought, wouldn't it be fantastic to make a sinfully sophisticated white and dark chocolate cheesecake, without the work? "In your dreams," I was told, until this recipe came along. Everyone who tastes this asks me for the recipe. No way. After waiting all these years, it's mine, all mine. Well, OK, it's Kyle's recipe and she's a sharing person.

"Black Tie Cheesecake represents the very best components derived from a variety of other cheesecakes I have developed over the years for food-industry clients. It's decadent but easy, even for a novice." —Kyle Nagurny

Yield: *10 to 12 servings* **Preparation Time:** *20 minutes* **Chilling Time:** *6 to 12 hours total* **Baking Time:** *48 minutes total* **Bakeware Required:** *9-inch springform pan*

CRUST

1½ cups finely crushed chocolate wafer cookies (such as Nabisco Famous Chocolate Wafers) or chocolate sandwich cookies (such as Oreos) or Chocolate Teddy Grahams

¼ cup ground macadamia nuts

6 tablespoons unsalted butter, melted

FILLING

12 ounces white chocolate, broken into small pieces

Two 8-ounce packages cream cheese

½ cup heavy cream

1 tablespoon fresh lemon juice

¼ teaspoon salt

3 large egg whites

1 large egg

TOPPING

1 cup sour cream

1 tablespoon chocolate-flavored liqueur (such as crème de cacao)

GARNISH

White chocolate curls

To Make the Crust

1. In a medium bowl, mix all the crust ingredients together. Press firmly onto the bottom and about 1 inch up the sides of the springform pan. Cover with plastic wrap or wax paper and refrigerate for at least 1 hour.

To Make the Filling

Preheat the oven to 350 degrees.

1. Melt the white chocolate (for effective methods and instructions, see page 274).

2. In a large bowl, beat the cream cheese, cream, lemon juice, and salt until blended and smooth. Gradually add the melted white chocolate, beating well after each addition. Beat the egg whites and the whole egg into the mixture until well combined (see tips on page 167).

3. Pour the filling into the crust. Place the pan on a baking sheet and bake for 45 minutes, or until the cheesecake is almost set.

To Make the Topping

1. In a small bowl, combine the sour cream and liqueur.

2. Remove the baked cheesecake from the oven and carefully spoon and spread the sour cream mixture over the cheesecake. Return the cheesecake to the oven for 3 minutes.

3. Let the cheesecake cool to room temperature in the pan on a wire rack. Cover and refrigerate for 6 to 12 hours.

4. When ready to serve, remove the sides of the springform pan. Garnish the chilled cake with white chocolate curls.

Recipe Note: This recipe may encourage you to try other white chocolate recipes; turn to page 273.

Chocolate Pies

■ ■ ■

There is an excellent recipe for a homemade pie crust right at the beginning of this chapter for those of you who have the time and the desire to make your own pie crusts. If not, there are plenty of premade pie crusts just waiting in the freezer or dairy section of your grocery store. (This is what I call the take-and-bake pie crust method.) I think they work great.

Tips for Successful Pie Crust

- Handle the pie crust as little as possible.
- To mend a broken or cracked crust, press the dough together and moisten the broken area with a few drops of water while still pressing.
- Cover the edges with aluminum foil if the pie crust begins to brown while baking.

Myrth's Sweet Coco-Nut Pie with Homemade Pie Crust

Myrth Knighton · Salt Lake City, Utah

■ ■ ■

hoc Talk: This is a chocolate-pecan pie with a hint of coconut dream come true. Since my homemade pie crusts have been used in the discus tournament at the Olympics, I usually rely on somebody else's, such as the premade, even fluted-for-you pie crusts in the frozen foods section of the supermarket or Pillsbury's Pie Crust (both are great). But Myrth's technique of making a paste with the flour to avoid overhandling the pie crust is ⅛ of a teaspoon beyond brilliant. Even my pie crust turned out flaky.

Yield: *8 servings* **Preparation Time:** *15 minutes* **Baking Time:** *45 minutes* **Bakeware Required:** *10-inch pie pan, lightly greased*

CRUST
1½ cups sifted all-purpose flour, divided
¼ cup cold water
½ cup solid vegetable shortening
½ teaspoon salt

FILLING
4 ounces semisweet chocolate
¼ cup unsalted butter

One 15½-ounce can (1⅔ cups) evaporated milk
1½ cups granulated sugar
3 tablespoons cornstarch
⅛ teaspoon salt
2 large eggs
1 teaspoon vanilla extract
1⅓ cups sweetened flaked coconut
½ cup chopped pecans

To Make the Crust

Preheat the oven to 375 degrees.

1. Place ¼ cup of the sifted flour in a small bowl. Add the water and stir to make a paste. Set aside.

2. In a large bowl, add the remaining flour with the shortening and salt. Using a pastry cutter or two knives in a scissors motion,

cut the shortening into the flour until the mixture forms particles the size of peas.

3. Add the paste to the flour and shortening mixture and blend well with a wooden spoon or pastry spatula. Avoid touching the dough with your hands.

4. Form the dough into a ball and place it on a floured surface. With a rolling pin that is floured, roll the dough into a 12-inch circle. Place the pie pan upside down over the dough and flip the dough into the pan. Highly flute the edges. Set aside while you make the filling.

To Make the Filling

1. In a large bowl, melt the chocolate with the butter (for effective methods and instructions, see page 27). Set aside to cool completely.

2. Gradually add the evaporated milk to the cooled chocolate mixture, mixing well.

3. In a separate bowl, combine the sugar, cornstarch, and salt. Beat in the eggs and vanilla to the sugar-cornstarch mixture. Add the chocolate mixture to the sugar-egg mixture and blend well. Stir in the coconut and pecans until well combined.

4. Pour the filling into the prepared pie crust and bake for 45 minutes. Do not overbake. The pie may seem soft and moist when removed from the oven but will firm up as it cools.

Presentation Note: Fabulous with fresh whipped cream (see the flavored whipped creams on page 304).

Oh Henry's Chocolate Neapolitan Pie

Henry Siegel · Seminole, Florida

■ ■ ■

***C**hoc Talk:* Fashioned after Neapolitan ice cream, Henry's pie consists of three layers, each with a different color and flavor. Neapolitan ice-cream makers were famous in the nineteenth century, especially in Paris. One luminary in this ice-cream–making mecca was named Tortoni, celebrated as the creator of several Neapolitan ice-cream cakes. Now he has a rival.

"I had too many things left over from the holidays and used them to make this pie . . . then I froze it for the next holiday!"
—Henry Siegel

Yield: *8 servings* **Preparation Time:** *25 minutes* **Chilling Time:** *1 hour* **Baking Time:** *15 minutes* **Bakeware Required:** *9-inch purchased pie shell. (Lightly bake the pie shell acording to the pie shell's package directions.)*∗

2 large eggs,† separated
¼ teaspoon salt
½ teaspoon cider vinegar
½ teaspoon ground cinnamon, divided
¾ cup granulated sugar, divided
6 ounces semisweet chocolate chips

¼ cup water
1 cup heavy cream

OPTIONAL GARNISHES
Melted semisweet chocolate
Chocolate curls

Preheat the oven to 350 degrees.

∗Or make your own pie crust (see page 178). Make sure you use bakeware that can be refrigerated. (Nonstick pans should not be refrigerated.)

†The recipe calls for the use of uncooked egg yolks. If you prefer, substitute an equivalent amount of egg substitute, which is pasteurized.

To Make the Meringue

1. In a medium bowl, combine the egg whites, salt, vinegar, and ¼ teaspoon of the cinnamon. Whip the mixture until it is stiff. Gradually add ½ cup of the sugar, one tablespoon at a time, and beat until very stiff. (For instruction and tips on beating egg whites, see page 184.) Spread the meringue over the bottom and sides of the pie shell. Bake for 15 minutes, then set aside to cool.

To Make the First Layer

1. Melt the chocolate chips (for effective methods and instructions, see page 27). Set aside to cool completely.

2. In a large bowl, combine the water, egg yolks, and melted chocolate, in that order. Blend until the mixture is well combined. Spread 3 tablespoons of the chocolate mixture on top of the cooled meringue layer. Reserve the remaining chocolate mixture until ready to use.

To Make the Second Layer

1. In a small bowl, whip the heavy cream, the remaining ¼ cup sugar, and the remaining ¼ teaspoon cinnamon until the mixture is stiff. Spread half of this whipped cream mixture over the chocolate layer in the pie. Reserve the rest for use in the third layer.

To Make the Third Layer

1. Combine the reserved chocolate mixture with the remaining whipped cream mixture. Spread carefully over the second layer. Chill for at least 1 hour.

2. If desired, just before serving, drizzle melted semisweet chocolate (or use one of the chocolate glaze recipes recommended on page 299) in a decorative fashion over the chilled pie. Top with chocolate curls.

Recipe Note: Be your own Neapolitan creator. Replace the chocolate layer with other delicious mousses and puddings (recipes beginning on page 183). Or try adding a layer of the Grasshopper Pie filling (recipe on page 210). But why should I come up with all the ideas? Just flip through the book and come up with your own variations.

Kentucky Derby Pie

Kala Cartwright · Milan, Georgia

■ ■ ■

Junior Chocolate Lover Category

***C**hoc Talk:* A winner by a nose! That is, if your nose happens to love chocolate. This delectable blend of chocolate and pecans is where the phrase "easy as pie" comes from.

"I took Kentucky Derby Pie to school with me for dessert at lunch. I shared my piece of pie with several classmates sitting near me. Everyone liked it so much that I made five pies and brought them to my Christmas party at school." —Kala Cartwright

Yield: *8 to 10 servings* **Preparation Time:** *10 minutes* **Baking Time:** *45 minutes* **Bakeware Required:** *9-inch purchased pie shell**

½ cup unsalted butter or margarine, melted	*1 cup chopped pecans*
1 tablespoon vanilla extract	*1 cup semisweet chocolate chips*
2 large eggs, beaten	*½ cup all-purpose flour*
	½ cup granulated sugar

Preheat the oven to 350 degrees.

1. In a large bowl, combine all the ingredients and mix together with a spoon.

2. Pour the mixture into the pie shell. Bake for 45 minutes or until a toothpick inserted in the center of the pie comes out almost clean. Do not overbake. Allow the pie to cool before cutting and serving.

*Or you can make your own pie crust by using the recipe on page 178.

Chocolate Mousse, Trifle, and Tiramisù

...

Chocolate Mousse

From the classic mousse to the modernized mousse to the five-minute (that's all?) Milky Way Mousse created by one of our Junior Chocolate Lover contestants, Caitlin Keys (page 192), you'll find a galaxy of mousse variations and techniques in this chapter. Years ago, when all of us were still eating raw chocolate chip cookie dough and licking cake batter from electric beaters, the only rule was to wait until the beaters stopped rotating before we stuck our tongues in them. Now we have to be more careful because of salmonella, nasty bacteria that have ruined it for all of us who ate dough from our mixing bowls. There is a theory that salmonella is present only in the yolk and does not affect the egg white. That theory was put forth by a disgruntled chicken and is not true. The bacteria affect the entire egg.

Traditional mousses are made with uncooked egg yolks and egg whites. We do have those traditional recipes here, but we also offer alternatives. Carol Levin from Seattle, Washington, gives excellent, safe step-by-step instructions for making a mousse with fresh, uncooked eggs (Grand Ma' Mousse, page 187), using hot syrup to "cook" the eggs. And Lorraine Carr uses gelatin in her mousse recipe instead of egg in Bagging a Mousse on page 188.

Tips for Whipping Egg Whites

My mother complained she just couldn't beat the egg whites for her mousse properly. (My father claimed my mother was an excellent beater but still made a morose mousse.) I've heard many other people complain about their frustration with this process. So we're going to spend a little time on it. Then if beaten egg whites are called for in a flourless chocolate cake recipe (such as Fallen Cake by Vicky Victor on page 130), you can refer back here for the proper instructions.

- At the culinary school where I once worked, it was a beautiful sight to see nervous first-term students frantically whipping egg whites with wire whisks in copper bowls. But I'm here in my home kitchen with the copper hanging decoratively on the wall and no students to whip egg whites for me. Stainless steel bowls are fine. Glass and plastic are less desirable. Glass is too slippery and plastic is too porous.
- The eggs should be at room temperature (70 to 75 degrees). More air can be whipped into egg whites at this temperature, making them fluffier.*
- I could go into detail about separating eggs, but you can use your own method. Just make sure you don't get any egg yolk in the egg whites. That's why I separate eggs in individual cups and then pour them in with the rest of the egg whites.
- Be careful not to overbeat the egg whites so that they separate.
- I have found that a bit of broken shell is great for carefully removing a speck or two of egg yolk.
- For soft peaks, the egg whites are beaten (usually at high speed) until they have the consistency of shaving cream—that's the best way to describe it—and barely hold their shape.
- For firm or stiff peaks, the egg whites are beaten longer, until they are drier and stand up in stiff mounds.
- When sweetening egg whites, add the sugar 1 tablespoon at a time, while beating continuously.

*For a quick method to get eggs to room temperature, place them in a bowl of warm (not hot) water. It is easier to separate eggs when they are cold. If that is preferable, separate the eggs cold and then warm up the egg whites before using by placing them in a microwave-safe dish and setting them in the microwave on defrost for 30 seconds per egg white.

- A scant ⅛ teaspoon cream of tartar per egg white helps stabilize the eggs and will make it easier to beat them to the proper consistency. The same proportion of cider or white vinegar and lemon juice also can provide the acidity. Beat the egg whites until frothy, then add the acidic ingredient during beating. When beating meringues, use ⅛ teaspoon of the acidic ingredient for every two egg whites.
- After whipping the egg whites, use them immediately in your recipe. It is best to incorporate them into a cooled mixture. Fold them in with a rubber spatula using a broad cutting and mixing motion to maintain the air beaten into them.

Tips for Whipping Cream

- Use heavy cream or whipping cream and keep it chilled until ready to use.
- If you are whipping the cream on a hot day, you may want to chill the bowl and beaters. Use the whipped cream as soon as possible.
- Whip the cream using an electric mixer just until peaks form. Don't overbeat it, or you'll have whipped butter.
- Gently fold whipped cream into other mixtures in large sweeping motions in order to maintain its fluffy consistency.
- Overwhipping happens to all of us. If it happens to you, keep going and make butter. Add a little salt, a little confectioners' sugar or honey (if you want it on the sweet side), and continue to whip until the cream reaches butter consistency. Serve your homemade whipped butter with chocolate bread or muffins.

Trifles

Our trifles (beginning on page 198) are layer upon layer of luscious chocolate leftovers. They are dazzling to look at and make a festive centerpiece at holidays.

We offer a variety of trifles, from the easy-to-make and eat (Death by Chocolate by Mary-Lou Esposito, page 201) to the more elaborate Black Forest Trifle by Elizabeth Norris with a to-die-for homemade chocolate pudding (page 198).

Great Moments in Chocolate History
■ ■ ■

Berthadine Oxcart, a cook in an uppercrust English household, was known to have a snootful of brandy when her ailments flared up. (Although no one could figure out what did ail her.) On a particularly achy day, Berthadine was so wrapped up in easing her pain that she forgot to make the evening dessert, and the lord and lady of the manor were hosting a dinner party. Frantic, Berthadine found a stale cake and some leftover chocolate pudding. Grabbing the glass punch bowl, she crumbled the stale cake into the bowl, doused it with brandy, dumped the pudding on top, and topped it all with leftover marmalade from the still-cluttered tea tray. The dessert was presented and everyone raved. When asked to take a bow for her creation, Berthadine hiccuped, blushed, and said, "Ah, sir, 'twas but a trifle." That's why this creation is not called Brandied Berthadine or Loaded Oxcart.

Tiramisù

Tiramisù has become one of the biggest dessert sensations in restaurants everywhere. It has been scripted on menus in the fanciest establishments and scrawled on blackboards of we-serve-Bud-only dives. The name is Italian, meaning "pick-me-up," with coffee or chocolate providing the boost to a classic fluffy egg and cream (and sometimes sweet mascarpone cheese) mixture. Beginning on page 193 you will find a variety of chocolate "pick-me-ups."

Although ladyfingers are usually available in the baked goods section of your grocery store, if you have difficulty finding these delicate creations, call 1-800-755-9890. Specialty Bakers, ladyfinger specialists since 1901, will be happy to tell you where you can purchase them in your area or how you can buy them directly by the case.

Grand Ma' Mousse

Carol Levin · Seattle, Washington

■ ■ ■

***C**hoc Talk:* Here is a very easy way to "cook" raw eggs by using a hot syrup, yet still have the creamy benefit of the yolks in the mousse.

"This is a personal adaptation of a 'passed along' recipe. . . . I added the Grand Marnier and it's been a most-requested favorite ever since. It is very simple to prepare, and you can get really whimsical with garnish. I've been making it for special occasions for fifteen years!" —Carol Levin

Yield: *6 servings* **Preparation Time:** *20 minutes* **Chilling Time:** *3 hours*

4 ounces unsweetened chocolate	**GARNISH OPTIONS**
¾ cup granulated sugar	*Orange peel, cut in very thin*
⅓ cup water	*slivers*
4 large egg yolks	*Chocolate shavings (page 306)*
2 tablespoons Grand Marnier	*Chocolate designs (page 306)*
liqueur⁎*	
1 cup heavy cream	

1. Melt the chocolate (for effective methods and instructions, see page 27). Set aside to cool completely.

2. In a medium saucepan, combine the sugar and water and bring to a boil, stirring occasionally until the sugar dissolves and a syrup forms.

3. Place the melted chocolate in a food processor or blender (you can also use a wire whisk). Pour the hot syrup into the chocolate and blend. Drop in the egg yolks one at a time while continuing to blend, and then add the liqueur, blending everything together. Set aside to cool.

continued

⁎You may substitute your favorite liqueur and garnish appropriately. Or you can substitute orange juice, if you prefer. You may also omit the ingredient if you wish.

4. In a medium bowl, whip the cream until stiff peaks form. Fold the cooled chocolate mixture into the whipped cream until it is well blended.

5. Transfer the mousse to a 1-quart glass serving bowl or individual dessert cups and refrigerate for at least 3 hours. Garnish as desired.

Magnificent Mousse
Is in the Bag
Special Award

Bagging a Mousse

Lorraine Carr · Rochester, Massachusetts

■ ■ ■

Choc Talk: Lorraine actually sent two chocolate mousse recipes, and we combined them. Some assembly is required, but the fluffy mousse-filled chocolate bag is fun to make and delicious to destroy.

Yield: *4 to 6 servings* **Preparation Time:** *25 minutes* **Chilling Time:** *2 to 3 hours* **"Bakeware" Required:** *1 waxed or oiled paper bag about 4 × 6 × 7 inches high (a white bag from the bakery or doughnut shop is perfect, or coat the inside of a brown paper bag with vegetable oil)*

CHOCOLATE BAG
12 ounces semisweet chocolate chips
1 tablespoon solid vegetable shortening

MOUSSE
One 1-ounce package unflavored gelatin
2 tablespoons cold water
⅓ cup boiling water

¾ cup granulated sugar
½ cup unsweetened cocoa
1 tablespoon instant coffee granules (I recommend instant cappuccino-flavored powder)
1 pint (2 cups) heavy cream

GARNISH
Fresh whipped cream

To Make the Chocolate Bag

1. Melt the chocolate and shortening over low heat (for effective methods and instructions, see page 27). Using a clean pastry brush, coat the inside of the bag with a thin layer of chocolate. Chill the bag until the chocolate has hardened. Repeat the process until the coating is ⅛ inch thick. Refrigerate the bag again until the chocolate is very firm. Carefully peel away the paper from the chocolate and refrigerate until serving time.

To Make the Mousse

1. In a bowl, sprinkle the gelatin over the cold water. Let stand for 5 minutes.

2. Add the boiling water to the bowl and stir until the gelatin is fully dissolved.

3. In a large mixing bowl, combine the sugar, cocoa, and coffee granules. Add the cream and beat until stiff. Add the cooled gelatin mixture and beat until well combined. Cover the bowl and refrigerate for 2 to 3 hours.

To Assemble

1. Spoon the chilled mousse into the chocolate bag and garnish the top of the mousse with fresh whipped cream. Serve by spooning mousse into the dessert cups and have everyone break off pieces of the chocolate bag.

Presentation Idea: Instead of making one large chocolate bag, you can purchase small bags at candy stores and use the same method to coat them. That way, each person can bag his or her own mousse.

Just-Like-a-Restaurant Chocolate Mousse

Cami Neidigh · Kirkland, Washington

■ ■ ■

***C**hoc Talk:* After a tough day at the office, this is what angels dine on, I'm sure. A traditional mousse made with beaten egg whites, it will remind you of the heaven-on-earth desserts you've had at the best restaurants. Now you can make this one yourself.

"I come from a long line of serious chocolate lovers. When my family would gather for a special occasion, it was mandatory that the meal end on a chocolate note. I created this recipe because it is simple and quick, yet will please the hardest of hardcore chocolate lovers. It has now become a family favorite. I hope you enjoy it as much as my family has." —Cami Neidigh

Yield: *16 servings* **Preparation Time:** *30 minutes* **Chilling time:** *1 hour*

10½ ounces semisweet
   chocolate*
7 large eggs, separated
5 tablespoons granulated sugar
2⅓ cups heavy cream

GARNISHES
1 cup heavy cream, whipped
Chocolate shavings (page 306)
Ladyfingers

1. Melt the chocolate (for effective methods and instructions see page 27). Transfer to a large bowl and set aside to cool completely.

2. In a separate bowl, whip the egg whites until frothy. Add the sugar, 1 tablespoon at a time, while continuing to beat until soft peaks form. (For instructions on beating egg whites, see page 184.)

---

*For a darker chocolate mousse, you may wish to substitute a dark sweet chocolate like Baker's German's.

3. In another bowl, beat the egg yolks until they become lemon-colored and ribbons of egg yolk drip from the beaters. Using a wire whisk, mix the beaten egg yolks into the cooled chocolate mixture. Fold in the whipped egg whites.

4. In a chilled bowl, whip the cream into firm peaks. Gently fold the whipped cream into the chocolate mixture. Be careful not to overmix and deflate the mixture.

5. Spoon the mousse into champagne glasses or dessert cups. Refrigerate for at least 1 hour. Decorate with a swirl of fresh whipped cream and shaved chocolate and serve, with ladyfingers.

Recipe Note: This recipe can easily be reduced by half by using 3 eggs.

Milky Way Mousse

Caitlin Keys · Middlebury, Connecticut

■ ■ ■

Junior Chocolate Lover Category

***C**hoc Talk:* This deceptively easy creation is made with Milky Way bars, which melt beautifully; the caramel in the candy bar adds the extra flavor. This is a creative idea, but we encourage you to experiment with your favorite candy bar. Creamy bars melt the best.

"I created this recipe for my brother. I am eight and he is five. His favorite dessert is chocolate mousse. The first time he ate chocolate mousse was in a restaurant. When the waitress offered it to him, he said, 'I'm not eating any moose.' We all laughed."
—Caitlin Keys

Yield: *4 servings* **Preparation Time:** *10 to 15 minutes* **Chilling Time:** *1 to 2 hours*

> *9 fun-size Milky Way candy bars (available in 14-ounce bags)*
>
> *1¼ cups heavy cream, divided*
> *Fresh raspberries (optional)*
>
> **TOPPING**
> *½ cup whipped cream*

1. Chop 1 candy bar into small pieces and set aside.

2. Melt the remaining candy bars (for effective methods and instructions, see page 27). Make sure the bars are thoroughly melted.

3. In a chilled bowl, whip the heavy cream until stiff peaks form. Set aside ¼ cup whipped cream and refrigerate.

4. Stir ¼ cup whipped cream immediately into the warm, melted chocolate. Fold this mixture back into the remaining ¾ cup whipped cream.

5. Refrigerate the Milky Way Mousse for 1 to 2 hours. Before serving, whisk the reserved ¼ cup whipped cream into the mousse.

6. Spoon the mousse into 4 stemmed glasses. Garnish the mousse with the whipped cream for topping. Sprinkle the chopped Milky Way bar and raspberries, if desired, on top of each serving.

Sierra Sin

Bobbie "Buff" Hirko · Gig Harbor, Washington

■ ■ ■

Choc Talk: This sin-sationally rich chocolate buttercream served on bourbon-soaked ladyfingers is a tiramisù treasure.

"We formerly owned a cabin in the Sierras and regularly visited a favorite restaurant, where we dined on the chef's signature dessert. Repeated requests for the dessert recipe fell on stubborn ears, and when the restaurant closed in 1983, I decided to create my own version. . . . Whether or not it re-creates the original no longer matters; it is wonderful in its own right. I have been serving . . . it for nearly ten years, to unanimously rave reviews." —Bobbie Hirko

Yield: *20 servings* **Preparation Time:** *30 minutes* **Chilling Time:** *6 hours* **Bakeware Required:** *10-inch springform pan*

2 packages (approximately 24) ladyfingers, split in half
8 ounces unsweetened chocolate
1½ cups unsalted butter
2 cups granulated sugar
5 teaspoons vanilla extract, divided
½ cup bourbon*
8 large eggs

8 ounces almond paste (optional)
1 cup heavy cream
1 tablespoon confectioners' sugar

GARNISH
Chocolate shavings (page 306)

continued

*Although the bourbon has a definite presence in the recipe, for a nonalcoholic substitution, use your favorite juice or place 1 to 2 teaspoons rum extract or brandy extract in ½ cup water (or to taste).

1. Line the bottom and sides of the springform pan with the split ladyfingers.

2. Melt the chocolate (for effective methods and instructions, see page 27). Set aside to cool completely.

3. In a mixing bowl, using an electric mixer at high speed, cream the butter. Add the sugar, melted chocolate, and 4 teaspoons of the vanilla. Cream the ingredients together until well blended. At low speed, beat in the bourbon. Add the eggs and beat at high speed for about 3 minutes, until the mixture becomes light-colored, smooth, and very thick (if the mixture gets runny from overbeating, refrigerate and then beat it again).

4. Spread half the chocolate buttercream in the ladyfinger-lined pan. Crumble the almond paste, if using, evenly over the top. Spread the remaining buttercream over all, and smooth the top with a spatula.

5. Cover with plastic wrap and refrigerate for at least 6 hours or until ready to serve.

6. When you are ready to serve the tiramisù, whip the cream with the confectioners' sugar and remaining 1 teaspoon vanilla until stiff peaks form. Spread the whipped cream over the buttercream. Sprinkle chocolate shavings on top and remove the sides of the springform pan. Serve in slices no thicker than one ladyfinger wide. This dessert is very, very rich.

Recipe Note: If you are not a bourbon lover, substitute your favorite liquor or liqueur.

Heavenly Crown

Marjorie Ohrnstein · Los Angeles, California
■ ■ ■

***C**hoc Talk:* The cream cheese in this recipe adds a delicious and creamy oomph. The orange juice is subtle and refreshing.

Yield: *12 servings* **Preparation Time:** *20 minutes* **Chilling Time:** *6 to 12 hours* **Bakeware Required:** *9-inch springform pan*

16 ladyfingers, split in half	*1½ cups heavy cream*
½ cup orange juice	*1½ teaspoons vanilla extract*
6 ounces semisweet chocolate	
1 cup firmly packed light brown	**OPTIONAL GARNISHES**
sugar, divided	*Chocolate shavings (page 306)*
3 large eggs, separated	*Whipped cream*
One 8-ounce package cream	
cheese, softened	

1. Using a pastry brush, lightly coat the cut sides of the ladyfingers with the orange juice. Place the cut sides down in the springform pan, covering the bottom and sides.

2. Melt the chocolate (for effective methods and instructions, see page 27). Set aside to cool completely.

3. In a large bowl, cream ½ cup of the brown sugar and the egg yolks. Add the cream cheese and mix well. Add the melted chocolate and stir to blend. Beat the heavy cream into the chocolate mixture until soft peaks form.

4. In a separate bowl, whip the egg whites with the vanilla and the remaining ½ cup brown sugar, one tablespoon at a time, until firm peaks form. (For instructions on beating egg whites, see page 184.) Gently fold the egg white mixture into the chocolate mixture.

5. Spoon the mousse into the springform pan on top of the ladyfingers. Smooth the top with a spatula and refrigerate for 6 to 12 hours.

6. Remove the dessert from the refrigerator 30 minutes before serving. Garnish, if desired, with whipped cream and chocolate shavings.

Le Diplomat
à la Chocolat

Marie-Christiane Corbett · West Hartford, Connecticut

■ ■ ■

Professional Chocolate Lover Category

***C**hoc Talk:* Marie packages her own scone mixes—Christiane's Wooden Spoon Scone Mixes (all natural, with no preservatives). I especially recommend her chocolate cappuccino scones. She is also the creator of the award-winning Queen of Sheba meatloaf (made with lamb, sausage, pine nuts, and pistachios) from *The Great American Meatloaf Contest Cookbook*. And, with this recipe, she's done it again.

"This recipe belonged to my great-aunt, who passed it down to my mom for her first wedding anniversary thirty-nine years ago. As a tradition, it's been made for every anniversary since then. I also use it in my catering package—it makes for a very elegant cake. The name is derived from the fact that it is very smooth, tempting, and regal—just like a diplomat. Enjoy!" —Marie-Christiane Corbett

Yield: *15 to 20 servings* **Preparation Time:** *30 to 40 minutes* **Chilling Time:** *6 to 12 hours* **Bakeware Required:** *10 × 15-inch or 9 × 13-inch shallow serving dish*

MOCHA FILLING
½ cup unsalted butter, softened
2 cups confectioners' sugar
¾ cup unsweetened cocoa
1 tablespoon instant coffee granules or powder
¼ cup heavy cream
3 tablespoons brandy or 2 to 3 teaspoons brandy or rum extract
1 tablespoon vanilla extract

1 tablespoon hot water (optional)

LADYFINGER LAYERS
½ cup brandy or 4 teaspoons brandy or rum extract
1 cup milk
6 packages (approximately 72) ladyfingers

WHIPPED CREAM

1 pint (2 cups) heavy cream

Vanilla extract to taste (start with 1 teaspoon)

Confectioners' sugar to taste (start with 1 to 2 tablespoons)

GARNISH

Walnut halves

To Make the Mocha Filling

1. In a large bowl, cream the butter.

2. In a small bowl, combine the sugar, cocoa, and instant coffee granules.

3. Gradually add the cocoa mixture to the creamed butter, alternating with the heavy cream and mixing well after each addition. Add the brandy and vanilla. If the mixture is too thick, stir in the 1 tablespoon hot water. Refrigerate for 15 to 20 minutes.

To Soak the Ladyfingers

1. In a small bowl, mix the brandy and milk together.

2. Using a pastry brush, lightly coat the ladyfingers with this mixture. Brush some of the ladyfingers sparingly to use on the sides of the tiramisù. (If they are too soft, they will not stand up.)

To Make the Whipped Cream

1. In a large bowl, whip the heavy cream until stiff peaks form. Mix in the vanilla and confectioners' sugar to taste.

To Assemble the Dessert

1. Place a single layer of the soaked ladyfingers in the serving dish. Spread one fourth of the mocha filling over the ladyfingers.

2. Repeat step 1, alternating between ladyfingers and mocha filling to make 3 to 4 layers. End with a layer of ladyfingers.

3. Arrange the remaining ladyfingers around the entire tiramisù, standing them up to create a wall around it. This wall should be taller than the layered center.

4. Top the tiramisù with the whipped cream and garnish with walnut halves. Refrigerate Le Diplomat 6 to 12 hours before serving.

continued

Recipe Note: Rum will work in place of brandy, or substitute rum or brandy extract if you prefer a nonalcoholic version.

Black Forest Trifle

Elizabeth Norris · Oakland, California

■ ■ ■

Choc Talk: Before discovering this recipe, I always made chocolate pudding the old-fashioned way—in an "instant" from a box. This fabulous from-scratch chocolate pudding may take more time, but ooh, is it worth it! Use this pudding recipe in other desserts in this book that call for chocolate pudding.

"Creating desserts is my hobby. Once, when I made a trifle with plain custard, someone asked, 'Where's the chocolate?' So I created a chocolate version of my trifle—and it's even a bigger hit than the original. Real chocolate, not instant pudding or cocoa, is my secret. Real men eat real chocolate!" —Elizabeth Norris

Yield: *12 servings* **Preparation Time:** *30 minutes* **Baking Time:** *1 hour, if not using purchased pound cake* **Chilling Time:** *6 to 12 hours* **Cookware and Bakeware Required:** *2-quart trifle bowl or punch bowl; 9½ × 5¼ × 2¾-inch loaf pan, lightly greased, for the cake, if you decide not to purchase a prepared pound cake; double boiler with a large, deep top half (at least a 4-cup capacity)*

CHOCOLATE PUDDING	½ cup granulated sugar
3 ounces semisweet chocolate	¼ teaspoon salt
3 cups half-and-half	1 teaspoon vanilla extract
6 large eggs	

CHOCOLATE POUND CAKE*

4 ounces semisweet chocolate

One 16-ounce package plain
   pound cake mix,† plus
   necessary ingredients to
   prepare cake (listed on the
   package)

TRIFLE LAYERS

1 to 2 tablespoons cherry
   brandy

One 20-ounce can cherry pie
   filling

GARNISH

1 cup heavy cream

½ cup slivered almonds

To Make the Pudding

1. Melt the chocolate (for effective methods and instructions, see page 27). Set aside to cool completely.

2. In a large microwave-safe bowl, scald‡ the half-and-half in the microwave on high power for 3 to 5 minutes. Or place the half-and-half in a large saucepan over medium heat and scald it.

3. Fill the bottom of the double boiler with water to the correct level and, over low heat, bring to a gentle simmer. Combine the eggs, sugar, and salt in the top half and set it over the water. Immediately begin to add the scalded half-and-half gradually, stirring continuously until the custard thickens (do *not* let the water boil in the double boiler). Be patient.

4. When the pudding is thick, stir in the melted chocolate and remove from the heat. Set aside to cool completely.

5. When the pudding is cool, stir in the vanilla. Place plastic wrap right on the surface so that a skin will not form, and set in the refrigerator to chill slightly.

To Bake the Cake

1. Melt the chocolate (for effective methods and instructions, see page 27). Set aside to cool slightly.

continued

---

*You can purchase a prepared plain or chocolate pound cake and eliminate the pound cake preparation steps.

†Elizabeth Norris uses a brand called Dromedary, but any brand will do.

‡Scald means different things to different people. Culinarily, it means to heat to just below the boiling point. Small bubbles usually form around the edge of the liquid.

2. Prepare the cake batter according to package directions.

3. Stir the melted chocolate into the batter.

4. Pour the batter into the prepared loaf pan. Bake according to package directions (this may take as much as 1 hour). Let the cake cool on a wire rack for 15 minutes, then remove from the pan. Refrigerate until chilled.

5. Cut the chilled cake in half. Cut the half portion of the cake into small pieces, 1 to 2 inches in size.

To Assemble the Trifle

1. Line the bottom and sides of the trifle bowl with half the cake pieces. Reserve the rest for another layer. Sprinkle or douse the cake with the cherry brandy to taste.

2. Spread half the can of cherry filling on the cake. Spoon half the pudding over the cherry filling. Cover the pudding with the remaining pieces of cake and repeat the layering of the cherry filling and pudding. Place plastic wrap over the pudding surface and chill the trifle overnight.

3. When ready to serve, beat the whipping cream until stiff. Swirl the whipped cream over the trifle and garnish it with the almonds.

Presentation Idea: Spoon the trifle into wide-mouthed champagne or margarita glasses. Then your guests can spoon the trifle into *their* wide mouths.

Recipe Note: "This trifle uses only half of the pound cake. The rest may be frozen for later use. Or you can double the trifle recipe for a big crowd."—Elizabeth Norris

Death by Chocolate

Mary-Lou Esposito · Oakdale, New York

■ ■ ■

C̲hoc Talk: "I made this for one of my roommates on her twenty-first birthday. I have four roommates, but there was plenty for all five of us, plus enough for breakfast the next day. Since I was making this with hungry people watching, I baked the cake batter in muffin pans instead of cake pans to shorten the baking time [see Recipe Note]. This is an excellent recipe."
—Elizabeth Howard, Chocolate Heaven Assistant Chocolatier

Yield: *6 to 8 servings* **Preparation Time:** *15 minutes* **Baking Time:** *35 to 40 minutes* **Chilling Time:** *2 hours* **Cookware and Bakeware Required:** *1 large glass trifle bowl or punch bowl; two 9-inch round cake pans or 2 muffin pans, greased*

One 18.25-ounce chocolate cake mix, plus necessary ingredients to prepare cake (listed on the package)
Two 3.9-ounce packages instant chocolate pudding mix
4 cups milk

½ cup Kahlúa or other coffee-flavored liqueur or cold coffee, divided
One 12-ounce container Cool Whip
Four to six 1.55-ounce Nestlé's Crunch bars

To Bake the Cake

1. Prepare and bake the cake according to the package directions. Set aside to cool completely.

2. Meanwhile, mix both packages of pudding with the milk. Refrigerate until set.

3. Prick holes all over the top of the cooled cake or cupcakes with a toothpick or fork. Pour ¼ cup of the Kahlúa over each cake

continued

layer. If you are using cupcakes, spoon 1 teaspoon Kahlúa over each. Set the cake or cupcakes aside until the Kahlúa is completely absorbed.

To Layer the Trifle

1. Cut or crumble the Kahlúa-soaked cake into small pieces and cover the bottom of the trifle bowl. Spread one third of the pudding on the crumbled cake. Spread a third of the Cool Whip on top of the pudding. Crumble 1 or 2 Nestlé's Crunch bars, and sprinkle the pieces over the Cool Whip.

2. Repeat the layering for as many layers as you wish, ending with a top layer of Cool Whip garnished with crumbled candy bar. Chill the trifle for 2 to 3 hours and serve.

Recipe Note: To reduce the baking time, bake the cake in muffin pans (a typical cake mix batter will make 24 cupcakes). Cupcakes take about 15 minutes to bake and work just as well because the cake is crumbled anyway. ("I wanted less cake in the trifle, so I only used twelve muffins and gave the other twelve to my roommates to keep them quiet until the trifle was done." — Elizabeth)

Another Great Moment in Chocolate History: Death by Chocolate
■ ■ ■

In the 1600s the upper-class expatriate Spanish ladies of Chiapa Real, Mexico, would have their maids bring jugs of chocolate to church during the long hours of mass to revive them and keep them from fainting. But the chocolate sipping proved so disruptive in church, the bishop vowed to excommunicate anyone caught doing it. The ladies were more than miffed. And shortly after this chocolate ban, the bishop was mysteriously poisoned by a tainted cup of chocolate. He died a slow and miserable death.

Paula's Dirt Recipe

Paula Kravetz · Randolph, Massachusetts

■ ■ ■

*C*hoc Talk: This recipe is served in a flower pot and will bring out the kid in you. I served it to adults at a "Be a Kid Again" party. Other menu items included fluffer-nutter sandwiches and Kool-Aid. For a "Surfin' Safari" party, we substituted finely ground vanilla wafers for the Oreos and served the "sand" with little shovels.

"I developed this recipe about five years ago. It started out as little 'dirt cups' for my children, but we then got the idea to turn it into one large dessert for everyone to share. We particularly like the idea of using it as a centerpiece and then surprising everyone else when we start to spoon the 'dirt' onto each plate." —Paula Kravetz

Yield: *15 to 20 servings* **Preparation Time:** *20 minutes* **"Cookware" Required:** *2-quart plastic "terra-cotta" planter or other flower pot (please use one that is clean); artificial flowers* **Chilling Time:** *2 to 3 hours*

Two 1-pound packages Oreo cookies

Three 3.9-ounce packages instant chocolate pudding mix

6 cups milk

Four 1.55-ounce Heath English Toffee Bars, crushed

Two 12-ounce containers Cool Whip

OPTIONAL GARNISH

Gummy worms (a jelly candy found in most grocery stores)

1. Crush the Oreo cookies in a blender or food processor until fine.

2. In a large bowl, mix the 3 packages of pudding with the milk. Refrigerate for 15 minutes.

3. Place one third of the cookie crumbs in the flower pot. (It may be necessary to cover the hole in the bottom of the pot with

Chocolate Mousse, Trifle, and Tiramisù • 203

a layer of aluminum foil to prevent leakage.) Spread one third of the pudding on top of the crumbs. Follow with one third of the Cool Whip. Then sprinkle with one third of the crushed Heath bars.

4. Repeat each layer until the top of the pot is reached, ending with the cookie crumbs. Chill in the refrigerator for 2 to 3 hours.

5. Decorate with artificial flowers. If desired, add gummy worms or gummy frogs on top of the dirt layer. Serve with an unused or child's plastic garden trowel instead of a spoon.

Brenda's
Sugar-Free Dirt Cake

Brenda Webb · Clarksville, Arkansas

■ ■ ■

Professional Chocolate Lover Category

***C**hoc Talk:* You don't miss the sugar. Use this recipe as a guideline to trim the excess sugar from other trifle recipes.

"I adapted this recipe from one a friend gave me because my husband can't eat sugar. Hers called for Oreos and a cup of powdered sugar and regular pudding mix. We really like the sugar-free version better because it's not as rich. It's also quick and easy to fix if company drops in unexpectedly. At first they don't believe it's sugar-free. I always say 'sugar-free' not 'calorie-free.'"
—Brenda Webb

Yield: *8 to 10 servings* **Preparation Time:** *15 minutes* **Chilling Time:** *1 to 2 hours* **"Cookware" Required:** *2-quart trifle bowl*

2 packages Estee or other brand of sugar-free chocolate cookies with creme filling
½ cup margarine, softened
One 8-ounce package cream cheese, softened
3 cups low-fat (2%) milk

One 1.4-ounce package Jell-O sugar-free instant chocolate pudding mix
One 8-ounce container Lite Cool Whip

1. Using either a food processor or a blender, crush the cookies very fine.

2. In a large bowl, cream together the margarine and cream cheese.*

continued

---

*I microwave the margarine and cream cheese for about 20 seconds to soften before mixing.

3. In a separate bowl, combine the milk and pudding mix. Immediately add the Cool Whip and mix well. Add the cream cheese mixture to the pudding mixture and blend well.

4. Beginning and ending with the crushed cookies, layer the cookies and pudding mixture in thirds in a 2-quart bowl. Refrigerate for 1 hour before serving.

The Big Chill:
Chocolate Desserts

■ ■ ■

All of the desserts in this section are easy, delicious, and perfect for hot weather or when you're having a heat wave in the middle of winter because the radiator is blasting and the super can't be found or whenever you crave cool refreshment.

Convenience is the key. In many recipes, the whipped cream is already whipped, the pie crusts are already prepared, the puddings are instant, even the cookies are precrushed (this innovation came from a bagger in a supermarket who systematically crushed a lot of cookies in an attempt to disprove the theory that cans really do go on the bottom—another **Great Moment in Chocolate History**).

Do note that some of these desserts require chilling time. Although some of our contributors suggested overnight hibernation in the refrigerator for their creations, we experimented and found that 6 to 12 hours of chilling will work. If you're making the dessert at 10 P.M., I guess overnight would apply.

Another note, this time about bakeware: Most of these desserts are refrigerated in a baking pan. I strongly suggest glass, but in any case, *do not use* bakeware that has a nonstick coating—the moisture and chilly temperatures may harm the coating.

Cookie Crust Recipes with Variations

Chocolate-Covered Memory

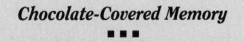

"Do you know exactly how to eat an Oreo,
Well to do it, you unscrew it, very fast.
'Cause the kid'll eat the middle of an Oreo first
And save the chocolate cookie outside for last."
—*Nabisco's Oreo cookie theme song, permission granted for reprint by Nabisco, Inc.*

Basic Chocolate Sandwich Cookie Crust

Make this Basic Chocolate Sandwich Cookie Crust or make the crust with the suggested variations ahead of time and have it on hand in the freezer for a quick Big Chill fix.

Combine 1½ cups of chocolate sandwich cookie crumbs (approximately 20 to 25 sandwich cookies such as Nabisco's Oreo cookies, finely ground) with ½ cup melted unsalted butter or margarine. Mix well and press into the bottom and up the sides of a 9 × 9-inch pan or 9-inch pie pan. Refrigerate for at least 20 minutes, then proceed with your recipe of choice for filling and topping.

For a crumbier crust, reduce the quantity of butter or margarine.

Hint: Crush extra cookies so that you have extra crumbs on hand. (You can also buy the crumbs already crushed if you really hate to watch the cookie crumble.) Place leftover cookie crumbs in a plastic bag and freeze them. They last for up to 3 months.

Variations:
Sandwich Cookie Crust: Using the Basic Chocolate Sandwich Cookie Crust instructions, substitute peanut butter sandwich cookies, vanilla sandwich cookies, or other filled sandwich cookies, for the chocolate sandwich cookies.

Nutty Cookie Crust: I use only 1 cup crushed cookies and add ½ cup crushed salted nuts* or salted sunflower seeds (lightly toast them for extra flavor).

Plain Chocolate Cookie Crust

For recipes that call for Nabisco Famous Wafers or for a chocolate graham cracker crust, try Chocolate Teddy Grahams (located near the graham crackers in the supermarket). Those little bears crush easily and make a delicious pie crust. Use the same ingredient proportions listed in the Basic Chocolate Sandwich Cookie Crust.

Vanilla Wafer Crust: See crust recipe in I Scream Mousse-Cream (page 217).

Top It with Flavor

Check out the flavored whipped cream ideas on page 304.

Be creative and have some fun with the festive ingredients available in the cake-decorating section of the grocery store. See page 306 for other garnishing ideas.

A Slice of the Big Chill Tip

Here's a tip from one of our contestants for slicing a frozen or chilled dessert. *"Before cutting the pie or bars, dip the knife (or server) into hot water for a minute or two. Repeat before cutting each piece. Use this method for all frozen or chilled desserts."* —Joel Crick Trimble, Choco-Peanut Butter Wowie (page 219).

*For extra nutty flavor, spread the nuts on a cookie sheet and toast them in a preheated 350 degree oven for 10 to 15 minutes. Stir the nuts occasionally to toast them evenly and prevent burning. Or, toast the nuts in the microwave (they will not change color but will taste toasted). Place 1 cup nuts on a paper plate and microwave uncovered on high power for 3 to 4 minutes, rotating the plate a half turn after 2 minutes.

Grasshopper Pie

Joann Gonzales · San Lorenzo, California

■ ■ ■

***C**hoc Talk:* A favorite after-dinner ice cream drink can now be enjoyed in a chocolate pie. What a great idea! Light green–colored clouds of mint-flavored whipped cream are studded with mini chocolate chips on top of a chocolate pudding layer in a crunchy chocolate crust.

"I wanted to get the flavors of chocolate cake and mint chocolate chip ice cream in a pie." —JoAnn Gonzales

Yield: *8 to 10 servings* **Preparation Time:** *10 to 15 minutes* **Bakeware Required:** *9-inch pie pan (if you don't use a purchased 9-inch chocolate crumb crust)*

1¾ cups milk
One 3.9-ounce package instant chocolate pudding mix
One 9-inch chocolate crumb crust (to make your own using crushed Nabisco Famous Chocolate Wafers or crushed Oreos, see page 208)
2 cups heavy cream
One 3.4-ounce package instant vanilla pudding mix

½ teaspoon crème de menthe liqueur or peppermint extract
⅓ cup mini semisweet chocolate chips
Green food coloring

GARNISHES
Whipped cream
Chocolate curls

1. In a bowl, combine the milk and chocolate pudding mix and beat for 1 minute with a wire whisk.

2. Pour the mixture into the prepared crust and refrigerate.

3. In a large bowl, combine the whipping cream, vanilla pudding mix, and crème de menthe and mix together until well blended. Add 3 drops of green food coloring. Beat the mixture until soft peaks form. Fold the mini chocolate chips into the whipped mixture.

4. Pour the mixture over the chilled chocolate layer of the pie. Garnish with whipped cream and chocolate curls. Chill until ready to serve.

Chocolate Déjà Vu Delight

Marceline Morris · King George, Virginia

■ ■ ■

Choc Talk: Crispy wafers and a creamy chocolate filling combine in this luscious, light, and refreshing dessert. The layers of chocolate and more chocolate create an attractive presentation, but there's no work involved. Take this dessert to a holiday office party, and you'll get a promotion.

Yield: *6 to 8 servings* **Preparation Time:** *15 minutes* **Chilling Time:** *8 to 12 hours* **Bakeware Required:** *8 × 4 × 3-inch loaf pan, lined with plastic wrap (allow some of the wrap to hang over the edge in order to lift the chilled loaf from the pan)*

4 ounces sweet dark chocolate	*2 large egg yolks*
(such as Baker's German's	*1 cup heavy cream*
chocolate)	*40 (approximately) Nabisco*
⅛ teaspoon salt	*Famous Chocolate Wafers*

1. Melt the chocolate (for effective methods and instructions, see page 27). Set aside to cool completely.

2. Stir the salt into the cooled chocolate. Add the egg yolks one at a time, beating well after each addition.

3. In a medium bowl, whip the cream until stiff peaks form. Fold ¼ cup of the whipped cream into the cooled chocolate mixture, blending well. Fold in the remaining whipped cream very gently until the two mixtures are completely blended.

4. Arrange a layer of the chocolate wafers on the bottom of the lined pan. Place the wafers upside down, with the tops touching the bottom of the pan. Spread one fourth of the chocolate mixture over the wafer layer.

continued

5. Continue to layer the wafers and chocolate mixture, ending with a top layer of wafers. Cover the dessert with plastic wrap and refrigerate for 8 to 12 hours.

6. When ready to serve, remove the dessert from the refrigerator and unmold it onto a serving dish. Slice into 6 to 8 servings.

Strawberry Fields with Chocolate

Jane Woods · Boca Raton, Florida
■ ■ ■

hoc Talk: "Strawberry Fields Forever"—like chocolate, strawberries are very much a part of our culinary culture. So it makes sense to merge two cultural legends in a strawberry-chocolate festival for the mouth. Try this one on a hot July Fourth weekend when beer and "pop" ("soda" on the East Coast) will not quench the thirst. If this dessert could be made the size of a swimming pool, I'd dive in face first.

"Chocolate has always been a family favorite, as have strawberries. What better treat than to combine the two? Trial and error allowed me to develop this wonderful 'family favorite.' " —Jane Woods

Yield: *6 to 8 servings* **Preparation Time:** *20 minutes* **Bakeware Required:** *9 × 9-inch baking pan, lightly greased* **Chilling Time:** *2 hours total*

6 ounces semisweet chocolate chips

1 cup Kraft marshmallow creme or any brand of marshmallow fluff

1 cup finely chopped pecans

1½ cups chocolate cookie crumbs (approximately 20 sandwich cookies such as Oreos, finely ground for crumbs, but grind more to add to the crust mixture for desired texture)

½ cup unsalted butter or margarine, melted

One 8-ounce container whipped topping (such as Cool Whip), thawed, or 2 cups fresh whipped cream, divided

1½ cups puréed strawberries* (approximately 1 pint fresh or frozen strawberries), divided

Fresh mint sprigs (optional)

1. Melt the chocolate chips (for effective methods and instructions, see page 27). When the chocolate is completely melted and still hot, add the marshmallow fluff and pecans, stirring until the marshmallow has melted into the chocolate. Set aside to cool while preparing the crust.

2. In a medium bowl, mix the cookie crumbs and melted butter until thoroughly blended. Press the mixture into the bottom of the prepared pan and slightly up the sides.

3. Stir 1½ cups of the whipped topping into the chocolate mixture and pour it into the crust. Cover the pan with plastic wrap and freeze for 1 hour, or until the chocolate mixture is set.

4. In a small bowl, combine 1 cup of the strawberry purée and the remaining whipped topping, stirring until well blended. Pour over the frozen chocolate mixture. Cover with plastic wrap and freeze until firm.

5. Remove the dessert from the freezer approximately 30 minutes prior to serving to allow it to soften slightly. Top with the reserved strawberry purée. Garnish with fresh mint sprigs, if desired.

*For instructions on making strawberry purée, see page 305

Silky Mousse Pie

Cynthia Blain · Taunton, Massachusetts

■ ■ ■

Choc Talk: This delicate, silky mousse is contrasted beautifully by the *crunch* of the chocolate cookie crust. The flavored whipped cream provides a tasty topping.

"Years ago a butter company printed a basic recipe for a chocolate pie. My mom and I loved it, and over the years we kept revising this dessert to suit different occasions and 'modern' times. It's a company favorite, and I never have to worry about leftovers!"
—Cynthia Blain

Yield: *8 to 10 servings* **Chilling Time:** *6 to 12 hours* **Bakeware Required:** *10-inch springform pan, greased*

CRUST
3 cups chocolate wafer crumbs (approximately 25 Nabisco Famous Chocolate Wafers, or use approximately 20 to 25 sandwich cookies, such as Oreos)
1 cup unsalted butter, melted

MOUSSE
8 ounces semisweet chocolate
2 extra large eggs
4 extra large eggs, separated
2 cups heavy cream

6 tablespoons confectioners' sugar
1 tablespoon crème de cacao liqueur*

TOPPING
2 cups heavy cream
2 tablespoons crème de cacao liqueur*
3 tablespoons confectioners' sugar

GARNISH
Grated chocolate or fresh fruit

To Make the Crust

1. In a large bowl, combine the crust ingredients and mix well. Press onto the bottom and sides of the prepared pan. Refrigerate for 30 minutes.

*For a nonalcoholic version, substitute unsweetened cocoa powder or instant cappuccino powder dissolved in 1 to 2 tablespoons hot water.

To Make the Mousse

1. Melt the chocolate (for effective methods and instructions, see page 27). Set aside to cool completely.

2. Add the 2 whole eggs to the cooled chocolate and mix well. Add the 4 egg yolks and blend well. Reserve the egg whites.

3. In a chilled bowl, beat the cream with the confectioners' sugar until soft peaks form. Add the crème de cacao and mix well.

4. In a separate bowl, beat the egg whites until soft peaks form, but do not let them get dry (for further instructions and tips on beating egg whites, see page 184).

5. Stir ⅛ cup of the whipped cream mixture and ⅛ cup of the egg whites into the chocolate mixture. Gradually fold the remaining whipped cream into the chocolate, alternating with the remaining egg whites.

6. Place the mixture in the prepared crust and refrigerate for at least 6 hours.

To Make the Topping

1. In a chilled bowl, beat the cream, crème de cacao, and confectioners' sugar until stiff peaks form.

2. Keep the pie chilled until serving time. Loosen the springform pan and remove the pie. Place it on a serving dish. Spread half of the topping over the chilled pie. Place the other half of the topping in a pastry tube and pipe a design of your choice onto the middle and edge of the pie. Or use the reserved topping to decorate as you wish without using a pastry tube.* Sprinkle the pie with shaved chocolate and/or fresh berries or other fruits. To serve, use a large, sharp knife to cut the pie cleanly into 8 to 10 wedges.

Recipe Notes: This pie can also be frozen for up to one month. Allow it to defrost 30 minutes before serving. • Substitute your favorite creamy liqueur (Irish cream, Kahlúa, etc.) for the crème de cacao.

---

*At Chocolate Heaven, when there's no time to pipe, we decorate using the "blob" technique. Perfect for whipped cream.

When the Mousse Meets the Pie . . . That's Chocolate Amore

Bette Gamash · Scottsdale, Arizona
■ ■ ■

***C**hoc Talk:* At your next garden party, serve thin slices of this frozen pie on your best china with little dessert forks. That way, you'll have a *huge* piece left for yourself after the last guest has finally departed.

"I've had this recipe for many years. 'Way back when,' I used real cream, coffee, baking chocolate, and my own pie crust. Now I've taken the 'easy way out' with store-bought crust, Cool Whip, Hershey bars, and instant coffee. It is a gourmet dessert requiring little effort. A perfect ending to a wonderful dinner." —Bette Gamash

Yield: *8 to 10 servings* **Preparation Time:** *15 minutes* **Chilling Time:** *6 to 12 hours* **Bakeware Required:** *9-inch pie pan (if you don't use a purchased 9-inch graham cracker pie crust)*

20 large marshmallows
½ cup milk
½ teaspoon instant coffee granules
One 7- or 8-ounce milk chocolate bar or six 1.55-ounce bars such as Hershey's milk chocolate, chopped into small pieces

One 8-ounce container Cool Whip
One 9-inch graham cracker pie crust

GARNISH
Chocolate sprinkles or chocolate curls

1. In a medium saucepan over moderate heat, combine the marshmallows and milk, stirring constantly until the marshmallows are melted. Add the instant coffee and pieces of chocolate and stir until the chocolate is melted and the ingredients are blended.

2. Transfer the mixture to a large bowl, cover, and refrigerate for 10 minutes to cool.

3. Fold three fourths of the Cool Whip into the cooled mixture, reserving the rest for decoration.

4. Pour the mixture into the prepared pie crust. Decorate with dollops of Cool Whip and chocolate sprinkles or chocolate curls. Refrigerate for 6 to 12 hours.

5. To serve, cut into small wedges, as this pie is very rich.

I Scream Mousse-Cream
Frozen Chocolate Mousse in a Vanilla Cookie Crust

Carolyn Coughlin · Carmichael, California
■ ■ ■

Choc Talk: Now make your own chocolate ice cream without the hassle. The frozen mousse is smooth and creamy. Keep this in the freezer for unexpected company.

Yield: *8 to 10 servings* **Preparation Time:** *15 minutes* **Baking Time:** *10 minutes* **Chilling Time:** *6 to 8 hours* **Bakeware Required:** *8-inch baking pan, lightly greased*

1 cup finely crushed vanilla wafers (about 25 wafers)	*1 cup semisweet chocolate chips*
¼ cup unsalted butter or margarine, melted	*5 cups miniature marshmallows*
	1 teaspoon vanilla extract
*1 cup slivered almonds, toasted, divided**	*½ teaspoon rum extract or 1 tablespoon rum (optional)*
¼ cup honey	*2 cups heavy cream, divided*
1 cup milk	*1 tablespoon confectioners' sugar*

continued

*For extra nutty flavor, spread the nuts on a cookie sheet and toast them in a preheated 350 degree oven for 10 to 15 minutes. Stir the nuts occasionally to toast them evenly and prevent burning. Or, toast the nuts in the microwave (they will not change color but will taste toasted). Place 1 cup nuts on a paper plate and microwave uncovered on high power for 3 to 4 minutes, rotating the plate a half turn after 2 minutes.

Preheat the oven to 300 degrees.

1. In a medium bowl, combine the vanilla wafer crumbs and the melted butter and mix well. Press into the bottom of the prepared pan. Sprinkle ½ cup of the toasted almonds on top of the vanilla wafer crust, pressing down lightly. Drizzle the honey over the almond layer. Bake for 10 minutes, then set aside to cool.

2. In a medium saucepan over low heat, combine the milk and chocolate chips, stirring constantly until the chocolate melts. Add the marshmallows and continue stirring until they are completely melted. Remove from the heat. Stir in the vanilla and the rum flavoring.

3. Transfer the mixture to a bowl and refrigerate briefly, just until the mixture has thickened.

4. In a small bowl, beat 1 cup of the cream until soft peaks form.

5. Fold the whipped cream into the chocolate mixture and pour it over the crust. Freeze for 6 to 8 hours, or until firm.

6. Remove from the freezer 10 minutes before serving.

7. Whip the remaining cream, sweetening it with the confectioners' sugar to taste.

8. To serve, cut the frozen mousse into squares. Dollop with whipped cream and sprinkle with the remaining toasted almonds.

Recipe Note: To make individual mousse-cream pies, place the vanilla wafer crumb crust in miniature aluminum pie pans.

Choco-Peanut Butter Wowie

The Choco-Wowie Special Award

Joel Crick Trimble · Nags Head, North Carolina

■ ■ ■

*C**hoc Talk:** Chocolate and peanut butter, two great tastes . . . wait, it's been done. But not in this big chill form. If you love peanut butter, check out the Recipe Note.

"I lived in Louisiana for several years and am a great fan of no-bake desserts, especially in the summertime." —Joel Crick Trimble

Yield: *6 to 8 servings* **Preparation Time:** *15 minutes* **Chilling Time:** *1 hour* **Bakeware Required:** *8-inch pie pan, lightly greased. To make bars instead, use an 8 × 8-inch baking pan.*

COOKIE CRUST	CHOCO-CHEESE PEANUT BUTTER FILLING
1½ cups finely crushed chocolate sandwich cookies (such as Oreos)	8 ounces semisweet chocolate
½ cup margarine or unsalted butter, melted	One 8-ounce package Neufchâtel cheese,* softened
	1¼ cups confectioners' sugar, divided
	1 cup creamy peanut butter (not chunky)
	12 ounces milk chocolate chips

To Make the Crust

1. In a large bowl, combine the cookie crumbs and melted margarine and mix well. Press evenly into the bottom of the pan and up the sides. Cover with plastic wrap and refrigerate to chill while preparing the filling.

To Make the Filling

1. Melt the semisweet chocolate (for effective methods and instructions, see page 27). Set aside to cool slightly.

continued

*A low-fat cream cheese.

2. In a large bowl, beat the softened Neufchâtel cheese with an electric mixer until smooth. Add ¾ cup of the confectioners' sugar and beat until smooth. Add the peanut butter and beat until well mixed.

3. Add the remaining ½ cup confectioners' sugar to the melted chocolate and stir until blended. Gently stir the chocolate mixture into the peanut butter–cream cheese mixture. Mix it lightly to create a rippled effect. Spread the mixture in the prepared crust.

4. Melt the milk chocolate chips (for effective methods and instructions, see page 27). Spread the melted chocolate over the pie. Chill for 1 hour before serving.

Recipe Note: This recipe inspired some creative license—a license that cannot be revoked. Substitute crushed peanut butter cookies (such as Nutter Butter) for the chocolate sandwich cookies. • Go nuts—add salted peanuts to the crust (½ cup chopped) and to the peanut butter filling (½ cup chopped). Sprinkle chopped peanuts on top.

Chocolate Candy

···

This was the last category we tested at Chocolate Heaven. Why? Because I was downright intimidated by the candy-making process. I never took chemistry in high school for the very reason I never made candy at home. It was scary. Very scary. Soft-ball stage (234 to 240 degrees Fahrenheit), hard-crack stage (300 to 310 degrees Fahrenheit), and I was at the beginning candy stage (0 degrees). I decided that the only way to learn how to make candy was to get out the old beaten-up pots and pans, take the phone off the hook, and follow the road into Candy Land.

Lessons Learned in Candy Land

- Candy making takes patience. Unlike the dump-and-bake cakes that I so enjoy, candy requires pounds and pounds of patience. But consider it an investment—with a big payoff at the end.
- Don't walk away while candy is simmering on the stove. Don't talk on the phone.
- Don't touch your face or hair.
- Don't pet your animals—your hand will have to be pried away with half their fur.
- Wear old clothes. Don't wear shorts. If something very hot and sticky drops on your bare leg, you'll know it. Take it from someone who knows.

- Never, ever test candy with your finger. This is not mousse—it's a chocolate concoction at *234 degrees*!
- Use a candy thermometer. It is great for accuracy, especially until you become more experienced.
- Use wooden spoons. Set out old saucers or spoon holders on which to rest utensils. The first wooden spoon I used to make candy will have to be sold with the house as a fixture.
- Review the recipe instructions completely. The great thing about candy making is that most recipes require few ingredients.
- When a recipe says let it sit for 20 minutes, that means *20 minutes*. No more. Don't take a shower or talk to a friend on the phone, or you will discover the rock stage in candy making, a phenomenon that results in the creation of delicious paperweights.
- Most candy and fudge need to be chilled, so don't use your nonstick bakeware or cookware. The nonstick finish can be marred by the cold temperature and moisture. Even if you only have a 9 × 13-inch baking dish, you can change its size by creating a temporary wall with a piece of rolled foil cut to the width of the pan. Place it where needed to shorten the length of the pan.

We're going to start off easy with some fast but yummy recipes that will build your confidence. Then we'll progress to Terri's Terrific Truffles with Almonds on page 232. Next, we'll try a variety of fudge recipes, and, finally, candy molds. Remember, if an anxiety-ridden candy-making novice can do it, you can too. That's why they call it *can*-dy.

Taking a Chocolate Dip

■ ■ ■

C*hoc Talk:* This is the simplest chocolate recipe on the planet, yet people ooh and aahh when I serve chocolate-dipped fruits and nuts on silver trays. I have learned to dip every food item halfway so that chocophiles know what they are eating. Leave the stems on strawberries or other stemmed fruit.

- Dunk your cookies (either freshly baked or fresh from the store) halfway in the chocolate dip for an extra chocolate surge. Use the optional garnishes to give some dowdy cookies pizzazz!

Yield: *30 servings* **Preparation Time:** *10 minutes* **Bakeware required:** *Cookie sheets lined with wax paper*

CHOCOLATE DIP	NONTRADITIONAL DIPPERS
8 ounces dark sweet chocolate	*Pretzels*
(such as Baker's German's)	*Potato chips*
or semisweet chocolate	*Tortilla chips*
2 tablespoons oil	*Crackers*

TRADITIONAL DIPPERS	OPTIONAL GARNISHES
Strawberries	*Sprinkles*
Banana chunks	*Jimmies*
Kiwi slices	*Toasted chopped nuts*
Orange slices	*Melted white chocolate (see*
Pineapple chunks or slices	*page 274 for instructions on*
Maraschino cherries	*melting white chocolate)*
Dried fruit	
Nuts	
Cookies	
Cake	

1. Melt the chocolate and oil together (for effective methods and instructions, see page 27).

continued

2. Using a toothpick or fork, dip the fresh or dried fruit. Then roll the fruit in the desired garnish.

3. Place on a cookie sheet lined with wax paper and set aside to harden.

Shortcut Candy: Do you love chocolate-covered toffee bars but want one *now*? Here's a shortcut. Take hard candy such as English toffee or peanut brittle and dip it in chocolate. Use 2 large spoons to dip and turn the candy until coated. After dipping, you can roll English toffee in finely chopped roasted pecans.

Banana Pops:
1. Cut a just ripe (not too ripe) banana in half crosswise. Insert a wooden popsicle stick in the center of each banana half and dip the halves in the melted chocolate (we rolled the banana using 2 large spoons).

2. Roll the chocolate-covered banana in chopped toasted nuts (almonds or pecans).

3. Place the banana pops on a cookie sheet lined with wax paper and either refrigerate or freeze until ready to serve.

Nutty Clusters:
1. Place 2 cups walnuts, pecans, peanuts (unsalted or salted), and/or my favorite, macadamia nuts, in a bowl.

2. Pour the Chocolate Dip over the nuts and mix well to coat thoroughly.

3. Drop clusters of the mixture onto wax paper or mini paper muffin cup liners. Refrigerate about 30 minutes, until firm.

Nuts About Chocolate Chinese Noodle Candy

Simi Turchin · Brooklyn, New York

■ ■ ■

***C**hoc Talk:* This is a quick-fix candy with crunch. The creative combination of chocolate, Chinese noodles, and peanuts may seem implausible at first, but give it a try. Simi's "Nuts About Chocolate Chinese Noodle Candy" has become a classic candy here at Chocolate Heaven, and there are always chunks of it around for chocolate lovers who drop in to say hi.

"Someone brought a batch to the nail salon. We all loved it and she gave us the recipe. I varied it with matzo and walnuts for Passover use." —Simi Turchin

Yield: *20 servings* **Preparation Time:** *10 minutes* **Chilling Time:** *30 minutes* **Bakeware Required:** *Cookie sheet, lined with foil and lightly greased with butter or nonstick cooking spray*

12 ounces semisweet chocolate chips	*2 tablespoons creamy peanut butter*
2 cups thin and crunchy chow mein noodles	*2 cups unsalted dry-roasted peanuts*

1. Melt the chocolate chips (for effective methods and instructions, see page 27). Place in a large bowl and set aside to cool slightly.

2. Break the noodles in half.

3. While the chocolate is still warm, mix the peanut butter into the melted chocolate until well blended. Then carefully mix the broken noodles and peanuts into the chocolate–peanut butter mixture.

continued

4. Place the mixture on the prepared cookie sheet and spread it out. It does not have to cover the entire cookie sheet. Cover and chill for 30 minutes.

5. Remove the hardened candy from the cookie sheet. Break into chunks and place in a plastic bag to keep fresh. This candy may be frozen for up to 1 month.

Chocolate-Covered Memory

■ ■ ■

"I'm gonna eat that chocolate.
Oh, I love you
'cause I'm gonna eat it all,
'til my chocolate's all gone."

—*Savvy (I Want Treat) Woods, age four, singing on a swing in Nantucket while eating Going Crackers Candy*

Going Crackers Candy

Roberta Mills · Bristol, Connecticut

■ ■ ■

hoc Talk: In this recipe, good old unpretentious saltines are all dressed up. You can also try it with other crackers.

"Every time I used to make this candy, it was chewy. So I thought I'd try adding something crispy, and saltines worked! This candy tastes like toffee, but it has many more possibilities for variations, such as using different nuts or milk chocolate chips." —Roberta Mills

Yield: *10 servings* **Preparation Time:** *10 to 15 minutes* **Baking Time:** *15 minutes* **Chilling Time:** *1 hour* **Bakeware Required:** *Cookie sheet, lined with foil that is well greased with butter. Make sure the edges of the foil extend about 2 inches beyond the cookie sheet to provide handles for lifting.*

1 sleeve (approximately 40 to 45) saltine crackers

1 cup unsalted butter, cut into pieces

1 cup granulated sugar

12 ounces semisweet chocolate chips

*1 cup finely chopped pecans, toasted**

Preheat the oven to 375 degrees.

1. Place the saltines in a single layer on the prepared cookie sheet. Completely cover the cookie sheet, even if you have to break a few crackers in half. Set aside.

2. In a medium heavy-bottomed saucepan, combine the butter and sugar and bring the mixture to a boil. Continue to boil, stirring

---

*For extra nutty flavor, spread the nuts on a cookie sheet and toast them in a preheated 350 degree oven for 10 to 15 minutes. Stir the nuts occasionally to toast them evenly and prevent burning. Or, toast the nuts in the microwave (they will not change color but will taste toasted). Place 1 cup nuts on a paper plate and microwave uncovered on high power for 3 to 4 minutes, rotating the plate a half turn after 2 minutes.

occasionally, until the mixture turns medium brown in color and becomes foamy.

3. Remove from the heat and spread evenly over the crackers.

4. Bake until the crackers bubble and "wiggle." This can take up to 15 minutes. Watch carefully.

5. Remove the crackers from the oven and sprinkle the chocolate chips evenly on top. Wait about 2 minutes to make sure the chips are heated through. Then, with a spatula or flat knife, gently spread the melted chocolate evenly over the crackers.

6. Sprinkle the pecans on top of the melted chocolate and press them down with your hands or the back of a spatula so they stick to the chocolate.

7. Cover and place in the refrigerator for about 1 hour to cool completely.

8. Carefully lift the edges of the foil and remove from the baking sheet. Then peel off the foil. Break into jagged chunks and place in candy dishes throughout the house, so that you're never far from a chocolate candy crunch.

Recipe Notes: Try other crackers, even gourmet varieties. • You can also create a rocky road effect by sprinkling 1 to 2 cups of mini marshmallows over the semisweet chips and returning the candy to the oven to let everything melt. • We even put this version under the broiler for about as long as it takes to say "I love going crackers on a rocky road" three times. This will brown the marshmallows.

Buckeyes

a.k.a. Pat's Chocolate-Covered Peanut Butter Perfection

Patricia Buie · Lees Summit, Missouri

■ ■ ■

Family and Friends Chocolate Lover Category

hoc Talk: I've received many memorable recipes from Pat Buie since meeting her fifteen years ago when we were just two young babes dating the Buie brothers. Buckeyes were (and still are) one of my favorite candies at holiday celebrations at the Buies'. I went from my own family, who never cooked or baked with chocolate, to the Buie household, where homemade chocolate in all forms was everywhere. How could I not marry into this chocolate-loving family?

"When I was a little girl, it was a holiday tradition for me to make this candy with my mother [Virginia Johnson], who received the recipe from Letha Lieb of Enid, Oklahoma (a favorite aunt and a great family recipe source). Now my mom and I still take the time out of our busy schedules to make this candy together because it just wouldn't feel like Christmas if we didn't. What's even more fun is that my two kids, Cameron and Alana, now join in the tradition." —Pat Buie

Yield: *50 servings* **Preparation Time:** *20 minutes* **Chilling Time:** *1 hour* **Bakeware Required:** *Cookie sheet, lined with wax paper*

1 cup unsalted butter, softened	1½ pounds confectioners' sugar
2 cups creamy peanut butter	12 ounces semisweet chocolate chips

1. In a large bowl, combine the butter and peanut butter. Add the confectioners' sugar and mix well. Form the mixture into small balls (the size of walnuts or buckeyes). Place on the prepared cookie sheet. Cover and refrigerate for 1 hour.

continued

2. Melt the chocolate (for effective methods and instructions, see page 27).

3. Dip each peanut butter ball into the melted chocolate, coating it completely, and place back on the wax paper–lined cookie sheet. If you'd like to keep your hands free of chocolate, cover them with plastic bags, or pick up the balls with toothpicks or forks.

4. Let the chocolate-covered buckeyes harden. Cover and refrigerate them until ready to serve.

Recipe Note: This recipe can easily be doubled. The hard part is not making one, then eating one, then making one. Grandma Edna Buie likes to add some crunch to her Buckeyes and stirs 1 to 2 cups Rice Krispies into the mixture. According to my Ohio sources, however, that makes them crispy buckeyes, which are not authentic.

The Easiest Fudge Ever

■ ■ ■

***C**hoc Talk:* If you're in a hurry and need a fudge fix fast, this is the perfect recipe. The sweetened condensed milk provides the shortcut. More traditional fudge recipes start on page 235.

Yield: *24 to 36 servings* **Preparation Time:** *15 minutes* **Chilling Time:** *2 to 4 hours* **Bakeware Required:** *8 × 8-inch baking pan, lined with well greased wax paper*

One 14-ounce can sweetened condensed (not evaporated) milk

12 ounces semisweet chocolate chips

½ cup unsalted butter, cut into pieces

3 to 4 ounces (half of a 7½-ounce jar) Kraft Marshmallow Creme or any brand of marshmallow fluff

1 teaspoon vanilla extract

1 cup chopped pecans or walnuts

1. Melt the chocolate with the condensed milk (for effective methods and instructions, see page 27).

2. While the chocolate is still hot, stir in all the remaining ingredients.

3. Spread in the prepared pan and refrigerate for 2 hours, or until firm.

Recipe Note: Substitute peanuts (salted or unsalted) for the pecans or walnuts and add 1 to 2 cups of miniature marshmallows for a rocky road version. Add the marshmallows when the fudge is slightly cool so they don't melt too much.

Terri's Terrific Truffles with Almonds

Terri Spencer · Cambridge, Massachusetts

■ ■ ■

Professional Chocolate Lover Category

*C**hoc Talk:* The ephemeral truffle is brought down to earth by the addition of chopped almonds. Make sure you chop them small, but don't pulverize them. Terri the Truffletier, who is, among many things, a chocolate instructor in the Boston area, uses fine-quality chocolate such as Lenôtre, a French brand. Cacao Barry and Valrhona are other brands of gourmet chocolate that aficionados appreciate like fine wines. These brands are available at specialty food stores and candy stores, but they are only recommended, not required. Use what is available in your area.

"My chocolate recipes are the result of my training with great French chefs and the assistance of Sally Pasley and Lani Baker, fellow pastry chefs. We all worked at Ridi Foods, creating new and exciting formulas for different product lines, using only natural ingredients. (Sally was trained by Albert Kumin, who was the chef at the White House!)" —Terri Spencer

Yield: *20 truffles* **Preparation Time:** *20 to 30 minutes* **Chilling Time:** *1 to 2 hours* **Bakeware Required:** *9 × 5 × 3-inch loaf pan*

CHOCOLATE GANACHE*	*1 cup heavy cream, room*
10 ounces bittersweet (such as	*temperature*
Baker's German's or a	*2 tablespoons unsalted butter,*
premium variety—Lenôtre or	*softened*
Lindt) or semisweet chocolate	

*Pronounced "Ge-NOSH," this is the center of the truffle.

1 teaspoon vanilla extract, room temperature	1½ cups chopped almonds, toasted*
1 tablespoon amaretto (almond-flavored) liqueur or 1 teaspoon almond extract	½ cup unsweetened cocoa

Preheat the oven to 250 degrees.

1. Break the chocolate into pieces. Put them in the loaf pan and place in the oven. Stir every 5 minutes, scraping down the sides of the pan with a rubber spatula, until the chocolate is completely melted.

2. After the chocolate has melted, set it aside to cool for 5 minutes, then stir in the heavy cream and butter. Whisk in the vanilla and amaretto or almond extract, then stir in the almonds. Let the chocolate ganache sit at room temperature for 1 to 2 hours, or until set.

3. After the ganache is somewhat hardened, place the cocoa on a plate. Using either a melon baller or a teaspoon, scoop up the ganache and form small balls. (Dip the utensil in boiling water and tap dry on a towel for easier scooping.) Place the balls in the cocoa and roll them around. You should use 2 forks or spoons to do this. Why? The heat from your hands may encourage the truffles to start melting. Place the coated truffles on wax paper or in a plastic lined container and cover. Store in a cool place. You may refrigerate them if necessary, but this may cause slight discoloration of the chocolate.

Recipe Note: Instead of using cocoa to coat the truffle center, you can melt more bittersweet or semisweet chocolate for a different coating. (For effective alternative methods for melting chocolate, see page 27.) Then temper the chocolate to make a couverture, or shiny coating. To temper the chocolate, see page 241 in this chapter.

continued

*For extra nutty flavor, spread the nuts on a cookie sheet and toast them in a preheated 350 degree oven for 10 to 15 minutes. Stir the nuts occasionally to toast them evenly and prevent burning. Or, toast the nuts in the microwave (they will not change color but will taste toasted). Place 1 cup nuts on a paper plate and microwave uncovered on high power for 3 to 4 minutes, rotating the plate a half turn after 2 minutes.

Even More Options: Roll the chocolate-coated truffle in more finely chopped toasted almonds. Or melt some white chocolate (see page 274 for effective methods) and drizzle some of it in a decorative fashion on a truffle that has been coated in melted dark chocolate. Place the melted white chocolate in a small heavy-duty plastic zipper bag, cut off a very small corner with scissors, and drizzle the chocolate through the hole. Then sell these precious truffles at the office or around town for a lot of money.

Variations:

Raspberry Truffles: Substitute 2 tablespoons framboise (raspberry-flavored liqueur) for the amaretto. Add ½ cup strained raspberry preserves to the ganache mixture and refrigerate until firm. Make a truffle by forming the ganache around a raspberry.

Use this method with other berries. Purée the fruits if you don't have preserves.

White Truffles: Substitute white chocolate for the dark chocolate and make a white ganache.

Truffle Cornucopia: For the amaretto in the basic ganache recipe, substitute other liqueurs like Grand Marnier, Frangelico (coat the truffle with toasted chopped hazelnuts), Irish cream, cherry-flavored brandy, and so on.

Fudge Rests and Restores
■ ■ ■

"I know a woman in the country who is a very busy housewife. . . . I was once amused to have her tell me that at times during the latter part of the day when she found herself too exhausted to carry on, she would promptly drop everything she was doing and make a 'batch of fudge.' After eating some of the fudge, she would find herself rested and able to carry on once more."

—*Francesca V. Balch, "The Health Value of Candy with a Few Hints on How to Make It,"* American Cookery Magazine *(formerly* The Boston Cooking School Magazine*), January 1934*

Dropped Not-on-the-Floor Fudge

Donna Wheeler · Levelland, Texas

■ ■ ■

*C*hoc Talk: FUDGE! Before I made fudge for the first time, I just used the word as an expletive-not-deleted around small children and my parents.

"My mother has made this fudge all of my life (I'm thirty-six). It is a family favorite and requested at all family reunions."
—Donna Wheeler

Yield: *50 servings* **Preparation Time:** *1 hour* **Cookware Required:** *8-quart heavy-bottomed saucepan*

4 cups granulated sugar	*⅛ teaspoon salt*
1 cup evaporated (not sweetened condensed) milk	*½ cup light corn syrup*
	½ cup unsalted butter or margarine
5 heaping tablespoons unsweetened cocoa	*2 teaspoons vanilla extract*

1. In the saucepan, combine the sugar, evaporated milk, cocoa, salt, corn syrup, and butter. Cook the mixture over moderate heat, stirring occasionally, until it reaches the soft-ball stage (see page 238). Remove the pan from the heat and add the vanilla.

2. Fill the kitchen sink one third full with cold water and set the saucepan in the water. (If it's inconvenient to use your kitchen sink, use a dishpan or other container large enough to hold the cold water and the saucepan.) While the saucepan is sitting in the cool bath, beat the fudge mixture vigorously with a wooden spoon until it thickens. Periodically scoop up spoonfuls of the warm fudge mixture, drop them back into the fudge mixture, and continue beating. Be careful not to get any water into the fudge. As Lucile Doyle explains in her "I Love Lucile's Chocolate Pecan Fudge" recipe (page 236), this makes a creamier fudge, and most important, it's fun.

3. When the fudge begins to hold its shape, spoon it onto wax paper and shape it into a square. Cover and refrigerate, or set aside at room temperature for 15 minutes before cutting the fudge into small squares.

I Love Lucile's Chocolate Pecan Fudge

Lucile Doyle · Lubbock, Texas

■ ■ ■

***C**hoc Talk:* Warning—don't walk away from the stove while the fudge is cooling. Oprah was talking about women who love men who love other men, and I wasn't watching the candy. It now serves as one of my leg weights when I exercise to a Richard Simmons tape. Candy is the Dennis the Menace of the chocolate-making world—it needs constant supervision.

This is an "I-can't-stop-eating-this" kind of fudge.

"I have made this candy for so long, it is hard to remember where I received the recipe. My four girls think it is very special."
—Lucile Doyle

Yield: *10 servings* **Preparation Time:** *1 hour* **Cookware Required:** *2-quart heavy-bottomed saucepan; large serving platter, well greased with butter*

3 cups granulated sugar	*½ cup light corn syrup*
6 tablespoons unsweetened cocoa	*2 cups chopped pecans*
¼ teaspoon salt	*¼ cup unsalted butter*
1 cup low-fat (2%) milk	*1 teaspoon vanilla extract*

1. In the saucepan, combine the sugar and cocoa. Add the salt and mix well. Add the milk and corn syrup and mix well.

2. Start cooking over low heat; in 3 to 4 minutes, increase the heat to medium-high and stir with a wooden spoon. When the mixture begins to boil, reduce the heat to medium-low.

3. When the mixture reaches the soft-ball stage (see page 238), remove the pan from the heat and let it sit for 20 minutes,* or

*You may use the cold water bath method to quickly cool the fudge (see page 235, step two).

until the mixture has cooled to 110 degrees (use a candy thermometer).

4. Add the pecans, butter, and vanilla and cook over low heat for 20 minutes.

5. Remove from the heat and beat vigorously with a wooden spoon until the mixture holds its shape. As you are beating, Lucile suggests you use the drop-it method, which is to periodically take spoonfuls of the mixture, let them drop back into the fudge mixture, and continue beating. This method helps to make a creamier fudge.

6. Spread the fudge on a large buttered platter and set aside to cool, about 15 minutes. To serve, cut the fudge into small squares.

Now that I've made fudge a few times, let me pass on some tips:
■ ■ ■

1. Most fudge mixtures must be heated to the soft-ball stage (234 to 240 degrees Fahrenheit). I recommend you use a candy thermometer. Otherwise, to test it, drop a bit of the mixture into a glass of ice-cold water; if it forms a—you guessed it—soft ball that does not hold its shape too well and is soft to the touch, then the mixture is at the right temperature.

2. Everyone has a secret technique for making smooth, creamy fudge. First of all, use a heavy-bottomed saucepan to prevent scorching. The key is to combine the ingredients well and heat the mixture to the correct temperature, so that no sugar crystals remain to spoil the texture. Crystals usually form on the sides of the pan, so scrape the sides frequently with a rubber spatula. Most people will tell you not to stir the fudge mixture at all while it is cooking. But since I'm not most people and you are dealing with a temperamental ingredient called chocolate, stir the mixture occasionally using a wooden spoon in slow, wide stirs, so as not to disturb the heating process. This will also help prevent scorching.

3. Before beating, it's important to let the fudge cool to at least 110 degrees (use your thermometer if you wish). The cooling usually takes 20 to 30 minutes, but a few of our contestants suggested giving the fudge a nice cool bath in order to speed up the process (see page 235, step 2 of "Dropped Not-on-the-Floor Fudge").

4. After the fudge has cooled, get your aggressions out by beating it vigorously. You can try using an electric mixer if you wish, but this is my upper-torso exercise, so I prefer doing it by hand.

Mabel's Chocolate Peanut Butter Fudge

Tammy L. Miller · Columbus, Ohio

■ ■ ■

*C**hoc Talk:*** This fudge recipe shocked me. I could actually make candy-store quality fudge with my own two hands. The peanut butter flavor is very subtle.

"This recipe came from my mother, Mabel. She learned to make it when she was a girl in home economics class in school. Over the years she modified the recipe to suit her taste, and it became an all-time favorite with her children and grandchildren. When I married and became a mother myself, I decided it was time for my mother to teach me her recipe. It was not easy because, like most 'old-time' cooks, she never measured or timed anything. I did finally master it and have made a few tiny changes to suit myself." —Tammy L. Miller

Yield: *10 to 12 servings* **Preparation Time:** *1½ hours* **Bakeware Required:** *9 × 9-inch baking pan, lined with well greased wax paper*

1½ cups granulated sugar	2 tablespoons unsalted butter or
2 tablespoons unsweetened	margarine
cocoa	1 teaspoon vanilla extract
⅛ teaspoon salt	2 tablespoons creamy peanut
1½ cups milk (2% low-fat	butter
works best), divided	

1. In a medium heavy-bottomed saucepan, mix the sugar, cocoa, and salt. Add 1 cup of the milk and place it on the stove over medium-high heat. Bring to a boil, stirring constantly.

2. Add the butter and reduce the heat to medium-low. Let the mixture boil for about 30 minutes, stirring occasionally. Remove from the heat and stir in the remaining ½ cup milk.

continued

3. Place the pan back on the burner and continue boiling for another 30 minutes. Do not stir.

4. When the candy reaches the soft-ball stage (see page 238), remove from the heat. Stir in the vanilla and peanut butter until well combined. Once the peanut butter has completely melted, set the mixture aside to rest 5 minutes.

5. Beat the fudge vigorously with a wooden spoon approximately 3 to 5 minutes, until it thickens and loses its gloss. Turn out quickly into the prepared pan and set aside to cool for 15 minutes. To serve, cut the fudge into small squares.

Recipe Note: Go nuts. To enhance the peanut flavor, add ¼ to ½ cup unsalted peanuts along with the peanut butter. And for an even nuttier fudge, roast the peanuts on a baking sheet in a 400 degree oven for 10 minutes. Add the nuts after the peanut butter has completely melted in the fudge mixture.

Chocolate Candy Molds

I've received a lot of instructions from the pros on this and I'd like to pass on their tips for making delicious and creative chocolate molds. If you've never done it before, start off easy. In the chocolate class where I received instruction, I watched with envy as everyone calmly unmolded their chocolate Valentine's boxes. I smacked mine, knocked it several times, bent and twisted it, and received about twenty pieces of advice from my classmates on what I should or should not do. While everyone in the class took home a lovely chocolate candy box filled with delicious truffles, I had to request a doggy bag for my chocolate scraps. They tasted good anyway, and I could always melt them and start over again.

You can usually get a variety of molds at party stores and kitchenware shops. To begin, I suggest you purchase molds that are shallow and not too intricate. I made chocolate circles and gave them to my friends in the computer business and told them they were chocolate microchips. They were impressed.

Melting and Molding

1. Select a high-grade baking chocolate, but something you enjoy eating and feel comfortable working with that isn't going to cost you a chocolate arm and leg. Melt the chocolate according to the directions given on page 27.

2. Make sure the mold is clean and very dry. Pour the melted chocolate so that it comes up to the very rim of the mold. Tap the mold a few times to rid the melted chocolate of any air bubbles. Place the mold in the refrigerator on a flat shelf away from the garlic (chocolate absorbs odors).

3. Check the mold in 15 to 20 minutes. If the chocolate is completely firm, take it out of the refrigerator. Turn the mold over on a hard, flat surface and smack it once or twice. The chocolate creation should come out easily. Certain molds may need a little more work, which is why I suggest starting out simple.

Temper, Temper

When making molds, you may want to "temper" the chocolate to give it a more professional-looking, glossy appearance. Oh, no, not that—it's hard. Actually, people have made tempering a more mysterious process than it really is. To temper simply means to add cold to hot.

Here is a basic easy method for tempering semisweet or bittersweet chocolate (based on 3 pounds of chocolate; you may reduce this proportionately):

Divide 2 pounds of chocolate, and melt each pound in a separate bowl (for effective methods and instructions, see page 27). Finely chop the third pound, but do not melt it. When the melted chocolate reaches 115 degrees (use a candy thermometer), remove it from the heat. Take half of the melted chocolate and slowly stir the unmelted chocolate bits ¼ cup at a time into the melted and still warm chocolate. The solid chocolate cools the warm chocolate and melts into it. Keep the rest of the melted chocolate warm in an oven on very low (150 to 200 degrees). After you have stirred in the chocolate bits and the chocolate has cooled, check the temperature. If the chocolate is not between 86 and 90 degrees, warm it up again by slowly adding the other pound of melted chocolate ¼ cup at a time. When the temperature is between 86 and 90 degrees, the chocolate is ready to pour into molds or cover truffles.

White chocolate is tempered the same way, except the temperatures are lower. When you melt it initially, it should reach 110 degrees, and after tempering, it should reach between 86 and 89 degrees. (This temperature also applies to milk chocolate.)

You can always reheat tempered chocolate if it cools too much, using the microwave or oven at 250 degrees.

Another popular method is table-top tempering. This involves melting all the chocolate at once, placing it on a marble slab, and, using two spatulas (the pros use their hands), moving the chocolate in sweeping motions on the cool marble. This cools the chocolate slowly.

The great thing about chocolate is that if you make a mistake, you can melt it again for a second chance. Too bad life doesn't always imitate chocolate.

Savory Chocolate

■ ■ ■

"Those happy days when Nacha was with her seemed so distant now
. . . her seasoning, her atole drinks, her teas, her laugh,
her herbal remedies, the way she braided her hair and tucked Tita
in at night, took care of her when she was sick and cooked what
she craved and whipped the chocolate!"

—From **Like Water for Chocolate** *by Laura Esquivel (Doubleday, 1989)*

exicans have been cooking with chocolate for hundreds of years—long before sugar and chocolate met in a cup of hot milk.

Unsweetened chocolate adds a richness to salsas, bisques, and *mole* sauces. When someone says "chocolate salsa," does a vision of candy bars stuck in a jar of Old El Paso Spicy Salsa come to mind? Well, *¡Viva Zapata!* The revolution is here in these recipes. Try the Santa Fe Salsa by Rebecca Covalt on page 244, which will convince you that chocolate is really a multifaceted gift from the gods. Lotte Mendelsohn, who has lived in Mexico, shares her recipe for a comforting chocolate soup, Chocolate Bisque a la Mexicana (page 246).

When I first read about *mole* sauce, I had no idea what it was. Had a mole met his demise on a busy highway? No. The secret ingredient in this flavorful sauce is chocolate, which lends richness and color.

I love history and actually did a little research on *mole* sauce. Remember how the Toll House cookie was invented by accident (see page 48)? Well, *mole poblano* was made under the pressure of unexpected company. In the sixteenth century, the nuns of the convent at Puebla, Mexico, received a surprise visit from their bishop. Unable to drive down to the corner for a bucket of the Colonel's Extra Crispy, they pounced on the only turkey around, and he was not a young Tom, or so the story goes. They served the tough turkey as a stew smothered in an Aztec sauce that combined chiles and chocolate. Thus was born *mole poblano*, also known as "Nun of Us Knew the Bishop Was Coming to Dinner" or "Unexpected Guests? No Problemo, Serve the Poblano." The *mole* versions on pages 248 and 250 are sensational. Use your favorite chiles in the amount you desire to control the hotness of the dish.

Can't Stop Eating This Chocolate Salsa Special Award

Santa Fe Salsa con Chocolate

Rebecca Covalt · Albuquerque, New Mexico
■ ■ ■

***C**hoc Talk:* This is a refreshing, addictive salsa. The cocoa adds a smoky flavor.

Yield: *6 servings* **Preparation Time:** *10 to 15 minutes*

3 cups chopped fresh tomatoes, divided	*½ cup green chiles**
1 tablespoon balsamic vinegar	*1 tablespoon red chile powder*
1 tablespoon unsweetened cocoa	*1 teaspoon salt*
½ cup chopped fresh cilantro	*½ cup fresh lime juice (add*
½ cup chopped red Bermuda onion	*more or less to achieve desired tartness)*

1. In a blender, purée 1 cup of the chopped tomatoes with the balsamic vinegar and cocoa.

*Try Bueno brand frozen or canned roasted, seeded, and chopped chiles, or use fresh. Jalapeños may be substituted, but check the degree of "hotness" first. You my want to adjust the quantity depending on the hotness of the chile and your personal preference.

2. In a large bowl, combine all the remaining ingredients. Stir in the puréed mixture.

3. The salsa may be served chilled or at room temperature.

Cooked Variation:

Rio Grande Salsa con Chocolate

1 batch Santa Fe Salsa
¼ cup homemade or canned
  chicken broth

2 tablespoons honey (add more
  to taste)

1. In a 2-quart saucepan over moderate heat, combine the Santa Fe Salsa, chicken broth, and honey. Heat for 10 minutes, or until the salsa becomes slightly thickened.

2. Serve immediately while still warm, or, if you prefer, chill for 1 hour and serve cold.

Presentation Ideas: Salsa for dipping with chips • Condiment for burritos, tacos, and tostadas • Condiment for broiled steak, chicken, or fish • Condiment for eggs • Salad dressing • Potato or pasta topping

Recipe Notes: Because I have tons of chocolate in my house, I experiment all the time. I substituted ½ ounce semisweet chocolate, melted, for the cocoa, and thought it brought out more of the natural sweetness in the tomatoes. You may want to try this in a future batch. • Add 2 cups mashed or chunked avocado to the recipe for more of a guacamole-style dip.

Chocolate Bisque
a la Mexicana

Lotte Mendelsohn · Wayland, Massachusetts
■ ■ ■
Professional Chocolate Lover Category

***C**hoc Talk:* We refer to this recipe as our chocolate soup. It is so simple and delicious that you will want to make it again and again. Lotte is a great cookbook author and food writer in the Boston area. Her knowledge and enthusiasm for food are reflected in this delightful recipe.

"Unsweetened chocolate is used in Mexico as a savory base seasoning not only in the famous mole poblano *but also throughout the Republic in a variety of dishes. This soup is my own creation using the classical dish from Puebla as inspiration. It is a great 'dunker' for little rounds of crisp, crusted French bread."*
—Lotte Mendelsohn

Yield: *Six 1-cup servings* **Preparation Time:** *20 minutes* **Cooking Time:** *45 minutes total*

1 tablespoon peanut or sesame seed oil	One 28-ounce can whole plum tomatoes
1 large onion, chopped	1½ tablespoons firmly packed light brown sugar
3 whole cloves	
½ teaspoon ground cinnamon	2 chipotle chiles,* drained, rinsed, and seeded
¼ teaspoon ground cumin	5 cups chicken broth, divided
⅛ teaspoon aniseed	2 ounces unsweetened chocolate

*Chipotle chiles are conical, brick-red, and very spicy. They are usually available in cans in gourmet specialty markets. If you like things spicy, add an extra pepper, but handle with care, as the seeds are especially hot! If you cannot locate these chiles, use an equivalent amount of green chiles or jalapeño peppers. Adjust the quantity to achieve the hotness you desire.

⅓ cup Quaker masa harina* *or*
   3 tablespoons cornstarch
½ teaspoon vanilla extract
1 teaspoon salt

GARNISHES
Sour cream to taste
½ cup almond slivers, toasted†

1. In a large saucepan over low heat, combine the oil and onion and sauté until the onion is translucent, about 5 minutes. Add the cloves, cinnamon, cumin, and aniseed and cook for 1 minute. Add the canned tomatoes with their juice and continue cooking for 10 minutes.

2. Add the brown sugar and chiles and simmer for 5 minutes. Remove from the heat and set aside to cool slightly.

3. Transfer the cooled mixture to a blender or food processor and purée until smooth. Blend in 4 cups of the chicken broth.

4. Melt the chocolate (for effective methods and instructions, see page 27).

5. In a small bowl, mix the *masa harina* with the remaining cup of broth. Blend until smooth. Gradually add this mixture to the purée, alternating with the melted chocolate and incorporating the ingredients well after each addition.

6. Return the soup to the stove and simmer for 20 to 25 minutes, or until the soup has a gravy or bisque consistency. Stir in the vanilla and salt.

7. Pour into heated bowls and swirl a tablespoon of sour cream into each. Garnish with toasted almond slivers.

Masa harina is a corn flour traditionally used for making tortillas. It can be found in larger grocery stores as well as gourmet specialty markets.

†For extra nutty flavor, spread the nuts on a cookie sheet and toast them in a preheated 350 degree oven for 10 to 15 minutes. Stir the nuts occasionally to toast them evenly and prevent burning. Or, toast the nuts in the microwave (they will not change color but will taste toasted). Place 1 cup nuts on a paper plate and microwave uncovered on high power for 3 to 4 minutes, rotating the plate a half turn after 2 minutes.

Mole Poblano de Pollo

(Chile-Chocolate Sauce of Puebla for Chicken)

Marion Karlin · Waterloo, Iowa

■ ■ ■

***C**hoc Talk:* Don't be daunted by the list of ingredients. This is a spice-rich dish that reflects true (not Tex-Mex) Mexican cuisine. It's worth the effort. I will confess to you, I am a chile pepper lightweight (what aficionados would call a "wimp"). While others are gulping down the jalapeños and chipotles with a chuckle, "Water!!!" crackles from my throat and my eyes gush with tears. I've finally learned to reduce the amount of chiles or use "mild" or "wimpy" chiles to suit my fire-in-the-mouth capacity.

*"My memories of this recipe bring me back to the Mexican town of Puebla (about 130 miles southeast of Mexico City). The people there make a chili-chocolate sauce for chicken of which they are justifiably proud. Unsweetened chocolate is always an ingredient in this dark, spicy sauce." —*Marion Karlin

Yield: *6 main-dish servings* **Preparation Time:** *45 minutes* **Cooking Time:** *1½ hours* **Bakeware Required:** *9 × 13-inch baking dish, lightly greased with lard or shortening*

> *¼ cup lard or solid vegetable shortening (lard is authentic to the traditional dish)*
> *2 tablespoons crushed red pepper flakes*
> *6 boneless, skinless chicken breast halves (about 2 pounds)*
> *3 cups homemade or canned chicken broth, divided*
>
> *4 corn tortillas* (7 to 8 inches in diameter), cut into small pieces*
> *¼ cup tomato sauce*
> *¼ cup minced onion*
> *4 cloves garlic, finely minced*
> *1 tablespoon unsweetened cocoa, or more to taste*
> *1 tablespoon raisins*
> *1 tablespoon chopped almonds or walnuts*

*If you can't find corn tortillas, feel free to use flour tortillas. They are less authentic but maybe easier to find.

1 tablespoon sesame seeds

1 tablespoon shelled pumpkin seeds

1 tablespoon peanut butter or chopped peanuts

1½ teaspoons granulated sugar

1½ teaspoons dried oregano leaves, crushed

½ teaspoon aniseed

¼ teaspoon ground cinnamon

¼ teaspoon ground nutmeg

¼ teaspoon ground allspice

¼ teaspoon ground ginger

¼ teaspoon ground cumin

OPTIONAL GARNISHES

Fresh cilantro sprigs

6 ounces semisweet chocolate, melted

To Make the Mole Poblano

Preheat the oven to 325 degrees.

1. Heat the lard in a large skillet over moderate heat until melted. Stir in the crushed red pepper flakes and sauté for 1 minute.

2. Add the chicken breasts and lightly brown each side. Remove from the pan and set aside. Using a strainer, remove any remaining crushed red pepper from the lard in the skillet. Reserve the red pepper for later use.

3. Add 2 cups of the chicken broth to the skillet. Stir in the remaining ingredients except for the garnishes and reserved broth. Heat the mixture to boiling, then reduce the heat, cover, and simmer, stirring occasionally, for 30 minutes. Remove from the heat and set aside to cool.

4. Pour a small amount of the cooled sauce into a food processor or blender and purée on high speed until the mixture is fairly smooth. Repeat with the remaining sauce.

To Make the Pollo

1. Combine the puréed sauce and the remaining 1 cup chicken broth in the prepared baking dish and mix well. Add the browned chicken breasts in a single layer, turning them over to coat each side well with the sauce. Sprinkle the breasts with the reserved crushed red pepper.

continued

2. Bake for 20 to 25 minutes, or until the chicken is tender and the juices run clear when pierced with a fork.

3. Serve the *mole poblano* with a garnish of fresh cilantro sprigs or melted chocolate spooned on the side, if desired.

Recipe Note: You must try this with spoonfuls of melted semi-sweet chocolate on the side. Either mix the chocolate into your serving, or dip forkfuls of the dish into the chocolate.

Mexican Chocolate Mole Poblano *Sauce*

Diana M. Padilla Hanau · West Palm Beach, Florida
■ ■ ■

*C*hoc *Talk:* Diana's sauce differs from Marion's *mole* sauce (page 248) in using a few less seasoning ingredients and melted semisweet chocolate instead of cocoa. Diana also uses fresh cilantro. There are several serving suggestions in the Presentation Ideas for this versatile *mole* sauce.

"This recipe was created by my brother-in-law, who lives in Mexico City and is an excellent amateur cook. I made minor adjustments (fewer hot peppers) to please the taste of my American family and friends. We particularly love this recipe as a dip for duck-breast fajitas, but it is equally good with any poultry dish." —Diana Hanau

Yield: *12 servings* **Preparation Time:** *20 minutes* **Cooking Time:** *30 minutes* **Cookware Required:** *4-quarts stockpot*

27 ounces canned green (poblano) chiles (or substitute your chile preference)	1 tablespoon minced fresh garlic
	1/4 cup minced fresh cilantro
	3 ounces shelled, salted peanuts
	3 ounces raisins
1/2 teaspoon aniseed	1 1/2 cups peeled and seeded fresh
4 taco shells	tomatoes or 12 ounces canned tomatoes drained

¼ cup sesame seeds, toasted*
1 teaspoon ground cinnamon
1 teaspoon black pepper
1 teaspoon sea salt†
¼ cup chopped red onion
3 ounces semisweet (preferably Mexican‡) chocolate, cut into small chunks
2 ounces unsalted butter or margarine

6 cups chicken broth (sodium-free chicken broth is preferred)

GARNISHES

Toasted sesame seeds (approximately ½ cup)
Sliced oranges (24 slices in round)
Sliced avocados (3 avocados, 8 slices each)

1. In a blender, combine the chiles, aniseed, taco shells, garlic, cilantro, peanuts, raisins, tomatoes, sesame seeds, cinnamon, pepper, sea salt, and onion. Purée until the mixture is almost smooth.

2. Pour into a saucepan over moderate heat. Add the chocolate chunks and butter and cook, stirring constantly, until the chocolate is completely melted. Stir in the chicken broth and simmer, uncovered, for 30 minutes, stirring often.

3. Sprinkle the sauce with sesame seeds and garnish with orange slices and avocado slices.

Presentation Ideas: Serve the sauce hot over cooked chicken breasts, cooked turkey breasts or whole turkey, sautéed duck breasts, roasted game hens, or any other roasted poultry. • Or use the sauce as a dip for tortilla chips or over fajitas.

Recipe Note: You may increase or decrease the number of chiles according to your preference. This recipe can easily be reduced by half.

---

*Spread the seeds on a cookie sheet and toast them in a preheated 350 degree oven for 5 to 10 minutes. Stir the seeds occasionally to toast them evenly and prevent burning. Or, toast the seeds in the microwave (they will not change color but will taste toasted). Place the seeds on a paper plate and microwave uncovered on high power for 2 minutes, rotating the plate a half turn after 1 minute.

†Sea salt is unrefined coarse salt. It is great for cooking and for coating the rim of margarita glasses when you are imbibing. Use table salt if that is easier.

‡Mexican chocolate is available at specialty food stores.

Chocolate, Etc., Etc.

∎∎∎

Weird, wacky, wonderful. Use any euphemism you wish: unusual, off-center, nontraditional. This is one of my favorite chapters because the recipes here just wouldn't fit into any one category. "Different," my mother always said, "means very special." That was in response, of course, to my older brother claiming his younger siblings were "just plain weird." Therefore these "very special" recipes have their own category. You'll find Chocolate Chip Cheese Fritters on page 258, Chocolate Double Dumplings on page 267, and other fun recipes. There are more traditional recipes too, but they're also special and cannot be defined as a cake or a brownie. So if your chocolate tastes are a little "different," you will appreciate this "very special" chapter.

Hot Chocolate Soufflés with Cherry Cream

Diane Halferty · Tucson, Arizona

■ ■ ■

Professional Chocolate Lover Category

***C**hoc Talk:* I had my first chocolate soufflé on my sixteenth birthday at a fabulous restaurant in Kansas City, where we lived. I felt so grown up. In addition to my Sweet Sixteen birthday dinner, I also received Janice Ian's life-is-a-bummer *At 17* album (something to look forward to). Quick, waiter, the soufflé!

Diane's soufflé recipe reminds me of that dinner.

"This is a fun and easy recipe to make. My family and friends not only enjoy it but are impressed with it as well. Chocolate fudge sauce may be substituted for the cherry cream, if desired. Garnish with cherries or sprigs of fresh mint. Try it, you'll love it!"
—Diane Halferty

Yield: *4 servings* **Preparation Time:** *15 minutes* **Baking Time:** *15 minutes* **Cookware Required:** *four 1-cup individual soufflé dishes, greased and dusted with sugar*

SOUFFLÉS	CHERRY CREAM
1 cup milk	*1 cup heavy cream*
4½ ounces unsweetened	*1 tablespoon cherry brandy or*
chocolate, chopped	*1½ teaspoons cherry extract*
¼ cup unsalted butter	*2 drops red food coloring*
1 tablespoon cornstarch	
2 tablespoons all-purpose flour	
¾ cup granulated sugar	
4 large eggs, separated	

To Make the Soufflés

Preheat the oven to 350 degrees.

1. Combine the milk and chocolate in a saucepan over low heat and cook without boiling. Stir constantly, until the chocolate is melted and the mixture is smooth.

2. In a small bowl, lightly beat the egg yolks and set aside.

3. Melt the butter in another saucepan over low heat and add the cornstarch and flour. Cook, stirring constantly, for 1 minute. Add the chocolate mixture and sugar and continue to cook, stirring constantly, until the mixture bubbles and thickens. Remove the pan from the heat.

4. Stir a few tablespoons of the heated chocolate mixture into the beaten egg yolks. Then add this to the rest of the chocolate mixture.

5. In a small bowl, beat the egg whites until soft peaks form (for further instructions on beating egg whites, see page 184). Gently fold the beaten egg whites into the chocolate mixture.

6. Pour into the prepared dishes and bake for 15 minutes. (The soufflés should be puffed up slightly beyond the edges of the dishes.) Serve immediately garnished with the Cherry Cream.

To Make the Cherry Cream

1. Whip the cream and brandy in a medium bowl until stiff peaks form. Stir in the food coloring. Use the cream to garnish the soufflés.

Recipe Note: As Diane suggests, you can also try a hot fudge sauce (see page 297) with the soufflé instead of or in addition to (why not?) the cherry cream. Or try the Grand Marnier sauce (see the recipe on page 299).

Double-Chocolate Strawberry Shortcake

Wolfgang Hanau · West Palm Beach, Florida

■ ■ ■

Professional Chocolate Lover Category

*C**hoc Talk:*** These shortcakes are outrageously good. Dark chocolate abounds, and they're not overly sweet, which allows the natural sweetness of the strawberries to come through. Fortunately, somewhere in the world strawberries are growing, and you can usually find fresh ones at the market any time of year. You may substitute frozen if necessary, but drain them very well. I also have used fresh peaches.

"I created this for a strawberry festival at the old Park Lane Hotel in New York. Since then, I have made this recipe in many hotels and restaurants. It's always a success. Chocolate and strawberries—what a great combination!" —Wolfgang Hanau

Yield: *8 shortcakes* **Preparation Time:** *30 minutes* **Baking Time:** *10 to 12 minutes* **Bakeware Required:** *Cookie sheet, greased*

4⅓ cups buttermilk baking mix (such as Bisquick), sifted	*3 ounces unsalted butter, melted*
2 ounces Dutch-process unsweetened cocoa*	*2 large egg whites, lightly beaten*
½ cup granulated sugar, plus extra for dusting shortcakes	*4 cups heavy cream*
1½ cups semisweet chocolate chips	*¼ cup confectioners' sugar, approximately*
1 cup buttermilk	*1½ pounds fresh strawberries, washed, stemmed, and cut in half*

*Dutch-process cocoa has alkali in it and more cocoa butter, producing a darker, richer cake. An example of a brand is Droste. If you can't find Dutch-process cocoa, use unsweetened cocoa such as Hershey's.

GARNISHES

1 cup chocolate syrup, chocolate   *8 whole strawberries with stems*
glaze (see recipe suggestions
on page 299), homemade
fudge sauce, or other topping
(see chocolate sauces on
page 297)

Preheat the oven to 400 degrees.

1. In a large bowl, combine the baking mix, cocoa, ½ cup sugar, and chocolate chips. Stir in the buttermilk and melted butter and blend thoroughly.

2. Using a ½-cup measure (Wolfgang suggests using ¾ cup for *big* shortcakes), scoop up the batter and place on the prepared cookie sheet, spacing each cake about 3 inches apart. Flatten the batter slightly with the back of a spatula.

3. Brush each shortcake with the egg white and dust with additional granulated sugar. Bake for 12 minutes, or until the cakes are just set and the tops are crinkly (like a worried brow). Set aside to cool.

4. In a large bowl whip the cream and add confectioners' sugar to taste.

5. Split each shortcake horizontally. Place the bottom half on a plate and spoon on ¼ to ½ cup whipped cream and a layer of sliced strawberries. Cover with the top half of the shortcake, and garnish with a dollop of whipped cream. Drizzle chocolate syrup or glaze over the cream and top with a whole strawberry.

Chocolate Chip Cheese Fritters

Patricia Amadure · Carlisle, Pennsylvania
■ ■ ■

***C**hoc Talk:* I am and have always been a fritter fiend, and this chocolate chip version, fried to a golden brown, is terrific.

"The original version of this recipe was given to me by a friend and was called ricotta balls. It was made with whole-milk ricotta and whole eggs. I took out the egg yolks, substituted part-skim ricotta, and since I am a chocolate lover, added the chocolate chips." —Patricia Amadure

Yield: *46 to 50 cheese fritters* **Preparation Time:** *10 minutes* **Chilling Time:** *1 hour* **Cooking Time:** *15 to 20 minutes for the entire batch* **Suggested Cookware:** *Best to use an electric wok or an electric skillet to control frying temperature*

One 15-ounce carton part-skim
   ricotta cheese
6 large egg whites
$^{1}/_{4}$ cup granulated sugar
1 teaspoon vanilla extract
1 cup all-purpose flour
$^{1}/_{4}$ teaspoon salt
4 teaspoons baking powder

$^{1}/_{2}$ to $^{3}/_{4}$ cup semisweet mini
   chocolate chips
4 cups canola oil

GARNISH
Sifted confectioners' sugar or
   granulated sugar

1. In a large bowl, combine the ricotta cheese, egg whites, sugar, and vanilla and mix until smooth. Refrigerate for 1 hour.

2. In a separate bowl, combine the flour, salt, and baking powder. Add this mixture to the chilled cheese mixture and blend well. Stir in the chocolate chips.

3. Heat the oil in the suggested cookware to 350 degrees. You can use a candy thermometer for accuracy. Be careful that the oil does not get so hot that the fritters burn. To make sure the oil

is hot enough for frying, drop in ½ teaspoon of the batter. If the oil is hot enough, the batter will fry immediately.

4. Drop the batter by rounded tablespoons (about 3 at a time) into the oil and fry for approximately 1 minute. Turn over and continue frying for another minute. Remove and drain on paper towels.

5. When the fritters are slightly cooled, roll them in sifted confectioners' sugar.

Recipe Note: One fun Friday at Chocolate Heaven, we experimented with this newly discovered recipe. We added chopped fresh bananas and apples (about 1 cup) to the batter and, as always, more chocolate chips.

Black and White Burritos
Peace, Love, and Chocolate

Roxanne Chan · Albany, California

■ ■ ■

Choc Talk: What a chocolate fiesta! *¡Olé!* Serve this dessert after one of the Mexican dishes presented in the "Savory Chocolate" chapter starting on page 243.

Yield: *8 servings* **Preparation Time:** *15 minutes* **Baking Time:** *15 minutes* **Bakeware Required:** *9 × 13-inch baking pan, lightly greased*

11 ounces cream cheese, softened	½ cup grated white chocolate
½ cup sour cream	¼ cup lemon juice
¾ cup confectioners' sugar	**OPTIONAL GARNISHES**
½ teaspoon grated lemon zest	Grated bittersweet or semisweet chocolate
½ cup semiswe mini chocolate chips (optional)	Lemon twists
Eight 6-inch flour tortillas	Fudge sauce (see Presentation Idea)
1 cup grated semisweet chocolate	Fruit Salsa (recipe opposite)

Preheat the oven to 350 degrees.

1. In a large bowl, beat together the cream cheese, sour cream, confectioners' sugar, and lemon zest. Stir the mini chocolate chips into the filling, if desired.

2. Lay the tortillas out on a clean, flat surface. Spread half of the filling over the tortillas. Sprinkle the grated semisweet chocolate on top. Set the remaining filling aside.

3. Roll up the tortillas and place in the prepared pan. Cover with foil and bake until the tortillas are warmed through, about 15 minutes.

4. Melt the white chocolate (for effective methods and instructions, see page 274). Set aside to cool slightly, then add to the reserved cream cheese filling. Stir in the lemon juice.

5. Top each burrito with some of the white chocolate mixture. Garnish with grated bittersweet or semisweet chocolate and lemon twists, or fudge sauce and Fruit Salsa (see Presentation Idea).

Fruit Salsa: Chocolate Heaven Creation

2 cups fresh or frozen strawberries or raspberries (reserve juice if frozen)	*½ cup pineapple chunks*
	2 tablespoons lime juice, or more to taste
½ cup chopped apples	*2 tablespoons sugar*
½ cup cubed bananas	
½ cup orange slices cut into bite-size pieces	

1. Place 1 cup of the strawberries and the apples, bananas, oranges, and pineapple in a glass bowl. Sprinkle with the lime juice and toss gently.

2. Purée the remaining berries and sugar in a blender or food processor, adding in some of the reserved juice or water to achieve a thinner consistency. Strain the purée to remove the seeds.

3. Stir the purée into the fruit. Serve alongside the burrito or spooned on top.

Presentation Idea: Use one of the homemade fudge sauces on page 297 or use bottled fudge sauce, heated. Place about ¼ cup of the sauce on a dessert plate and set a burrito on top of the chocolate sauce. Or simply melt semisweet chocolate, place 1 to 2 tablespoons on each plate, and drizzle the top of the burrito with some more melted chocolate. Serve this recipe with Fruit Salsa (recipe above), just a little something we whipped up.

Chocolate Raspberry Pizza

Roxanne Chan · Albany, California

■ ■ ■

Choc Talk: Mozzarella, pepperoni, and chocolate do not mix! That's why this combination is *not* in this pizza recipe. But now chocolate lovers can enjoy their favorite ingredients on pizza, complete with cheese. The homemade crust is easy and delicious, and you can add your own pizza-like decoration. This is fun party food.

Yield: *8 servings* **Preparation Time:** *25 minutes* **Baking Time:** *25 minutes* **Bakeware Required:** *10- or 12-inch pizza pan, lightly greased*

DESSERT PIZZA CRUST

1²/₃ cups all-purpose flour

1 tablespoon granulated sugar

³/₄ cup solid vegetable shortening

¹/₄ cup cold water

CHOCOLATE PIZZA TOPPING

1 cup grated bittersweet or semisweet chocolate

³/₄ cup sour cream

8 ounces cream cheese, softened

2 tablespoons unsweetened cocoa

¹/₄ cup confectioners' sugar

¹/₂ teaspoon vanilla extract

2 cups fresh strawberries, raspberries, or fruit of your choice

¹/₂ cup currant jelly

1 tablespoon water

GARNISH

Chocolate curls

To Make the Crust

Preheat the oven to 375 degrees.

1. In a medium bowl, combine the flour and sugar. Using a pastry cutter or 2 knives, cut in the shortening until the mixture resembles coarse crumbs. Sprinkle the dough with water and stir with a fork until it forms a ball.

2. Transfer to a lightly floured surface and roll out to form a 14-inch circle. Fit the circle into the prepared pizza pan. Turn the overhanging dough to the inside and press against the edge of the pan to form a ridge.

3. Bake for 25 minutes, or until golden brown.

To Top the Pizza

1. Sprinkle the grated chocolate over the warm pizza crust. Use a spatula or flat knife to spread the chocolate over the entire surface. If the chocolate does not melt readily, place the pizza in the oven for a few minutes to speed it along. Set aside to cool.

2. In a large mixing bowl, beat the sour cream, cream cheese, cocoa, confectioners' sugar, and vanilla until smooth.

3. Spread this mixture evenly over the chocolate-coated crust and attractively arrange the berries or other fresh fruit on top.

4. In a small pan, heat the jelly and 1 tablespoon water together until the jelly melts. Or place in a microwave-safe bowl and heat in the microwave until the jelly melts.

5. Spoon the melted jelly over the fruit. Garnish with chocolate curls and chill until serving time. Cut with a pizza cutter.

Recipe Notes: For garnish, you may wish to drizzle melted chocolate and/or melted white chocolate (for a melted mozzarella look) as the final touch over the entire topping. • Go crazy—unleash your creativity and add on or substitute other dessert topping ideas.

Eat-Your-Vegetables Chocolate Cake

Marion Karlin · Waterloo, Iowa

■ ■ ■

*C*hoc Talk: For those of you freaking out about how much you hate vegetables, your taste buds will never detect what's holding this moist chocolate chip cake together. No frosting needed, and it's great for the lunchbox too!

"My memories of this chocolate vegetable Bundt go back to the 1940s. My mother, a very creative person, was not afraid to try unusual combinations of food, and if her ingenuity got me to eat my vegetables, so much the better! This is an adaptation of my mother's recipe, which she called her chocolate carrot ring."
—Marion Karlin

Yield: *8 servings* **Preparation Time:** *20 minutes* **Baking Time:** *40 to 45 minutes* **Bakeware Required:** *2-quart (8-cup) Bundt pan or tube pan, greased and floured*

1½ cups all-purpose flour	*¾ cup vegetable oil*
¾ cup firmly packed light brown sugar	*2 teaspoons vanilla extract*
	¾ cup grated carrot
½ cup granulated sugar	*½ cup grated zucchini*
1 teaspoon ground cinnamon	*½ cup grated apple*
1 teaspoon ground cloves	*¾ cup semisweet chocolate chips*
1¼ teaspoons baking soda	
¼ teaspoon salt	*½ cup chopped pistachios*
4 large eggs	

Preheat the oven to 350 degrees.

1. In a large bowl, combine the flour, sugars, spices, baking soda, and salt and mix well.

2. In a smaller bowl, beat together the eggs, oil, and vanilla. Add this mixture to the flour mixture and stir until well blended.

Stir the carrot, zucchini, apple, chocolate chips, and pistachios into the batter.

3. Pour into the prepared Bundt or tube pan and bake for 40 to 45 minutes, or until a toothpick inserted in the cake comes out clean. Let the cake cool on a wire rack for 30 minutes, then carefully remove from the pan.

Poires Chocolat Amandine, S'il Vous Plaît

The Pearfect Chocolate Dessert Special Award

(Chocolate-Covered Pears with Almonds, Please)

Amelia Meaux · Crowley, Louisiana

■ ■ ■

***C**hoc Talk:* This is a refreshing chocolate dessert. Pears and chocolate are made for each other. The chocolate sauce is superb.

"This recipe is one I created to indulge my chocolate fantasy with other flavors that are some of my favorites. It's a dessert that is very easily made, and the warm sauce and cold pears present an interesting contrast. It receives rave reviews when I serve it to guests." —Amelia Meaux

Yield: *8 servings* **Preparation Time:** *15 minutes* **Chilling Time:** *1 hour*

8 canned pear halves, well
  drained, or 4 fresh pears,
  peeled and halved
¼ cup amaretto liqueur

¾ cup heavy cream
6 tablespoons firmly packed
  light brown sugar
¼ cup sliced almonds, toasted*

CHOCOLATE SAUCE
6 ounces semisweet chocolate
  chips

GARNISH
Mint sprigs (optional)

continued

*For extra nutty flavor, spread the nuts on a cookie sheet and toast them in a preheated 350 degree oven for 10 to 15 minutes. Stir the nuts occasionally to toast them evenly and prevent burning. Or, toast the nuts in the microwave (they will not change color but will taste toasted). Place 1 cup nuts on a paper plate and microwave uncovered on high power for 3 to 4 minutes, rotating the plate a half turn after 2 minutes.

1. Place the pear halves in a flat serving dish, cut side up, in a single layer. Sprinkle evenly with the amaretto. Cover and refrigerate until chilled, at least 1 hour.

2. When ready to serve, make the chocolate sauce by combining the chocolate, cream, and brown sugar in a small saucepan over low heat. Stir constantly until the chocolate is melted and the mixture is smooth.

3. To serve, place about 2 tablespoons of the chocolate sauce on the bottom of each dessert plate. Spread the sauce around to cover the bottom of the plate.

4. Place a pear half on each plate, cut side up, and spoon an equal portion (about 1½ tablespoons) of the chocolate sauce on each pear half. Sprinkle each serving with 1½ teaspoons almonds. Garnish with mint sprigs, if desired.

Recipe Note: If available, use fresh ripe pears, peeled. Be creative with your garnish. Fill the center of the pear with fresh berries.

Best Dessert for a Cold Winter Night Special Award

Chocolate Double Dumplings

Lynda Sarkisian · Salem, South Carolina

■ ■ ■

Choc Talk: Brrrr. Time to cover yourself in a warm, comforting dessert, and here it is: chocolate chip dumplings baked in a chocolate sauce. Add that extra topping of ice cream or whipped cream for real comfort.

Yield: *8 to 10 servings* **Preparation Time:** *20 minutes* **Baking Time:** *30 minutes* **Bakeware Required:** *10 × 15-inch baking dish*

DUMPLING DOUGH

1 cup all-purpose flour

½ teaspoon salt

¼ cup unsweetened cocoa

½ cup granulated sugar

1¼ teaspoons baking powder

½ cup minus 1 tablespoon half-and-half

3 tablespoons margarine, melted

½ cup semisweet chocolate chips

½ cup chopped pecans

CHOCOLATE SAUCE

¾ cup granulated sugar

⅓ cup unsweetened cocoa

⅛ teaspoon salt

3 cups half-and-half

½ cup unsalted butter or margarine, melted

1 teaspoon vanilla extract

GARNISH

Fresh whipped cream

To Make the Dumpling Dough

Preheat the oven to 375 degrees.

1. In a medium bowl, combine the flour, salt, cocoa, sugar, and baking powder and mix well.

2. In a small bowl, combine the half-and-half and melted margarine and stir all at once into the flour mixture, making a soft dough. Stir in the chocolate chips and pecans. Set aside.

To Make the Sauce

1. In a large heavy-bottomed saucepan, combine the sugar, cocoa, and salt and mix well. Over moderate heat, gradually stir in the half-and-half until the mixture is smooth. Add the butter and bring to a boil, stirring often. Allow the mixture to boil about 3 minutes, stirring constantly.

2. Remove it from the heat, stir in the vanilla, and pour into the baking dish.

3. Drop the dumpling dough by heaping tablespoons into the baking dish on top of the sauce. Bake for 30 minutes. Serve the dumplings and sauce warm with whipped cream.

Chocolate Bread Pudding

■ ■ ■

*C**hoc Talk:* Chocolate is comforting. Bread pudding is comforting. The two are deliciously doubled in this combination, which may prove medicinal.

Yield: *8 servings* **Preparation Time:** *20 minutes* **Baking Time:** *30 to 40 minutes (15 to 20 minutes for muffins)* **Bakeware Required:** *Cookie sheet and 9 × 13-inch baking pan, well greased, or 8-cup muffin pan (for individual servings), well greased*

³⁄₄ loaf French or Italian bread,
   cut into cubes (about 4 cups)
¹⁄₃ cup butter, melted
3 tablespoons granulated sugar
10 ounces semisweet chocolate,
   finely chopped, divided
2 cups heavy cream, scalded

4 large eggs
1 teaspoon vanilla extract
¹⁄₄ teaspoon ground nutmeg

GARNISH
Fresh whipped cream

Preheat the oven to 350 degrees.

1. Toss the bread cubes in the melted butter to coat lightly. Spread on the cookie sheet in a single layer and sprinkle with the sugar. Place in the oven and bake for 10 to 15 minutes, stirring occasionally to ensure even toasting. (To crisp the cubes further, place them under the broiler for just a few minutes but watch them carefully!)

2. Melt 1 cup semisweet chocolate (for effective methods and instructions, see page 27). Set aside to cool.

3. In a large bowl, combine the cream, eggs, vanilla, and nutmeg and mix well. Stir in the melted chocolate. Add the toasted bread cubes and set aside to soak for 10 minutes.

4. Pour the mixture into the prepared pan and sprinkle the remaining chocolate on top.

5. Bake for 30 to 40 minutes, or until the pudding puffs like a soufflé and pulls away slightly from the pan. Let the pudding cool slightly before cutting into squares. Serve warm with fresh whipped cream.

Recipe Note: See page 297 for more topping or chocolate glaze ideas you may find interesting to try.

Black Forest Brunch Pancakes

Norine Casale · Flushing, New York

■ ■ ■

***C**hoc Talk:* These simple chocolate pancakes will really wake everybody up on a Sunday morning. Or serve them as dessert pancakes and fill them with a variety of sautéed fruit (like apples with sugar and cinnamon).

"I wanted a compromise between dessert and serious food, and my chocolate pancakes are the happy result. They taste just as good cool as hot, so brunch can be relaxed and gabby." —Norine Casale

Yield: *12 medium pancakes* **Preparation Time:** *15 minutes* **Cooking Time:** *10 to 15 minutes* **Cookware Required:** *Griddle or large frying pan, well greased*

1½ cups all-purpose flour
½ cup instant chocolate milk powder or sweetened cocoa mix
2 tablespoons baking powder
¼ teaspoon instant coffee granules
2 large eggs or equivalent egg substitute

1 cup milk
¼ cup unsalted butter or margarine

TOPPINGS

2 cups cherry pie filling
Confectioners' sugar to taste

continued

1. In a large bowl, stir together the flour, chocolate milk powder, baking powder, and instant coffee.

2. In a separate bowl, beat the eggs until lemon-colored and light in texture (about 2 to 3 minutes). Add the milk to the eggs and beat again.

3. Pour the milk and egg mixture into the dry ingredients and blend until smooth. Stir in the melted butter.

4. Heat the greased griddle or frying pan over medium-high heat. The griddle is hot enough when a few drops of cold water sprinkled on the griddle bounce and sputter. Ladle large spoonfuls of the batter onto the surface and cook for 2 to 3 minutes. Turn over and cook for about 2 minutes more.

5. Top the cooked pancakes with the cherry pie filling and sprinkle with confectioners' sugar.

Recipe Note: If you wish to vary the Black Forest touch, substitute another type of fruit for the cherries. For dessert, serve with one of the wonderful chocolate sauces starting on page 297. Or dress up the pancakes with a creative topping (page 299) and call them crêpes. Ooh-la-la!

Oh, Poppycock! Chocolate-Covered Popcorn

Chocolate Heaven Creation

■ ■ ■

Choc Talk: This is a chocolate twist on traditional caramel corn. When I was in high school, I ate a lot of Fiddle Faddle and always wondered how it would taste if it were covered in chocolate. I would have been better off if I had wondered more about how I was going to pass algebra.

Yield: *8 to 10 servings* **Preparation Time:** *30 minutes* **Baking Time:** *1 hour* **Bakeware Required:** *Large roasting pan; 2 large cookie sheets, lined with foil, lightly coated with nonstick cooking spray*

8 cups popped corn	*½ teaspoon salt*
1 to 2 cups almonds, pecans,	*2 tablespoons butter*
and peanuts (or nut mixture	*6 ounces semisweet chocolate,*
you prefer), toasted∗	*chopped*
1 cup granulated sugar	*1 teaspoon vanilla extract*
½ cup light corn syrup	

Preheat the oven to 250 degrees.

1. Place the popped corn and nuts in the roasting pan and mix together.

2. In a medium saucepan over medium heat, combine the sugar, corn syrup, salt, and butter. Bring to a boil, stirring constantly. Stir in the chocolate. Continue to cook, stirring constantly, until the chocolate is completely melted and the mixture becomes very thick. Remove from the heat and stir in the vanilla.

3. Pour the chocolate syrup over the popcorn and nuts in the roasting pan and stir to coat evenly. Bake for 1 hour, stirring occasionally. Place the hot poppycock on foil-lined cookie sheets to cool. Store Poppycock in a plastic Ziploc bag.

∗For extra nutty flavor, spread the nuts on a cookie sheet and toast them in a preheated 350 degree oven for 10 to 15 minutes. Stir the nuts occasionally to toast them evenly and prevent burning. Or, toast the nuts in the microwave (they will not change color but will taste toasted). Place 1 cup nuts on a paper plate and microwave uncovered on high power for 3 to 4 minutes, rotating the plate a half turn after 2 minutes.

Chocolate Fondue

■ ■ ■

Choc Talk: Dust off the avocado green fondue pot you received as a wedding present in the sixties, or go to a flea market and find one, and have yourself a chocolate fondue party.

Yield: *10 to 12 servings* **Preparation Time:** *15 minutes*

FONDUE	DIPPERS
1 cup granulated sugar	*Fresh fruit, cut into bite-size*
½ cup water	*chunks (oranges, pineapple,*
3 ounces semisweet chocolate	*apples, bananas)*
3½ ounces unsweetened	*Dried fruit (dates, apricots,*
chocolate	*pineapple)*
¼ cup unsalted butter	*Marshmallows*
2 tablespoons heavy cream	*Brioche or croissants, cut into*
	pieces
	Plain doughnuts, cut into pieces

1. Place the sugar and water in a medium saucepan over medium heat and bring to a gentle boil. Lower the heat and simmer until the mixture thickens to a syrup, stirring constantly. Set aside.

2. Melt the chocolate with the butter (for effective methods and instructions, see page 27).

3. Stir the chocolate and butter mixture into the syrup until blended. Stir in the heavy cream and transfer to the fondue pot.

4. Use long fondue forks to spear the dippers and immerse them in the chocolate.

The Great White Lie—White Chocolate Cakes, Candy, and Desserts

...

They lied. We lied. I lied. There is no such thing as white chocolate. Because by law (believe it or not there are chocolate police), a product identified by the word "chocolate" must contain cocoa solids, according to the FDA. (If you're really interested, check back to the beginning of the book to read all about chocolate.) White chocolate has not one speck of cocoa in it. So technically it should be called white anti-chocolate or fool's chocolate.

White chocolate is also the perfect dessert to make for those who are allergic to chocolate (a horrible disease for which we are now seeking a cure). The content of this ingenious invention is cocoa butter, milk, sugar, and vanillin. It melts like chocolate, and you can probably substitute equivalent quantities of white chocolate for any of the dark chocolate recipes in this book. Try it.

I will admit to you, I was a white chocolate skeptic. But while there is no substitute for chocolate, white chocolate in cakes, mousses, and even crème brûlée is really fabulous and deserves its own unique dessert category.

White chocolate can be found in most grocery stores (look for the brands Tobler, Lindt, and Droste), but the best source I found was my neighborhood candy store. They buy their chocolate in blocks and sell it by the pound. The chocolate is usually of a high grade, such as Callebaut or Cacao Barry, which is what the professionals use.

The finer the grade of white chocolate, the easier it is to work with. Why? Because the higher the grade, the higher the cocoa butter content, which means the white chocolate will melt better. I have also used white chocolate chips, which are perfect if you want the chips to remain somewhat intact, but they may not be the best for melting.

Tips for Working with White Chocolate

- If using the microwave, melt the white chocolate on defrost for 2 minutes, stirring after each minute until melted. White chocolate is more temperamental than traditional chocolate and can scorch or seize (see page 27) more readily.
- If you prefer the double-boiler method, make sure you set the stove heat on low to moderate. Do not let the water in the lower pot boil, since any steam or moisture that hits the melting chocolate will just aggravate it into a belligerent, stiff white blob. Be patient and take it slow.
- The oven method is effective as long as you maintain a constant temperature of 250 degrees. Place the broken or chopped chocolate in a standard (9 × 5 × 3-inch) loaf pan or baking pan and stir frequently to prevent scorching until it is completely melted.
- Make sure to let the white chocolate cool before adding any other liquid ingredients, unless the ingredients are meant to cook with the melted white chocolate.
- If the white chocolate seizes, stir in 1 tablespoon of solid shortening or vegetable oil and place it back in the microwave or on very low heat in the double boiler to bring it back to a smooth consistency. Add more shortening or oil 1 tablespoon at a time as needed.

White Chocolate Adds the Yin to the Yang or Vice Versa

- Melted white chocolate is a beautiful garnish for dark chocolate desserts. Melt 2 to 4 ounces of white chocolate according to the instructions above. Place the melted white chocolate in a small plastic Ziploc bag. Cut off a very small corner of the bag at an angle. Gently squeeze the melted white chocolate and drizzle it over the dessert. Or draw designs on parchment paper, drizzle on the chocolate, and allow it to harden to create your own garnishes. For other garnishing ideas, see page 306.
- Melted white chocolate is also great for chocolate dipping.

I Love These Recipes . . . But I Want Chocolate Chocolate

You can substitute equivalent amounts of semisweet or unsweetened dark chocolate in the recipes in this chapter. See the Recipe Notes for advice.

Whitie* with Caramel Sauce

Mary LaFleur · Grand Rapids, Michigan

■ ■ ■

***C**hoc Talk:* What a tantalizing combination. The caramel sauce is great on its own, and you can serve it on everything (including your finger). It's especially elegant to serve after dinner with the White Mousse with a Red Swirl on page 284.

Yield: *10 to 12 servings* **Preparation Time:** *20 to 30 minutes* **Baking Time:** *35 minutes* **Bakeware Required:** *10-inch round baking pan, lined with greased parchment paper*

WHITIES
3 tablespoons instant coffee granules
1 tablespoon hot water
¾ cup unsalted butter
1 pound dark brown sugar
2 cups all-purpose flour
2 teaspoons baking powder
½ teaspoon salt
2 large eggs
2 tablespoons Kahlúa liqueur or brewed coffee

1 cup white chocolate, chopped into ½- to 1-inch pieces†
¾ cup pecans, coarsely chopped

CARAMEL SAUCE‡
2 cups granulated sugar
½ cup unsalted butter, cut into 8 pieces
1 cup heavy cream

GARNISH
Vanilla ice cream

To Make the Whities

Preheat the oven to 350 degrees.

1. Dissolve the instant coffee granules in the hot water.

2. In a medium saucepan over moderate heat, melt the butter and dark brown sugar. Add the dissolved coffee and mix well. Pour into a large bowl and set aside to cool to room temperature.

*A white chocolate brownie.

†The chocolate pieces must be fairly large. If chopped too small, they'll melt into the brownie as it bakes. As an alternative, use white chocolate chips.

‡See page 297 for instructions for making chocolate caramel sauce.

3. In a separate bowl, sift together the flour, baking powder, and salt.

4. Beat the eggs and Kahlúa into the cooled butter-sugar mixture. Add the sifted ingredients and mix well. Gently stir in the white chocolate chunks and chopped pecans.

5. Spread the batter in the prepared pan and bake for 35 minutes. Let the whitie cool in the pan, then gently remove it to a plate and chill before cutting into wedges. Serve at room temperature or slightly rewarmed, topped with a scoop of vanilla ice cream and drizzled with warm caramel sauce.

To Make the Caramel Sauce

1. In a heavy saucepan over moderate heat, heat the sugar without stirring. As the sugar begins to melt around the outside edges, shake the pan gently to mix. As the sugar becomes darker, shake the pan over the heat more frequently.

2. When the sugar is a medium-brown caramel color (after approximately 5 minutes), remove from the heat and whisk in the butter pieces. Just before the butter is blended, whisk in the cream, return to the heat, and let the mixture come to a boil. Remove from the heat and gently stir with a wooden spoon to dissolve the sugar on the bottom. Store covered in the refrigerator. Reheat before serving.

Recipe Note: This recipe is very easy, absolutely fantastic, and everyone loves it. There are several recipes in this book that call for bottled caramel sauce, but why not try this one instead? It freezes well, so now I double the batch when I make it.

White Chocolate Crunchies

Christine Farneti · Deland, Florida

■ ■ ■

Professional Chocolate Lover Category

*C***hoc Talk:** My husband, Tim Buie, has a secret love. A veteran member of the meatloaf staff at World Meatloaf HQ and a drafted member of the Chocolate Heaven crew, he can live without chocolate and barely touched the stuff until he was forced to test ten recipes a day. (How I've stayed married to a guy who is dispassionate about chocolate, I'll never know.) But, I discovered the secret passion of this restrained man. I had placed a batch of the White Chocolate Crunchies in the refrigerator, and when I went to serve them to some of the chocolate-tasting panel, they were *gone*. And, so was Tim. He surfaced later on in the evening looking like he had just returned from an Arctic expedition: His almost-black mustache was sprinkled like a white frosted Christmas tree. Guilty. "I couldn't stop eating the crunchies. I love white chocolate!" he confessed.

"This recipe came from a friend I used to work with. As a single working mother, I was (and still am) always pressed for time. Yet I wanted to contribute to holiday parties, both mine and my daughter's. This candy has never failed to delight holiday snackers, and it's sinfully easy to make." —Christine Farneti

Yield: *20 servings, or one Tim Buie* **Preparation Time:** *10 minutes* **Chilling Time:** *15 to 20 minutes* **Bakeware Required:** *Cookie sheet, lined with foil*

1 pound white chocolate, chopped into small pieces for melting	*1½ to 2 cups salted peanuts*
	3 cups Rice Chex cereal
1 cup small (mini size) pretzels	

1. In a medium glass bowl in the microwave, melt the chocolate for 2 minutes on defrost, stirring after 1 minute. (White chocolate is temperamental, so be careful not to overcook or burn it.)

2. Pour the melted chocolate into a large bowl and add the rest of the ingredients. Toss together well using 2 spatulas, so that the mixture is completely covered with the melted white chocolate.

3. Spread the chocolate-covered mixture on the prepared cookie sheet to cool. It may be placed in the freezer for 15 to 20 minutes to cool rapidly. Break into pieces like peanut brittle. Store in a cool place.

Recipe Note: You die-hard dark chocoholics may substitute equivalent amounts of semisweet chocolate for the white. Or try using half white chocolate and half semisweet chocolate melted separately but mixed with the Chex mix in various decorative methods.

Cumulus Cloud Cake

Lorraine Langlois · Newark, Ohio

■ ■ ■

Choc Talk: This truly beautiful white chocolate cake is what I imagined it would be like to eat a fluffy white cloud. I had no idea clouds were so moist and flavorful.

"Here in Newark there is a very fine chocolate candy shop called Goumas. It is owned and managed by the Goumas family, who immigrated here from Greece. They come from a family of Greek candy makers. Mrs. Goumas developed the white chocolate cake recipe herself and keeps it posted in their candy shop, where she makes and sells white chocolate by the pound." —Lorraine Langlois

Yield: *12 servings* **Preparation Time:** *20 minutes* **Baking Time:** *25 minutes* **Bakeware Required:** *Three 9-inch round cake pans, well greased*

CAKE	WHITE CHOCOLATE ICING
4 ounces white chocolate, chopped into small pieces for melting	4 ounces white chocolate, chopped into small pieces for melting
1 cup unsalted butter	½ cup unsalted butter, softened
2 cups granulated sugar	1 large egg yolk
4 large eggs	½ teaspoon vanilla extract
1 teaspoon vanilla extract	3 tablespoons heavy cream
2½ cups sifted all-purpose flour	3 cups confectioners' sugar, approximately
1 teaspoon baking powder	
½ cup sweetened flaked coconut	
1 cup buttermilk	
1 cup chopped pecans	

To Make the Cake

Preheat the oven to 350 degrees.

1. In a medium glass or microwave-safe bowl in the microwave, melt the chocolate for 2 minutes on defrost power, stirring after 1 minute. (White chocolate is temperamental, so be careful not to overcook or burn it.) Set aside to cool completely.

2. In a large bowl, cream the butter with the sugar and beat until light and fluffy.

3. Add the eggs one at a time, beating well after each addition. Add the vanilla and mix thoroughly.

4. In a separate bowl, mix together the flour and baking powder. Gradually beat into the sugar-butter mixture. Mix in the coconut and buttermilk. Add the melted white chocolate and mix well. Stir in the chopped pecans.

5. Divide the batter evenly among the prepared pans. Bake for 25 minutes, or until a toothpick inserted in the center of the cakes comes out clean. Be careful not to overbake the cakes. Let them cool on wire cooling racks for 5 minutes, then carefully remove them from the pans. Let the cakes cool completely on wire racks before covering with the White Icing.

To Make the White Chocolate Icing

1. In a medium glass or microwave-safe bowl in the microwave, melt the chocolate for 2 minutes on defrost, stirring after 1 minute. (White chocolate is temperamental, so be careful not to overcook or burn it.) Set aside to cool completely.

2. In a medium bowl, combine the melted white chocolate, butter, egg yolk, vanilla, and cream. Beat together until creamy.

3. Add the confectioners' sugar a little (⅛ cup) at a time, until the icing reaches a spreadable consistency. This icing recipe should be enough to fill and frost a 3-layer cake.

A White Mercedes Birthday Cake

Paula Anderson · Tierra Verde, Florida

■ ■ ■

***C**hoc Talk:* "Lord, won't you buy me a Mercedes Benz," and if that doesn't happen, just make your own with this recipe. The luxurious interior satisfies the most discriminating tastes. The cake was actually developed to celebrate a white dog's birthday.

"I have two dogs—a black Pomeranian (Taboo) and a white Pomeranian (Mercedes). In honor of Mercedes making it to her first birthday (since she had several near-death accidents when she was a puppy), we decided a special cake was in order. Since Mercedes is white, my daughter and I decided to come up with a white chocolate cake to celebrate. Too bad Mercedes only got a very small bite of her cake; dogs are not supposed to have chocolate, and we didn't want to push her luck anymore." —Paula Anderson

Yield: *8 to 10 servings* **Preparation Time:** *20 to 30 minutes* **Baking Time:** *30 minutes* **Bakeware Required:** *Three 8-inch round cake pans, bottoms lined with lightly greased wax paper or parchment paper*

CAKE

½ cup water
4 ounces white chocolate, chopped into small pieces
1 cup unsalted butter, softened
2 cups granulated sugar
4 large eggs, separated
1 teaspoon vanilla extract
2½ cups sifted cake flour
½ teaspoon salt
1 teaspoon baking soda
1 cup buttermilk

WHITE CHOCOLATE GLAZE

4 ounces white chocolate, chopped into small pieces for melting
¾ cup confectioners' sugar
⅛ teaspoon salt
2 tablespoons hot water
1 large egg yolk
2 tablespoons unsalted butter
½ teaspoon vanilla extract

To Make the Cake

Preheat the oven to 350 degrees.

1. In a medium glass or microwave-safe bowl, boil the water in the microwave on high power. Add the white chocolate pieces and microwave for 2 minutes on defrost, stirring after 1 minute. Heat again and stir, until the chocolate is completely melted. (White chocolate is temperamental, so be careful not to overcook or burn it.) Set aside to cool completely.

2. In a large bowl, cream the butter and sugar until fluffy. Add the egg yolks one at a time, beating well after each addition. Add the cooled melted white chocolate and the vanilla and mix well.

3. In a separate bowl, sift together the cake flour, salt, and baking soda.

4. In another bowl, beat the egg whites until they form stiff peaks (for instructions and tips on beating egg whites, see page 184).

5. Gradually add the sifted ingredients to the creamed mixture, alternating with the buttermilk and beating well after each addition. Gently fold in the egg whites.

6. Divide the batter among the prepared pans. Bake for 30 minutes, or until a toothpick inserted in the center of the cakes comes out relatively clean. This cake is moist, so be careful not to overbake it. Let the cakes cool on wire racks for 5 minutes, then carefully remove them from the pans. Peel the wax or parchment paper from the bottoms and let the cakes cool completely on the wire racks before frosting.

To Make the White Chocolate Glaze

1. In a medium glass or microwave-safe bowl in the microwave, melt the white chocolate pieces for 2 minutes on defrost, stirring after 1 minute. (White chocolate is temperamental, so be careful not to overcook or burn it.) Continue heating in this manner until the chocolate is fully melted. Set aside to cool completely.

2. Blend the sugar, salt, and hot water into the cooled white chocolate. Add the egg yolk and beat well. Add the butter 1 tablespoon at a time, beating thoroughly after each addition. Stir in the vanilla.

continued

3. When the cakes are cooled, frost each layer with the glaze and set 1 layer on top of the next. This is a thin icing and should cover the cake lightly.

A White Mousse with a Red Swirl

Marilou Robinson · **Portland, Oregon**

■ ■ ■

*C***hoc Talk:** White chocolate makes a light and just-sweet-enough mousse. A flying red swirl of raspberry purée streaks through the mousse.

"A chef on TV demonstrated a basic chocolate mixture using this technique. I found it easy and delicious. To make it even more festive, I decided to use white chocolate and contrast it with a swirl of red berries for color. Guests are generally surprised when the first bite turns out to be white chocolate instead of whipped cream or ice cream." —Marilou Robinson

Yield: *6 to 8 servings* **Preparation Time:** *20 to 30 minutes* **Chilling Time:** *6 to 12 hours total*

6 ounces white chocolate, chopped into small pieces for melting

2 cups heavy cream, divided

1 tablespoon almond-flavored liqueur (such as amaretto) or 1 teaspoon almond extract

*1 cup fresh raspberries**

1 tablespoon raspberry liqueur (such as Chambord; optional)

GARNISHES

White chocolate shavings

Fresh raspberries

Mint leaves

*Use strawberries if raspberries are not available. The purée can also be made with thawed frozen berries or canned berries, which may require more time to thicken.

1. In a medium heavy-bottomed saucepan over low heat, combine the white chocolate and 1 cup of the cream, stirring until the chocolate is melted and the mixture is smooth. Bring just to a boil (the mixture will bubble around the edges of the pan), remove from the heat, and set aside to cool at least 2 hours (or refrigerate for 1 hour).

2. Whip the cooled white chocolate mixture until stiff peaks form. Stir in the almond liqueur and refrigerate, covered, for 6 to 12 hours.

3. Place the raspberries in a blender or food processor and purée until smooth. Press the puréed raspberries through a strainer to remove the seeds and place in a small saucepan. Simmer over low heat for 20 to 30 minutes, or until the raspberry purée is thick and syrupy and coats the back of a spoon. Cover and refrigerate for 6 to 12 hours.

4. When ready to serve, whip the remaining cream until stiff peaks form and fold it into the chilled raspberry purée. Stir in the raspberry liqueur.

5. To serve, swirl the chilled white chocolate mousse and the raspberry cream together to create a marbled effect. Spoon into glasses and garnish as desired.

Recipe Note: This recipe can be made a day ahead and chilled overnight.

White Wonder Pavlova

Anne Woolf · Clearwater, Florida

■ ■ ■

*C**hoc Talk:** This is *Swan Lake* performed as a dessert. The meringue shell holds the delicate white mousse with sweet elegance. Your guests will be yelling "Encore!" after one slice of this glamorous creation.

Yield: *4 to 6 servings* **Preparation Time:** *45 minutes* **Baking Time:** *1½ hours* **Chilling Time:** *1 hour (during baking)* **Bakeware Required:** *Large cookie sheet, lined with parchment paper or wax paper*

PAVLOVA

4 large egg whites

1 cup granulated sugar

1 tablespoon cornmeal

2 teaspoons white vinegar

¼ teaspoon vanilla extract

**WHITE CHOCOLATE
MOUSSE**

4 ounces white chocolate,
chopped into small pieces for
melting

2 cups plus 3 tablespoons heavy
cream, divided

¼ cup granulated sugar

2 tablespoons rum or 1
teaspoon rum extract

2 tablespoons cognac or 1
teaspoon brandy extract

2 large egg whites

OPTIONAL GARNISHES

White chocolate curls

1 cup fresh berries

To Make the Pavlova

Preheat the oven to 300 degrees.

1. In a large bowl, beat the egg whites until stiff peaks form. Add the sugar 1 tablespoon at a time while continuing to beat until the meringue is very stiff. Mix in the cornmeal, white vinegar, and vanilla.

2. Pile the meringue onto the prepared cookie sheet and spread into a 9-inch round. Hollow out the center of the meringue so that

it resembles a doughnut with a large (5-inch) hole. Bake for 1½ hours, or until hard and very lightly browned. Set aside to cool. Peel the meringue from the paper and place it on a large serving platter.

To Make the Mousse

1. In the top half of a double boiler over hot water, melt the pieces of chocolate (do *not* let the water in the bottom pot boil).

2. Stir 3 tablespoons of the cream into the melted white chocolate and blend well. Add the sugar, rum, and cognac, stirring constantly, until all the ingredients are well combined. Simmer for 2 to 3 minutes. Remove from the heat and set aside to cool.

3. In a separate bowl, beat the egg whites until stiff peaks form (for further instructions and tips on beating egg whites, see page 184). Gently fold the beaten egg whites into the cooled white chocolate mixture.

4. In another bowl, beat the remaining 2 cups cream until soft peaks form. Gently fold the whipped cream into the white chocolate mixture. Cover and refrigerate for at least 1 hour.

5. To serve, spoon the chilled white chocolate mousse into the center of the Pavlova. Garnish, if desired, and just wait to hear the oohs and aahs.

Recipe Notes: Instead of making this as one large Pavlova, you can also divide the meringue evenly and make individual baby Pavlovas, hollowing the centers and filling them with the white chocolate mousse. • Drizzle melted dark chocolate over the dessert for a dramatic presentation (see chocolate glazes on page 299). Or fill the Pavlova with one of the dark chocolate mousses starting on page 187.

White Chocolate Crème Brûlée

Diane Halferty · Tucson, Arizona

■ ■ ■

Professional Chocolate Lover Category

Choc Talk: I used to think I had to go to an expensive restaurant for a good crème brûlée. Not anymore. Save the cash and make this dessert at home. Diane uses a blowtorch to caramelize the sugar. But since my sad stint in shop in junior high, when I set Patty Shubnosky's hair on fire while trying to weld a warped jewelry box, I have stayed clear of blowtorches. Broiling is a fine idea.

"My husband and I had this dessert at a very famous and expensive cafe. We thought it was really good, so I created my own version at home. I use a hand blowtorch to brown the sugar, but it is tricky if you have not learned how to use it." —Diane Halferty

Yield: *4 servings* **Preparation Time:** *20 minutes* **Baking Time:** *1 hour plus 2 minutes broiling time* **Chilling Time:** *6 to 12 hours total* **Bakeware Required:** *Four 10-ounce custard or individual soufflé cups and 1 large baking dish*

5 large egg yolks
½ cup plus 1 teaspoon granulated sugar, divided
2 cups heavy cream

3 ounces white chocolate, chopped into small pieces for melting
1 teaspoon vanilla extract

Preheat the oven to 300 degrees.

1. In a medium bowl, combine the egg yolks and ¼ cup of the sugar and mix well.

2. In a medium heavy-bottomed saucepan, combine the cream and another ¼ cup sugar and simmer over low heat. Gradually add the white chocolate pieces and stir until the chocolate is melted and the mixture is smooth. Remove from the heat and set aside to cool slightly.

3. Using a wire whisk, combine the cooled white chocolate mixture with the egg yolk mixture. Stir in the vanilla.

4. Spoon the mixture evenly into the individual custard cups. Place the cups in the baking dish. Pour enough hot water into the baking dish to come halfway up the sides of the custard cups.

5. Bake for 1 hour, or until the custard is set in the center and a knife inserted in the center comes out clean. Remove the custard cups from the water bath and set aside to cool.

6. Cover the custards and refrigerate for 6 to 12 hours.

7. Before serving, preheat the broiler. Sprinkle the remaining sugar (about ¼ teaspoon per cup) over the top of each custard. Place under the broiler for about 2 minutes to caramelize the sugar. Watch closely, because sugar burns quickly. Serve immediately or refrigerate for up to 1 hour.*

Recipe Note: How is it possible so few ingredients can make something so fabulous? You can substitute semisweet chocolate for the white to make Dark Chocolate Crème Brûleé.

*We here at Chocolate Heaven prefer the crème brûlées right from the broiler. We also believe in this simple KLK rule when cooking: Keep Lips Kissable—cool this dessert slightly before serving.

Choco-Licious Drinks

Elizabeth Howard

■ ■ ■

Chocolate Heaven Assistant Chocolatier

Before working on this chapter, the only chocolate beverage I knew about was Nestlé's Quik. All of my friends loved it and I hated it. I wondered if there was something missing in my genetic makeup. Perhaps I was lacking that recently discovered gene—chocodium. I had nightmares of staying over at a friend's house and having to drink instant chocolate milk and pretending to like it. Horrors! Thank goodness for this chapter. My eyes are open and I see the chocolate-brown light.

Chocolate beverages are as old as the Aztecs. They would literally die for a drink of chocolate. The Europeans discovered their little secret, added sugar, and the rest is chocolate history. Isn't it right to pay homage to history and toast the Aztecs with a steaming cup of homemade hot chocolate?

The beverages in this chapter can be altered to suit your personal tastes. The more creative you are, the more fun you'll have.

Old-Fashioned Hot Chocolate

■ ■ ■

*C**hoc Talk:** This is a real hot chocolate that will melt those winter chills. In the mid-seventeenth century, drinking chocolate as a hot beverage became popular. Chocolate paste was dissolved in boiling water with some sugar. This mixture was then whipped with a *molinillo* (still used today in parts of Mexico), a wooden stick with loose rings around the end. It created a swirling motion, which resulted in a foaming mixture. During Montezuma's time, the chocolate drink was made with bitter chocolate, water, and a little cornmeal (thrown in to absorb the fat). If you're craving more history on Montezuma and this beverage, see "More Than You Ever Really Wanted to Know About Chocolate" on page 13.

Yield: *2 servings*

1 to 2 ounces semisweet chocolate, chopped	**GARNISHES**
	Whipped cream
1 cup milk	*Grated semisweet chocolate or*
⅛ teaspoon vanilla extract (optional)	*ground cinammon*

1. Place the chopped chocolate and milk in a saucepan over moderate heat. Stir periodically with a wire whisk to prevent a skin from forming. Remove from the heat and stir in the vanilla, if using.

2. Pour into serving mugs and garnish with fresh whipped cream and a dusting of semisweet chocolate or a sprinkling of cinammon.

Recipe Note: For a more intense chocolate flavor, scald the milk (see footnote on page 199) before adding the chocolate.

Chocolate Milk Float

Nancy Luningham · Russellville, Arkansas

■ ■ ■

Chocolate Classic Revived Special Award

*C**hoc Talk:** This is a delicious classic chocolate milk float recipe, perfect on a lazy summer day. Although it is refreshing as is, we went a little crazy with our experiments. Try adding your favorite instant coffee or liqueur to the milk.

"This recipe was selected from my grandmother's very old cookbook." —Nancy Luningham

Yield: *6 servings* **Preparation Time:** *5 to 10 minutes*

CHOCOLATE SAUCE	*Chilled milk*
2 ounces unsweetened	*Chocolate ice cream*
chocolate, cut into pieces	
¾ cup water	
½ cup granulated sugar	
1 teaspoon vanilla extract	

1. In a small saucepan over moderate heat, combine the chocolate and water. Cook, stirring constantly, until well blended. Add the sugar, bring to a boil, and continue cooking for 1 minute. Set aside to cool and then stir in the vanilla.

2. For each serving, pour 8 ounces of cold milk into a 12-ounce glass. Stir in 3 tablespoons of the chocolate mixture and add a scoop of chocolate ice cream.

Variations:

Hot Chocolate: For homemade hot chocolate, heat or scald (see footnote on page 199) 2 cups of milk. Stir in 2 tablespoons of the chocolate sauce. Top the drink with marshmallows or whipped cream and sprinkle it with cinnamon.

Peppermint Patty: Add ¼ teaspoon of peppermint extract to the basic chocolate sauce after it has cooled. Heat the milk, stir in the chocolate sauce, and serve with a peppermint stick swizzler!

continued

Mocha-Licious: For a mocha chocolate drink, heat or scald 2 cups of milk. Add 2 teaspoons of instant cappuccino powder (such as General Foods International Coffees). Stir in 2 tablespoons of the chocolate sauce and top with whipped cream.

Monk's Cap: For a true winter warmer, add 2 teaspoons of Frangelico to the cappuccino hot chocolate above.

Recipe Notes: The chocolate sauce is super over ice cream or brownies. • Place the drink in an ice cube tray and make chocolate ice cubes. Or place it in plastic cups, and when it begins to freeze, insert a stick in the center of each cup to make your own ice pops.

Monkey in Heaven

Elizabeth Howard
■ ■ ■
Chocolate Heaven Assistant Chocolatier

hoc Talk: Give a monkey a banana and watch him dance. Give a monkey chocolate and a banana and hear him sing. Give the monkey crème de cacao and watch him sleep till Tuesday.

Yield: *Three 6-ounce servings* **Preparation Time:** *5 minutes*

1 medium ripe banana, sliced	**GARNISHES**
1 ounce crème de cacao	*Whipped cream*
1 cup French vanilla ice cream	*Chocolate sprinkles*
½ cup milk	
1 teaspoon chocolate syrup	

1. Combine all the ingredients in a blender. Blend until the mixture is thick and the ingredients are well mixed.

2. Serve in wineglasses and top with whipped cream and chocolate sprinkles.

Recipe Notes: You can make this a nonalcoholic drink simply by eliminating the crème de cacao and adding another teaspoon of chocolate syrup. • Instead of ice cream, use 6 to 8 ice cubes and ½ cup skim milk. Or try 1 cup of vanilla frozen yogurt and ½ cup skim milk.

Bahia Chocolate Chuckle

Sue Siegel · Seminole, Florida

■ ■ ■

*C*hoc Talk: This drink will leave you laughing all the way through the evening! It is very thick—like egg nog with chocolate—and makes a great after-dinner drink, especially following the *Mole Poblano* on page 248.

"I learned about this drink during a visit to Brazil during Mardi Gras. After too much Brazilian coffee, I welcomed this festive chocolate drink, which now brings back happy memories of dancing and parades. Mugs of this delicious chocolate drink highlighted those events." —Sue Siegel

Yield: *5 to 6 servings* **Preparation Time:** *5 minutes* **Cooking Time:** *30 minutes*

2 ounces unsweetened chocolate

½ cup hot water

½ cup superfine sugar*

½ teaspoon ground cinnamon, or to taste

¼ teaspoon salt

3 cups milk

1 cup light cream

1 large egg, beaten

1 teaspoon vanilla extract

½ cup orange juice (optional)

OPTIONAL GARNISH

Orange peel twists

1. In the top of a double boiler over simmering water, combine the chocolate and hot water. Cook, stirring constantly, until a smooth paste is formed. Add the sugar, cinnamon, and salt. Stir in the milk, cream, and beaten egg and cook for 30 minutes, beating frequently with a wire whisk.

2. Just before serving, stir in the vanilla and orange juice, if using. Serve in mugs, garnished with a twist of orange peel, if desired.

*Superfine sugar is available at the grocer store, or just place 1½ cups granulated sugar in the food processor, grind the sugar to a finer consistency, then measure for the 1¼ cups needed in the recipe. Superfine sugar makes a finer-textured cake.

Gilligan's Mint Mud Slide

Lauren Gilligan · Harriman, New York
■ ■ ■
Family and Friends Chocolate Lover Category

Choc Talk: "Lauren is my roommate here at Boston University. Her parents will be so proud to see what she spends her free time doing—creating drinks for us." —Elizabeth Howard, Chocolate Heaven Assistant Chocolatier

Yield: *Three 6-ounce servings* **Preparation Time:** *5 minutes*

1 tablespoon Silver Palate After Dinner Mint Fudge Sauce,* plus extra to coat the glasses
6 to 8 large ice cubes
2 ounces Kahlúa
2 ounces vodka
2 ounces Baileys Irish Cream
⅔ cup milk

GARNISHES
Whipped cream
3 maraschino cherries

1. Line 3 wineglasses with the mint fudge sauce. Do not cover the entire glass; instead, allow it to form patterns on the glass.

2. Place 1 tablespoon mint fudge sauce and all the remaining ingredients in a blender and blend until the ice is well crushed.

3. Divide the mixture evenly among the glasses. Garnish each Mud Slide with whipped cream and a cherry.

Variations:
Mocha Mud Slide: Add 2 teaspoons of instant coffee or cappuccino powder.
Amaretto Mud Slide: Substitute 2 ounces of amaretto for the Bailey's. Top with whipped cream and sprinkle with toasted almonds.

Recipe Note: For a thicker Mud Slide, use 1 cup vanilla ice cream and ½ cup milk.

---

*If you can't find this, you may use an equivalent amount of Hershey's syrup and ¼ teaspoon crème de menthe. Use extra Hershey's syrup to coat the glasses.

Topping It All Off

■ ■ ■

Here are some basic recipes and recipe references for super sauces, glossy glazes, fantastic frostings, flavored whipped creams, and berry purées. Use these recipes on chocolate creations throughout the cookbook.

Super Sauces

Many of the contestants contributed fabulous homemade sauces that deserve to be used on other recipes.

Saucy Hint: If a sauce separates or curdles for whatever reason, simply place the sauce in a blender, food processor, or electric mixer and beat until smooth.

Homemade Hot Fudge Sauce from Fudge Walnut Brownie Pie by Regina Albright on page 70.

Chocolate Sauce from *Poires Chocolat Amandine, S'il Vous Plaît* (Chocolate-Covered Pears with Almonds, Please) by Amelia Meaux on page 265.

Caramel Sauce from Whitie with Caramel Sauce by Mary LaFleur on page 276. If you wish to transform it into a chocolate caramel sauce, use the basic caramel sauce recipe and add 2 ounces melted unsweetened chocolate to the hot sauce.

Hot Fudge Sundae Sauce

Carol Robinson · Lubbock, Texas

■ ■ ■

***C**hoc Talk:* Serve this sauce hot with loads of salted peanuts and ice cream, as Carol suggests, to create your own version of a Peanut Buster Parfait, a favorite refreshment at my old summer hangout, the Dairy Queen. My friend who stumbled through— I mean "hiked"—the Grand Canyon with me (are we having fun yet?), Jim Hundrieser, was a veteran of the Dairy Queen workforce. While we were resting our thirty-pound backpacks against a steaming canyon wall with several miles still to go in hundred-degree heat and fantasizing about ice cream, I asked him the secret of getting that curly-Q on the chocolate dipped ice cream cone. He only smiled knowingly as if he held a precious state secret, either that or he was out of Gatorade.

"My mom, Barbara Atchley of Huntsville, Alabama, gave me this recipe, which she made when I was a child. She doesn't remember where she got it. We enjoy this over vanilla ice cream and include salted peanuts and bananas for a special sundae." —Carol Robinson

Yield: *12 servings, or 4½ cups* **Preparation Time:** *15 minutes*

4 ounces unsweetened chocolate	*⅛ teaspoon salt*
½ cup unsalted butter or	*One 12-ounce can evaporated*
margarine	*milk*
2 cups granulated sugar	

1. In a large saucepan over moderate heat, combine all ingredients. Cook, stirring occasionally, until everything is dissolved.

2. Bring to a boil, then cook for 2 minutes for a thin sauce or 3 minutes for a thicker sauce.

3. Remove from the heat and beat vigorously with a mixer for 10 seconds.

4. Serve over ice cream. This sauce keeps well in the refrigerator and can be reheated on the stove or in the microwave.

Grand Marnier Sauce

Chocolate Heaven Creation

■ ■ ■

Yield: *2 cups*

*1 egg yolk or equivalent egg
    substitute*
*1¼ cups sifted confectioners'
    sugar*

¾ cup heavy cream
*2 to 4 tablespoons Grand
    Marnier*

1. Beat together the egg yolk and confectioners' sugar.

2. In a separate bowl, stir the liqueur into the heavy cream.

3. Stir the cream into the egg mixture until smooth.

Toppings

Chocolate Glazes

These chocolate glazes will be the shining star on cakes, pies, and other chocolate creations. A chocolate glaze will not be as thick as a frosting but will delicately drizzle down a cake or other dessert and add an elegant sheen.

Outstanding, versatile glazes can be found in the following recipes:

Après Ski Chocolate Cake by Sharron Daily, page 114.

Camper's Chocolate Cake by Roberta Kelly, page 150.

Chocolate Mint Parfait Bundt Cake by Eleanor Norris Adams, page 155.

Chocolate Kahlúa Pound Cake Dream by Nikki Skelton, page 159.

Red Devil Cake Dressed in Satin Beige by Peggy Bolmgren, page 135.

Hazel Is Nuts—About Chocolate Torte by Kato Perlman, page 116.

Wilson's Wickedly Wonderful Cake by Margaret Wilson, page 148.

Frostings

Cream and sugar are the main building blocks here. Heavy cream, whipped or unwhipped, and brown sugar, granulated sugar, or confectioners' sugar combine to make fluffy, fabulous frostings that will out-frost anything from the can. Plus, they're easy. Frosting flavors go on forever, so substitute and add to the basic recipes to suit your whim.

In addition to the frosting recipes in this chapter, you'll find delicious frostings in the following recipes:

Bittersweet Frosting from Bittersweet Cake by Mary Ann Lee, page 124.

Sour Cream Choco Icing from Chocolate Sauerkraut Cake by Lorraine Langlois, page 108.

Texas Sheet Cake by Eleanor Cook, page 111.

Chocolate Mocha Frosting from Double-Chocolate Mocha Supreme Cake by Ann Marshall, page 126.

Chocolate Mocha Frosting from Double-Chocolate Tornado Cake by Josephine Piro, page 138.

Whipped Cream Frosting from Festive Choco-Cherry Torte by Eleanor Froehlich, page 120.

Other Not-Necessarily-Chocolate Frostings

Satin Beige frosting from Red Devil Cake Dressed in Satin Beige by Peggy Bolmgren, page 135.

White Chocolate Frostings/Icings

Try these white chocolate icings and frostings on dark chocolate cake for a delicious difference.

White Chocolate Glaze from A White Mercedes Birthday Cake by Paula Anderson, page 282.

Heavenly Devil's Food Surprise Cake by Sally-Mary Cashman, page 163.

White Chocolate Icing from Cumulus Cloud Cake by Lorraine Langlois, page 280.

Honey Frosting*

■ ■ ■

Yield: *Enough to frost one 9 × 13-inch cake* **Preparation Time:** *5 minutes*

One 8-ounce package cream
    cheese, softened
2 tablespoons honey (add more
    to taste)

1. In a medium bowl, combine the ingredients and cream until smooth.

*For more information on baking with honey, see page 23.

Heaven-on-Earth Mint Frosting

Teri Lindquist · Wildwood, Illinois

■ ■ ■

Choc Talk: This frosting creates a fun party cake especially appropriate for celebrating St. Patrick's Day or the birthday of someone named Green.

Yield: *Enough to frost one 9 × 13-inch layer cake* **Preparation Time:** *15 minutes*

½ cup unsalted butter, softened
2 cups confectioners' sugar
2 tablespoons milk, or more, if necessary, to achieve the right consistency

1 teaspoon peppermint extract
1 to 2 drops green food coloring

1. In a medium bowl, cream the butter and confectioners' sugar together. Beat in the milk until smooth. Add the peppermint extract and green food coloring and mix well. Spread over the cooled cake. Cover and refrigerate the frosted cake for at least 1 hour.

Recipe Note: Teri created this easy frosting and glaze to be used on a basic cake such as Aunt Fannie's Chocolate Cake or Cheap Chocolate Cake (see pages 101 and 102).

Coconut Pecan Frosting

Chocolate Heaven Creation

■ ■ ■

*C*hoc Talk: This simple frosting will give a basic chocolate cake fresh new taste.

Yield: *4 cups (enough to frost 3 cake layers)* **Preparation Time:** *20 minutes*

One 14-ounce can sweetened condensed milk	1½ teaspoons vanilla extract
4 egg yolks, lightly beaten	2 cups sweetened flake coconut*
¾ cup butter	1½ cups chopped pecans

1. In a medium saucepan over moderate heat, combine the sweetened condensed milk, egg yolks, and butter. Cook, stirring occasionally, for 10 to 15 minutes.

2. Remove from the heat and stir in the vanilla, coconut, and pecans. Stir vigorously with a wooden spoon until the mixture reaches spreading consistency.

*Toast the coconut for a more intense flavor if you wish. Spread the coconut on a cookie sheet and bake in a preheated 350 degree oven for 10 minutes, or until it toasts to a golden color. Stir the coconut occasionally to toast it evenly and prevent burning.

Flavored Whipped Creams

Here are some ideas for flavoring whipped cream using instant flavored coffees, liqueurs, and other ingredients.

*Basic Flavored Topping**

■ ■ ■

2 cups heavy cream
3 tablespoons confectioners'
  sugar

2 tablespoons selected liqueur:
  crème de cacao, crème de
  menthe, amaretto, Grand
  Marnier, kirsch, Frangelico,
  Irish cream, and framboise
  (raspberry) and other
  flavored brandies

1. Place all the ingredients in a large bowl and whip with an electric mixer until peaks form.

Variations:

- If you do not wish to use liqueur, substitute 1 teaspoon (or to taste) of extracts such as almond, rum, and peppermint.
- To give the topping a cappuccino flair, add 2 tablespoons instant flavored coffee powder and reduce the confectioners' sugar to taste.
- Add ½ teaspoon cinnamon (or to taste) to 2 cups heavy cream, then whip it into peaks.
- Mix in 1 to 2 tablespoons melted semisweet chocolate or chocolate syrup to taste.
- Tint the whipped cream with 1 to 2 drops of food coloring.
- If you're in too much of a hurry to whip cream, stir 1 to 2 tablespoons of liqueur or 1 to 2 teaspoons of extract (modified to taste) into one 8-ounce container of Cool Whip.

*Adapted from the crème de cacao topping in Silky Mousse Pie by Cynthia Blain, page 214.

How About Some Whipped Cream, Honey?*

■ ■ ■

1 cup heavy cream
2 to 3 tablespoons honey

1 teaspoon vanilla

1. Beat the heavy cream until soft peaks form. Gradually add the honey to taste and beat into the whipped cream until stiff peaks form. Fold in the vanilla.

Puréed Berry Topping

■ ■ ■

1 cup fresh or frozen berries
(raspberries, strawberries,
blackberries, blueberries)

1 teaspoon granulated sugar, or
to taste

1. If using frozen berries, thaw and drain them, reserving some of the juice for the purée.

2. Purée the berries in a blender or food processor. If using raspberries or blackberries, press the puréed berries through a strainer to remove the seeds.

3. Transfer the puréed berries to a small saucepan over medium-low heat and simmer for 15 to 20 minutes to thicken. Stir in sugar to taste. If using frozen berries, add the reserved juice and mix well. Continue to simmer to the desired consistency.

4. Serve with chocolate cakes, cheesecakes, and other chocolate desserts.

*For more information on baking with honey, see page 23. Remember that infants under the age of one year should not be fed honey.

Decorating with Chocolate

Shaved Chocolate: Use a vegetable peeler to shave chocolate from either baking chocolate or a favorite chocolate bar.

Grated Chocolate: Grate semisweet or Baker's German's sweetened chocolate with a hand grater. Chocolate bars do not grate well. Use the same method for white chocolate.

Drizzled Chocolate: Place melted* chocolate in a heavy-duty Ziploc sandwich bag. Cut a very small piece from the corner of the bag. Gently squeeze the bag to drizzle the chocolate over the dessert in a decorative fashion.

Chocolate Designs: Trace shapes with a pencil on a piece of parchment paper. Place the parchment paper on a cookie sheet. Drizzle melted* chocolate over the traced shapes on the parchment paper or drizzle the shapes freehand. Place in the refrigerator for 30 minutes, or until the chocolate designs are firm. Carefully remove and use as a garnish.

Chocolate Shapes: Line a cookie sheet with parchment or wax paper. Put melted* chocolate on the paper in an oblong shape at least ⅛ inch thick. Refrigerate the chocolate for about 15 minutes, or until firm. Using cookie cutters or hors d'oeuvres cutters, cut shapes to use as garnish.

Chocolate Painting: Using a small, flat knife or pastry brush, completely coat the inside of a small paper candy cup or a regular-size paper muffin cup with melted* chocolate. Make sure the chocolate is thickly applied and covers the cup completely. Refrigerate for 1 hour. Peel off the paper carefully from the chocolate cups and fill with chocolate-dipped fruits or mousse.

Chocolate Leaves: This is my favorite garnish because it is so easy. Using a pastry knife or small paintbrush, brush melted chocolate over nontoxic leaves such as rose leaves, painting the underside where the veins are most prominent. Be careful not to go too close to the edge of the leaf. Place the leaves chocolate side up on wax paper on a cookie sheet and refrigerate until firm. Carefully peel the leaves away from the chocolate. If you are caught without rose leaves, trace a leaf shape onto parchment paper, or use artifical leaves, and proceed as above.

*For effective methods and instructions on melting dark chocolate, see page 27. For white chocolate, see page 274.

Recommended Chocolate Reading List

■ ■ ■

You can never have enough chocolate cookbooks. Once you start collecting chocolate books, your appetite is forever insatiable. Here's at least a sampling to appease that appetite.

Chocolate Fiction

Dahl, Roald. *Charlie and the Chocolate Factory*. New York: Alfred A. Knopf, 1964. Children's book for the child in all of us. Made into a film starring Gene Wilder called *Willy Wonka and the Chocolate Factory*.

Davidson, Diane Mott. *Dying for Chocolate*. New York: Bantam, 1992. Delicious mystery with chocolate recipes.

Esquivel, Laura. *Like Water for Chocolate*. New York: Doubleday, 1989. A romantic novel about a family in turn-of-the-century Mexico, in which food is an integral part of the story. The book was made into a movie in 1993 and is also available in paperback (Bantam, 1994).

Goudge, Eileen. *Such Devoted Sisters*. New York: Penguin, 1992. Intriguing novel about two sisters involved in the chocolate industry.

Chocolate Books

Boynton, Sandra. *Chocolate, the Consuming Passion*. New York: Workman, 1982. A humorous look at chocolate with terrific cartoons and recipes.

Brody, Lora. *Growing Up on the Chocolate Diet*. New York: Stephen Greene/Pelham Press, 1990 (paperback edition). A humorous and informative firsthand account of the author's foray into the culinary world, with chocolate as a constant theme. Includes wonderful recipes. Also available in hardback (Little Brown, 1985) at libraries.

Coady, Chantal. *Chocolate, the Food of the Gods*. San Francisco: Chronicle, 1993. Excellent resource on chocolate history detailed in a well-told story of chocolate's growth into a major industry. Chantal Coady owns an exclusive chocolate shop in London and is the cofounder of the Chocolate Society. Includes recipes.

Waterhouse, Debra. *Why Women Need Chocolate*. New York: Hyperion, 1995. Nutritionist Debra Waterhouse explains why the female biology triggers a need for chocolate and other foods, and how women can enhance their well-being by responding to these food cravings.

Chocolate Cookbooks

Baggett, Nancy. *The International Chocolate Cookbook*. New York: Stewart, Tabori, and Chang, 1991. A chocolate cookbook filled with beautiful photographs and over one hundred recipes. Includes descriptive techniques for working with various types of chocolate.

Beranbaum, Rose Levy. *The Cake Bible*. New York: William Morrow, 1990. The book is exactly as the title implies and the perfect guide to making fabulous chocolate cakes in all forms.

Bernachon, Maurice and Jean-Jacques. *A Passion for Chocolate*. New York: William Morrow, 1989. The famous Bernachon chocolate recipes are divulged in this book, which has been translated and adapted for the American kitchen by Rose Levy Beranbaum.

Desaulniers, Marcel. *Death by Chocolate*. New York: Kenan Books, 1992. Beautiful chocolate book with photographs and recipes, by the chef at the Trellis Restaurant in Williamsburg, Virginia.

Henderson, Janice Wild. *White Chocolate*. Chicago: Contemporary Books, 1987. Paperback cookbook devoted entirely to white chocolate. Includes photographs and recipes.

Steege, Gwen. *The Search for the Perfect Chocolate Chip Cookie*. New York: Wings Books, 1988. Recipes are from contestants who entered the Chocolate Chip Cookie Contest. Includes prize-winning recipes and explicit instructions on how to make the perfect cookie.

Williams-Sonoma Kitchen Library. *Chocolate*. New York: Time-Life Books, 1993. Step-by-step guide to working with chocolate in a variety of forms. Recipes are by Lora Brody, author of *Growing Up on the Chocolate Diet*.

Zisman, Honey and Larry. *The 55 Best Brownies in the World*. New York: St. Martin's, 1991. Recipes were contributed by contestants who entered The Great American Brownie Bake. Includes prize-winning recipes.

Chocolate Publications

Chocolatier Magazine. Dept. A92, P.O. Box 333, Mt. Morris, Illinois 61054. Six glorious issues of this glossy, beautifully photographed magazine are published each year. Each issue is filled with chocolate recipes of varying levels of difficulty, presented in a detailed, clear form. Write to receive subscription information.

Stern, Lisë. *The Chocolate Report* (supplement to *The Cookbook Review*, a bimonthly newsletter). 60 Kinnard Street, Cambridge, Massachusetts 02139. *The Chocolate Report* reviews chocolate brands and includes an extensive list of chocolate cookbooks. Write to receive subscription information.

If you wish to send your cherished chocolate recipe to Chocolate Heaven in anticipation of *The Great American Chocolate Contest Cookbook*, Volume II, or just to keep us in the know with your chocolate tip, advice, or story, please contact us at:

Chocolate Heaven
P.O. Box 1500
Jamaica Plain, MA 02130

All those sending recipe submissions for future contest consideration will be contacted when the contest is officially under way.

Signs of a Great Chocolate Lover

Favorite designer: Coco Chanel

Favorite dog: Chocolate Labrador

Favorite eye color: Brown

Favorite detective: The chocolate-loving Belgian sleuth Hercule Poirot in the television mystery *The Chocolate Box*

Favorite soda (pop in the Midwest): Yoo Hoo

Favorite galaxy: The Milky Way

Favorite classic: *The Three Musketeers*

Favorite eye shadow color: Chocolate brûlée

Favorite song: "Chocolate Buttermilk" by Kool and the Gang

Favorite holiday: Valentine's Day

Favorite opera: *The Chocolate Soldier* (adapted from George Bernard Shaw's play *Arms and the Man*)

Favorite monster: Count Chocula

Favorite breakfast cereal: Cocoa Krispies

Favorite animal: Mousse

Favorite magazine: *Chocolatier*

Index

...

easiest fudge ever, 231
eat-your-vegetables chocolate cake,
264–265
eeee-zeee chocolate cake, 122–123
egg whites, tips for whipping of,
184–185
Eskimo Pie, 14
Esposito, Mary-Lou, 201
Esquivel, Laura, 243

fallen cake, 130–131
Farneti, Christine, 278
fastest chocolate chip cake in the
world, 100
fat-reduction, tips for, 19–21
"Fatso" (song), 95
fee-phy fillo bars, 86–87
Ferdinand, king of Spain, 13
festive choco-cherry torte, 120–122
fillo bars, fee-phy, 86–87
float, chocolate milk, 293–294
flower pots, for Paula's dirt recipe,
203–204
foggies, San Francisco fudge, 78–
79
Folsom, Nita, 86
fondue, chocolate, 272
freezing of bread, muffins, and
coffee cakes, 30
frenzied but saporous adventure in
cakery, a, 161–162
fritters, chocolate chip cheese, 258–
259
Froehlich, Eleanor, 120
frosting:
chocolate, for Texas sheet cake,
111–112
for chocolate Kahlúa pound cake
dream, 159–160
chocolate mocha, for double-
chocolate mocha supreme
cake, 126–127
chocolate mocha, for double-
chocolate tornado cake, 138–
139
coconut pecan, 303
heaven-on-earth mint, 302
honey, 301
malted milk, 133–134
satin beige, red devil cake dressed
in, 135–137
tips for, 97

whipped cream, for festive choco-
cherry torte, 120–122
see also glaze; icing; sauce;
topping
fructose, 25
fruits, for taking a chocolate dip,
223–224
fruit salsa, 261
Fry & Sons, 14
Fry family, 13
fudge:
dropped not-on-the-floor, 235
the easiest ever, 231
foggies, San Francisco, 78–79
I love Lucile's chocolate pecan,
236–237
Mable's chocolate peanut butter,
239–240
quick brudgies, 69
tips for making, 238
walnut brownie pie with
homemade hot fudge sauce,
70–71
fudge sauce, hot:
homemade, fudge walnut brownie
pie with, 70–71
sundae, 298

Gamash, Bette, 216
ganache, chocolate, for Terri's
terrific truffles with
almonds, 232–234
Gardner, Mavis, 110
Gardner's chocolate zucchini cake,
110–111
garnish:
for cakes, 98
for Hazel is nuts—about
chocolate torte, 116–117
German, Samuel, 14
German's Sweet Chocolate, 14
Gibbs, Gladys, 62
Gilligan, Laura, 296
Gilligan's mint mud slide, 296–
297
Ginny's "better than sex" cake,
104–105
give-them-the-raspberries chocolate
icing, 157–158
glaze:
for camper's chocolate cake, 150–
151

tips for, 148–149
Turchin, Simi, 225

unrefined sugars, 23–25
unsweetened chocolate, 8

vanilla:
 cookie crust, for I scream
  mousse-cream, 217–218
 Lizbeth's low-fat 'nilla-'nana
  chocolate chip muffins, 36–
  37
vegetables, eat-your-, chocolate
 cake, 264–265
Victor, Vicky, 130

Wakefield, Ruth, 14
walnut(s), fudge brownie pie with
 homemade hot fudge sauce,
 70–71
Walter Baker and Co., 14
Webb, Brenda, 205
Wheeler, Donna, 235
when the mousse meets the pie . . .
 that's chocolate amore, 216–
 217
whipped cream:
 frosting for festive choco-cherry
  torte, 120–122
 how about some, honey?, 305
white cake mix, chocolate
 checkerboard cake, 144–145
white chocolate, 9, 273–289
 black and white burritos, 260–
  262
 black tie cheesecake, 174–175
 crème brûlée, 288–289
 crunchies, 278–279
 cumulus cloud cake, 280–281

filling for seven sins chocolate
 torte, 141–143
Mercedes birthday cake, 282–284
mousse with a red swirl, 284–285
PMS cookies, 54–55
tips for, 274
white wonder Pavlova, 286–287
whitie with caramel sauce, 276–
 277
white wonder Pavlova, 286–287
whitie with caramel sauce, 276–
 277
Whitman's Sampler, 14
wicked good chocolate cake, 128–
 129
Willodean's cream cheese chocolate
 coffee cake, 38–39
Willour, Ginny, 104
Willour, Jean, 42
Wilson, Margaret, 148
Wilson's wickedly wonderful cake,
 148–149
Winter, Catherine, 92
Woods, Jane, 212
Woolf, Anne, 286

xocolatl, 13

yellow cake mix, chocolate
 checkerboard cake, 144–145

zucchini:
 chocolate bread, 45–46
 chocolate cake, Gardner's, 110–
  111
 in eat-your-vegetables cake, 264–
  265
 in heavenly devil's food surprise
  cake, 163–164